EXPLORATIONS IN FINANCIAL ETHICS

ETHICAL PERSPECTIVES MONOGRAPH SERIES

1

Explorations in Financial Ethics

Editors

Luc Van Liedekerke
Jef Van Gerwen
Danny Cassimon

PEETERS
2000

ISBN 90-429-0812-2
D. 2000/0602/17

© Peeters – Bondgenotenlaan 153 – B-3000 Leuven – Belgium

TABLE OF CONTENTS

INTRODUCTION

Jef Van Gerwen & Luc Van Liedekerke

Financial ethics, as any field of economic ethics, can be approached from various perspectives.

On the one hand, one can engage in a fundamental reflection on the basic institutional components of finance: i.e. on the functions and social meanings of money, of interest and savings, of loans and investments. These, however, are not purely technical instruments of economic transactions. They are, first of all, social realities, imbued with interpersonal meanings (trust and confidence; power and social status; value and well-being; estimates of future events, of risk and uncertainty; innovation and public choice) that touch upon the basic moral convictions and orientations of a society. Secondly, their administration and governance implies a series of policy choices and decisions that are of an eminently moral nature. Classic economic authors, such as John Maynard Keynes in his 'General Theory', or Amartya Sen in his essays 'On Ethics and Economics', and on 'Money and Value', have been well aware of this deep interrelation of ethics and economics at the level of fundamental theory.[1]

Such fundamental reflection can be pursued both on institutional and systemic levels, including reflection on financial markets and institutions, on the role of regulatory agencies such as central banks and Exchange Committees, or on the instruments and the objectives of monetary and financial policy. All these institutional agents are not merely obeying the standards of economic rationality and efficiency (which are themselves already expressions of specific moral values and preferences of economic agents), but are also responding

---

[1] John Maynard KEYNES, *The General Theory of Employment, Interest and Money*, Collected Writings, London, Royal Economic Society, 1936, vol. VII; Amartya SEN, *On Ethics and Economics*, Oxford, Blackwell, 1987; id., 'Money and Value. On The Ethics and Economics of Finance' reprinted in *Economics and Philosophy*, 9(1993), pp. 203-227.

to fundamental issues of equity, social responsibility (or the lack of it) and prudence.

On the other hand, one can also pursue a case-method approach, starting from concrete observations on recent developments, or crises, in the field of finance. The financial history of the post-Bretton Woods-era provides abundant material for such an applied ethics of finance, based on case-analysis: the processes of globalisation, of dis-intermediation and increased interconnection of financial markets; questions of deregulation and re-regulation of those markets as they emerged in the stock market crash of October 1987 or during the recurrent debt crises of less developed countries (LDC); questions of speculation and manipulation of information in derivative markets; critiques of debt and fiscal policies of contemporary governments, including the critique of international agencies such as the IMF and the World Bank. These are important issues that have been attracting growing attention during the last decennia, not only among specialists but also of the larger public. A true exercise of ethics, which is after all 'a part of politics' and 'a practical science', according to Aristotle, should not limit itself to a systematic reflection on the theoretical level, but also engage in the evaluation of concrete conduct, based on particular cases of recent financial history.

In the following contributions, the authors have made an attempt to combine both perspectives. In some contributions, the concreteness of case-analysis will certainly take the upper hand, as one is confronted with the peculiarities of Belgian sovereign debt management or micro-credit in Nicaragua (e.g. Cassimon & Van Gerwen, Bastiaensen). Other texts will rather start from a systematic and theoretical perspective (e.g. the contributions of Heremans and Erreygers). However, while we have not made an attempt to offer a complete or systematic coverage of all relevant items of financial ethics – we have been merely exploring a vast field of study –, we have tried to bridge the gap between theory and practical evaluation in each of our contributions. The authors have also been working in regular contact with each other, discussing and criticising preparatory drafts of each of the chapters of this book.[2] Therefore, we hope that the end

[2] This research project of the Centre for Ethics (U.F.S.I.A., University of Antwerp) was funded by the F.W.O. (Belgian Fund for Scientific Research) from January 1995

result of our research features greater internal consistency than a mere collection of essays by different authors could ever provide. At the same time, we do not pretend to speak with one voice, nor have we tried to present one single and uniform approach to the issues. Each author remained free to follow his personal insights and orientations in exploring a particular topic.

As this project reaches its closure, it is tempting to repeat the questions that have been driving the participants in this research from the beginning, namely: What are the major issues and the major orientations for a contemporary financial ethics? And what could be a conceptual framework that would offer an adequate common perspective for the contemporary debates? In this introduction, we will propose some tentative answers to these questions, without attempting to provide an exhaustive summary of all the contributions that are included in this work. After all, the reader cannot be dispensed from reading each of them. The following lines of orientation, however, might prove helpful in organising the field of study.

1. The Levels of Analysis

In order to delineate the different fields of research in applied ethics, we have found it useful to follow the classic sociological distinction between individual, organisational and systemic levels of conduct.

(i) Ethical responsibility can be defined, first of all, at the level of professionals, acting as individual agents: what are the moral norms or required virtues for the daily conduct of an investment banker, a stockbroker or a financial manager of a corporation? This is the level of individual ethics, though we are not merely interested in the virtues and vices of one particular individual, be it Nick Leeson or George Soros, but rather in the role of responsibility that financial agents should take into account when acting as bankers, investors, or financial experts. Professional deontology is what one is seeking at this level.

(ii) Ethical responsibility can also be defined at an institutional level: the 'rules of the game' may be obeyed or neglected by individual

to December 1998, under the heading "Ethics of International Financial Markets" (G003796). Promotors: J. Van Gerwen, T. Vandevelde and D. Cassimon. Assistent researcher: L. Van Liedekerke.

agents, but they are most often the product of organisational decision-making procedures and controls: standards of financial supervision are set by central banks, exchange committees and international bodies; financial regulation is defined by national laws and local customs; banking and non-banking financial institutions develop and adapt their own standard operating procedures for the training and coordination of their staff. This is the institutional level of analysis, searching after the ethical qualities of corporate conduct, of particular markets or regulators.

(iii) Finally, an ethical evaluation can be offered of the global system of financial markets and regulations: what are the moral qualities or injustices that are inherent in the present functioning of the international monetary system? How should one evaluate the unequal distribution of power and access which characterises global markets?

It would be a mistake to try to separate the different levels of analysis very neatly, since they often interact closely in particular issues. Avoiding systemic risk, for example, is not simply an issue which belongs to the systemic level of effective transnational regulation, but has direct roots and bearings upon the other levels as well. But the three level distinction may be helpful in order to direct our attention to the necessary conditions of professional action, both on the institutional and systemic levels. Accordingly, good intentions are not enough. An effective ethics of responsibility must rely upon the support of an adequate set of common procedures, institutional rules and objectives. This preferential attention for the institutional and systemic foundation of financial ethics has been with us from the beginning of this research project. We believe it is based both on observation (the urgency and present weakness of institutional guarantees and worldwide standards for regulating and supervising financial markets) and on moral convictions (the call for justice in the international monetary order, based both on a traditional 'common good' approach, or on more recent theories of justice.[3])

---

[3] The "common good" includes the sum total of structural and institutional conditions that have to be met by society as a pre-condition for the adequate exercise of free initiative by the individual agents. This includes the guarantee of a number of public goods (such as jurisprudence, security, the rule of law, a guaranteed minimum income, free access to information and jobs, etc.) under the control of public authorities. The "common good" concept has been derived from Aristotelian ethics, and has been developed in the tradition of Thomism and Catholic Social Teaching. For a

2. The Conceptual Framework

The typical ethical arguments for financial conduct do not differ from those that are used in economic ethics:
— Deontological arguments, defined in terms of rights and duties of agents.
— Consequentialist approaches, in terms of utility maximisation, or of orientation toward an end state of well-being (teleology, defined in terms of a common good, or of a just order).
— The latter types of consequentialism (teleological versions), which typically include an ethics of virtue (of prudence, justice, etc.).
Nevertheless, the combination of the different arguments, or, rather, the mere juxtaposition of them, represents some major pitfalls for economic ethics. In order to avoid the false dilemma of putting ethical rationality over against economic rationality as two separate species (profit maximisation versus regard for the other, rules versus discretion, markets versus regulation, etc.), an inclusive approach is required, which is able to situate the discernment of ethical values as an inherent component within economic rationality itself. In order to do so, the following process of ethical reflection seems most appropriate when studying finance, as any other field of economics:

(i) One should start from a consequentialist approach: focus on profit maximisation, on efficiency criteria, for evaluating particular transactions or strategies.

(ii) Then, in a second step, one can broaden the consequentialist approach, moving beyond narrow utilitarianism, by asking and answering questions such as:
— What are the conditions of the possibility of markets (equal access, fairness of information sharing, redistribution of wealth, public goods etc.)? How can they to be realised in a durable manner in the present institutional context?
— What are the goals of finance beside maximising shareholder value or capital accumulation (e.g. stability of wealth for depostors, reaching a particular rate of savings, long-term well-being)?
— What are the effects of financial transactions upon underlying markets of 'real' goods and services? What is their social surplus value?

functional equivalent, one should look at the theories of justice in the social contract tradition (e.g. John Rawls).

In this way, one is moving toward an inclusive evaluation of all consequences of financial management, including its societal responsibility and overall social utility.

3. Essential Aspects of Financial Markets

3.1. *The function of financial markets*

Basically, financial markets perform the economic function of channeling funds from people who have surpluses to people who have a shortage of funds. This can be done in two ways:

(i) *Direct finance*: borrowers borrow funds directly from lenders by selling them securities, which are claims on the borrower's future income or assets.

(ii) *Indirect finance*: a net-saver deposits his/her money with a financial intermediary, most notably a bank, who uses this money to lend it out to net-spenders either directly or via a particular financial market. Indirect finance is by far the most common funding approach and this immediately poses the problem of why we need this extra stage of going through an intermediate party. We shall return to this problem later on.

Why is the channeling of funds from savers to investors so important? The answer is that net-savers are not necessarily the persons with the most productive opportunities. Financial markets help us to develop productive ideas and are therefore essential to promoting economic efficiency. Economic efficiency need not only include profitable investments in business, it might also refer to the young couple that wants to buy an apartment. Though both have an income, they do not have sufficient funds to make the investment. At that point financial markets allow them to transfer future income and use this for present-day needs. This is clearly welfare enhancing.

3.2. *The structure of financial markets*

There are several possible categorisations of financial markets, we shall introduce three categorisations which are used below in the articles.[4]

---

[4] Another popular categorisation splits financial markets according to whether they trade in debt instruments or equity.

3.2.1. Primary and secondary markets

A *primary* market is a financial market in which new issues of securities, such as a bond or a stock, are sold to initial buyers by the corporation or government agency borrowing the funds. A *secondary* market is a financial market in which securities that have been previously issued (and are thus secondhand) can be resold.

Primary markets are limited and rather closed to the public. Investment banks are major players in these markets. They underwrite a new security, which means that they guarantee the corporation or government a certain price, and then sell the security to the public. Secondary markets are far better known to the public and are far larger. They involve at least 99% of all capital. This might seem strange given the fact that, as indicated above, the main function of financial markets is to channel funds to their most productive uses. But secondary markets are essential for the proper functioning of primary markets. They provide liquidity, which means that it is possible and easy to sell the newly issued security, which makes buying the new security less risky. Secondary markets also help us to determine the price of new securities and allow us to monitor the performance of corporations present in these markets. In this sense, conditions in the secondary market determine what happens in the primary market.

3.2.2. Exchanges and Over-the-counter (OTC) markets

Secondary markets can be organised in two ways. One is to organise *exchanges* where buyers and sellers of securities meet in one central location to conduct trades (e.g. stock market and futures market). The other method is to have an *over-the-counter* market, in which dealers stand ready to sell and buy securities 'over the counter' to anyone who is willing to buy at their prices. OTC markets are usually much more closed and personalised than exchange markets. However, some large OTC markets like the US government bond market are as competitive and open as an exchange market.

3.2.3. Money and capital markets

(i) *Money market*: The money market is a financial market in which only short-term debt instruments (maturity of less than one year) are traded. The most important instruments are:

Treasury bills: These are short-term debt instruments of governments. They are considered very safe and liquid and are therefore actively traded.

Commercial paper: Again a short-term debt instrument, but this time issued by large banks or well known corporations. The increase in commercial paper issues is part of the disintermediation trend in financial markets, which is explained below.

Repurchase agreements (repos): These are short-term loans (less than two weeks) often made by large colourations with a temporary surplus towards banks. The company provides the funds and accepts (mostly) treasury bills as collateral. The repurchase part consists in the repurchase of the colletaral by the bank, once the term of the loan has ended.

Eurodollars: All US dollars deposited in foreign banks or in foreign branches of American banks are called Eurodollars. It is a broad market and an important source of short-term funds for banks.

Banker's acceptances: These money market instruments are created in the course of carrying out international trade and have been in use for hundreds of years. Essentially a banker's acceptance is a sort of a check issued by a firm and guaranteed (accepted) by a bank.

(ii) *Capital market*: The capital market is defined as the market in which longer-term debt (maturity of more than one year) and equity instruments are traded. Again we provide a short-list of the most important capital market instruments.

Stocks: These are claims on the net income and the assets of a corporation. In recent decades the outstanding capital in stock markets all over the world has risen considerably. They are probably the best known financial markets to the public at large.

Bonds: Bonds are long-term debt instruments issued by local and national governments or big corporations. In terms of outstanding capital, the bond market is much bigger than the stock market. Also in terms of new issues (the primary market) the bond market is far more important than the stock market.

Commercial loans and mortgages: These are loans to consumers and businesses made principally by banks. In contrast with stocks and bonds, there are often no secondary markets for these loans, although this has been changing recently. Such loans are by far the largest source of funding for individuals as well as corporations.

3.3. *The function of financial intermediaries*

Why is indirect finance the primary route for moving funds from lenders to spenders? Or, put differently, why do we need financial intermediaries? Economists answer this question by referring to the role of transaction costs and information costs in financial markets. They provide the theoretical foundation for the existence of financial intermediation in a market economy.

Economies of scale and transaction costs: Transaction costs can be defined as the time and money spent in carrying out financial transactions, and they are a central problem for anyone wishing to lend or borrow money. Without financial intermediaries it would cost a potential lender or borrower a considerable amount of time to find a good counter party and to write up a reliable loan contract that protects your investment. Financial intermediaries pool borrowers and lenders and specialise in the matching of both. This allows them to benefit from economies of scale. Economies of scale, which express themselves in reduced transaction costs are therefore the first reason for the existence of financial intermediaries.

Asymmetric information: In financial markets one party often does not know enough about another party to make accurate decisions. This situation is called asymmetric information. Lack of information creates problems in the financial system on two fronts: before the transaction is entered into (adverse selection) and after (moral hazard). Again intermediary parties will specialise in the collection of information that allows you to break the asymmetric information situation and guarantees that good money goes to good creditors, who pay back their loans. From this point of view financial intermediaries are primarily information processing agents.

In this book the information economics framework is central to the contribution of Dirk Heremans on the role of regulation in the banking sector. Information problems and moral hazard in specific also play a crucial role in the contribution by Jef Van Gerwen on 'The ethical responsibilities in central banking'. Opening up the market, transparency, providing better and more up-to-date information will be an issue throughout the book. It is advanced by many controlling agencies like the IMF and BIS as the way forward. We recognise the importance of these initiatives for the proper functioning of financial markets. It nevertheless leaves one question open: how will this information be used by the participants in financial markets. In the contribution by Luc Van Liedekerke and Danny Cassimon on derivatives, it is argued that next to good information streams, we need to breed accountability on all levels in order to enhance stability in financial markets. That financial markets have somehow missed out on their vocation becomes painfully clear in the last contribution by Johan Bastiaensen on micro-credit in Nicaragua. The business of lending to the poor has been entirely neglected by developed financial markets, but as the Nitaplan initiative points out, it is probably one of the most successful strategies in the development of the institutional and social framework that form the necessary backbone for all well-functioning market economies.

3.4. *Principal financial intermediaries*

One can discriminate between three types of financial intermediaries: depository institutions, contractual savings institutions and investment intermediaries.

Depository institutions: Depository institutions are financial intermediaries that accept deposits and make loans. Banks are the most common type, though by no means the only one. The trade mark of depository institutions is that they play a part in the money creation process and co-determine the available money supply in the economy. It is this property which implies that they are closely watched by regulators.

Contractual savings institutions: Major examples here include insurance companies and pension funds. These institutions acquire their funds and determine their pay-outs on a contractual base. Liquidity is therefore not their major concern and they tend to invest in long-term securities like bonds, stocks and mortgages. The importance of these intermediaries in financial markets has increased considerably over recent decades.

Investment intermediaries: Well-known examples of investment intermediaries are mutual funds and investment banks. Despite their name, investment banks are not banks in the ordinary sense since they do not attract deposits. Their main task is assisting corporations or governments in attracting money, usually through the bond or stock market. Mutual funds pool the money of individuals in order to invest it.

3.5. *The function of financial regulation*

Governments regulate financial markets for three reasons: to ensure the soundness of the financial system, to increase the information available to other parties, and to improve control of monetary policy.

Systemic safety: In the modern market economy, money and stable prices allow one to compare the value of products and greatly facilitates the exchange of goods. A breakdown of the financial system – for example, the post-war hyperinflation in Germany and the Great Depression in the US – can bring considerable damage to the economy. Protection is gained by tight regulations as to who is allowed to set up a financial intermediary, limits on how much and which kinds of assets an intermediary can hold, depository insurance schemes and limits to competition.

Increasing information: In order to limit the asymmetric information problem, and also in order to guarantee investors a fair position, all kinds of information requirements are put in place. The recent trend in regulation is to enhance these requirements.

Monetary policy: Because banks, in combination with the central bank, determine the supply of money, governments regulate these banks closely. Reserve requirements, which make it obligatory to hold a certain fraction of deposits in accounts with the central bank, are the main instrument.

3.6. *The main regulators*

Concrete regulation schemes differ from country to country, but most of the time the parties involved will be: the central bank, the ministry of finance, a banking commission that oversees especially banks, and further down the line regulatory bodies of insurers, stock markets and other specific institutions.

4. Recent Developments in Financial Markets

Growth: The most striking feature of the financial system is probably its enormous growth. This applies to virtually all of the different markets, with the remarkable performance of the exchange markets and derivatives markets leading the way. Growth can be measured in different ways: one can refer to an increase in the volume of trade, in terms of amount of money or the number of transactions. One can also refer to increases on the input side where it seems that more and more savings are reaching the financial markets, particularly the stock markets. This has as a consequence that the relative importance of financial services for the GDP in many different countries has increased dramatically, with the financial economy growing at a much greater rate than the real economy, both in the established industrial nations as well as in the newer economic powers.

Innovation: Money is anything but a homogeneous product. Banks are the supermarkets of the financial world, where one can buy financial products perfectly suited to one's own preferences. The goods being offered differ in terms of liquidity, risk, sensitivity to inflation, expected return, etc. The derivatives markets, in particular, exhibit a continual stream of innovative products, with the risks connected to the newer, more exotic products often being greatly underestimated (see elsewhere in this issue). This continual product innovation has certainly contributed to the growth of financial markets and has also ensured more universal access to the markets. More and more people have gained admittance to capital markets by way of institutional investment, their own banks, and special products such as mutual funds. Herein, democratic capitalism has become a reality.

Deregulation: Since the Seventies, there has been a tendency toward liberalisation in the financial markets. Beginning in the United States, and moving into Europe by way of England, this tendency is now making itself felt in Eastern Europe, Asia and Latin America. Legislation applying to the financial markets is being scrapped everywhere. This reflects an ideological shift on the one hand, where the logic of the market imposes itself more and more as the only one possible, but on the other hand it can be seen as simply official confirmation of the actual situation. Financial legislation seemed to be rather ineffective, especially in the developed countries, and was for this reason easily scrapped, giving more impetus to the movement toward globalisation.

Globalisation and concentration: Globalisation is a growing trend throughout the entire economy, but it is nowhere more noticeable than in the financial sector. The introduction of the computer has been decisive in this regard. Digital communication has made it possible to be constantly informed about market situations on the other side of the world. Deals can be closed and contracts delivered at the click of a keyboard. The financial sector follows these developments closely and even reinforces them through its attempts at greater concentration. Large commercial banks buy out their smaller competitors or squeeze them from the market, and in doing so they have become active far beyond their national borders. Banks such as America's Citicorp have global aspirations with a network of branches spread over the entire world. Not only banks are following this trend, but insurance companies are merging into larger concerns with world-wide reach. The disappearance of national affiliations at the same time increases the gap between corporate interest and national interest even further, making the job of control organs much more difficult, since they still operate on a national basis.

Diversification: The clear distinction that used to exist between the operations of a commercial bank and those of an insurance company, for instance, has blurred considerably. Commercial banks now offer insurance, and insurance companies offer many different sorts of loans. Moreover, large companies are setting up divisions that are only concerned with financial activities, thus becoming competition for the banks. The line between commercial and investment banking is also being effaced, usually because large commercial banks are buying up smaller investment banks and, in this way, adding new divisions to their operations. This blurring of the boundaries even applies to the different kinds of financial markets. Theoretically a distinction can still be drawn between money markets and capital markets, but the links between the two have become so numerous that one should rather think of a single, large network where events in one market will have direct consequences for many other markets as well. This evolution hinders the task of control organs even further, and implies that the impact of a local crisis can have significant spill-over effects in other countries. A case such as the Mexican peso-crisis of 1994 would have remained merely local twenty years ago, but nowadays is a threat to the US and even the European economy.

5. Conclusion

According to information economists, the gathering and processing of information lie at the heart of the financial system. Adverse selection and moral hazard problems mould the concrete form of financial contracts and institutions. They form a natural barrier against the possibility of ever having a perfect capital market. And precisely because perfect capital markets are impossible, the actions of financial players become crucial. They play an active, perhaps dominant, role in the organisation of the economy. Their actions determine which investments can be made and which not, which organisations will survive and which will perish, which entrepreneurs will control the organisations and which will not. As a result, some have talked about the 'vocation' of financial markets (Dembinsky and Schoenberger, 1993). It is their mission to help us develop the economy, to open up new markets, to assist developing economies on their way to sustainable growth. It is unfortunate to see how in recent crises unaccountable conduct in financial markets has hampered rather than supported the economy.

EFFICIENCY AND RATIONALITY
IN FINANCIAL MARKETS

Guido Erreygers

1. Introduction

Does it make sense to examine whether financial markets are rational or not?[1] Individual rationality can be defined in terms of preferences and choices, but is the same possible with respect to aggregates such as the "market"? Although no precise definition of a rational financial market will be given here, I will suppose that two ingredients are in any case necessary: a financial market is rational only if (i) it transmits 'correct' price signals to market participants, and (ii) its evolution is not completely disconnected from the evolution of the 'real economy'. These two requirements are not independent of one another.

For economists markets are intimately related to efficiency: it can be demonstrated that if certain conditions hold, markets turn out to be the best instruments available for allocating scarce resources over different uses. It is not surprising, therefore, that financial economists make a connection between rationality and efficiency. Efficient financial markets are seen as markets in which prices adequately reflect the available information. The prices which are formed in an efficient market are thus reliable signs for investors and help them to make the right decisions. A non-efficient market sends out the wrong signals and obstructs the actions of rational investors. This may lead to mistakes and misallocations.

[1] I am grateful to Christian Bidard, Danny Cassimon, Toon Vandevelde, Jef Van Gerwen and Luc Van Liedekerke for comments on a previous draft of the paper; as usual, none of them is responsible for any remaining errors. During the preparation of this contribution I have been much inspired by Doug Henwood's book *Wall Street*. Henwood is the editor of the New York-based *Left Business Observer*; more information can be found at the following address: <http://www.panix.com/~dhenwood/LBO_home.html>.

Even the most casual observer of financial markets realises that they can be quite volatile, and that investing money in financial markets is always a risky business. From time to time this becomes visible in dramatic events such as the crash of the New York Stock Exchange in October 1929. No one knows for sure how the future will look, but it is safe to say that only fools and die-hard optimists would maintain that "it" can never happen again (I am paraphrasing here the title of Hyman Minsky's 1982 book on the 'financial instability' hypothesis). Some of the movements on financial markets, e.g. in daily stock market prices, often seem not to be at all related to any underlying evolution in the 'real economy', or if they do, to be grossly exaggerated reactions to minor real world events. If it were true that prices move erratically, following a logic of their own which nobody understands and which has scarcely anything to do with the real world, then one might reasonably doubt whether financial markets are always and everywhere rational.

In order to determine whether, or to what extent, financial markets are rational, one could try and determine whether the participants in these markets behave rationally. Could it not be that most of the time financial markets are dominated by prudent, rational economic agents, but every now and then are invaded and destabilised by the actions of foolish, risk-loving speculators? A powerful argument in favour of the assumption of rational behaviour in general is that individuals with intransitive preferences can be exploited by others, as exemplified by the 'money pump' argument (cf. Hausman & McPherson, 1996, p. 28). Surely, in the merciless world of financial markets agents who make decisions based upon inconsistent preferences will hardly ever survive: as vulnerable players they are bound to be outwitted by more intelligent traders, and will end up on the losing side of the market. This is the essence of Milton Friedman's Darwinian argument against the existence of destabilising speculators (Friedman, 1953). But the issue is not as simple as that. In today's financial markets practically all decisions have to be made under (heavy) uncertainty. It is not obvious how individual rationality under conditions of uncertainty should be defined. We will see that it is not always easy to distinguish rational from irrational behaviour in financial markets, and that even when all or most of the market participants might be termed rational, the market need not be rational.

Economic theorists routinely assume that indivuals are rational. Economists specialised in finance are no exception to this rule. The application of the rationality paradigm has, over the last thirty or fourty years, led to substantial progress in the branch of theoretical finance, as measured by the standards prevailing in economics. This is nicely illustrated by the fact that in the last decade, the Nobel prize in economics has been awarded twice to researchers for their contributions to finance: Merton Miller, Harry Markowitz and William Sharpe became Nobel laureates in 1990, and Myron Scholes and Robert Merton in 1997.[2] Two models have been especially popular in finance: the *capital asset pricing model*, or CAPM, which gives a formula explaining the price of a financial asset, and the *efficient market hypothesis*, or EMH, which holds that market prices 'fully reflect' available information. Empirical research on both of these models has strengthened the belief among finance economists that financial markets are on the whole 'well-behaved'.

This belief, however, is not shared by everyone in the field. There is a growing literature on different forms of 'market anomalies', revealing the existence of persistent inefficiencies in financial markets. Noise trading, speculative bubbles, January effects, etc., indicate that a whole array of phenomena have been identified which are difficult to reconcile with the efficient markets view. This literature seems to develop into a new research programme, called 'behavioural finance', based partly upon the psychological research of Daniel Kahneman and Amos Tversky. Remarkably, some economic historians have been writing about these anomalies for a long time, but have been largely neglected. The work of Charles P. Kindleberger deserves special mention in this regard.

In this contribution I will very briefly review some of the contributions that have been made.

2. The CAPM and EMH

Assuming financial markets to be efficient, different models have been proposed to explain prices of financial assets. The most influential model has been the one developed by Sharpe (1964), Lintner (1965) and Black (1972), known as the 'SLB'-model or 'CAPM'.

---

[2] The reputation of Scholes and Merton has, however, been seriously damaged by their involvement in the near-colllapse of the hedge fund *Long-Term Capital Management (LTCM)*, in September-October 1998. For more details on the LTCM-story, cf. Lenzner (1998).

According to this model, in equilibrium the expected return (and hence the expected price) of an asset depends upon its 'risk'. When faced with the choice between a risk-free and a risky asset, investors are willing to hold the riskier asset only if they receive compensation in the form of a higher expected return. The risk, or β, of an asset is defined as the covariance of the asset's return with the market return, divided by the variance of the market return. The CAPM states that the expected return will be a linear function of this β (see Box A). An alternative model has been developed by Ross (1976): this is the 'Arbitrage Pricing Theory' or APT-model (cf. Connor and Korajczyk, 1995, for a review.)

Box A: The CAPM formula

In formal terms, the CAPM can be expressed as follows. The return R_0 of the risk-free asset 0 between t and $t+1$ and is defined by the following equation:

$$R_0 = \frac{d_{0,t+1} + p_{0,t+1}}{p_{0,t}} \qquad (A.1)$$

where $d_{0,t+1}$ is the dividend paid at $t+1$, and $p_{0,t}$ and $p_{0,t+1}$ are the prices of the asset at times t and $t+1$. (The rate of return is equal to the return minus one.) The return R_i of the risky asset i is not known with certainty at time t; it is a random variable with an expected value equal to $E(R_i)$ and a volatility measured by the variance $Var(R_i)$. The expected value of the return of the risky asset can be expressed in similar terms as the one of the risk-free asset:

$$E(R_i) = \frac{E(d_{i,t+1} + p_{i,t+1})}{p_{i,t}} \qquad (A.2)$$

Let $E(R_m)$ be the expected return of the market portfolio, i.e. the weighted average of the expected returns of the individual portfolios. Then the CAPM states that in equilibrium the following condition holds:

$$E(R_i) = R_0 + [E(R_m) - R_0]\beta_i \qquad (A.3)$$

where the coefficient β_i is defined as:

$$\beta_i = \frac{Cov(R_i, R_m)}{Var(R_m)} \qquad (A.4)$$

But are financial markets really efficient? The question has been thoroughly discussed in the literature on the EMH. Two excellent reviews of this literature have been written by Eugene Fama (1970, 1991); they summarise the state of the art both at a relatively early stage, when optimism prevailed, and at a much later time, when the hypothesis was increasingly criticised. As mentioned in the introduction, finance theorists interpret efficiency as 'informational efficiency': in an efficient financial market equilibrium prices 'fully reflect' available information. Three variants of efficiency are distinguished, according to the set of information market prices are assumed to reflect. The *weak form* means that current prices fully reflect the information contained in the history of past prices. The *semi-strong* form states that prices incorporate all publicly available information, such as annual reports. And finally the *strong* form asserts that prices also reflect information that is available to some market participants only. Common to all these forms is that they are based upon the hypothesis of rational expectations.

The *weak form* implies that it is impossible to beat the market, i.e. to obtain a better than normal return without higher risk, simply by looking at past prices and trying to discern a trend in the data. In other words, 'technical analysis' cannot predict the future better than the market does. If you think of it, it is almost self-evident that financial markets must be efficient in this sense: if a model existed which could predict the future better than the market, everybody would use it. As a result prices would immediately adjust and the opportunities for extra-profits disappear. The argument has been known to economists for ages; Adam Smith (1976, Book I, Chapter VII) already used it when he explained the gravitation mechanism by which market prices are drawn towards natural prices. Research on the weak form of market efficiency has often been done in connection with models in which price changes of financial assets are described as 'random walks'. This means that the change in price between today and, for example, one month from now, cannot be predicted on the basis of past prices; the change is truly random. The first to observe this phenomenon in financial markets was the Frenchman Bachelier, who published about it in 1900.

The *semi-strong* form goes a step further: it is also impossible to beat the market by looking at all kinds of public information that is available to market participants, such as balance sheets, annual reports, etc. Hence, if financial markets are efficient in the semi-strong sense, 'fundamental analysis' will not allow anyone to get rich faster than others do. The argument is, again, quite plausible: if there were an investor who could interpret the data in such a way as to obtain a huge profit, he/she would surely be imitated, leading to a correction of prices which would wipe out his/her profit opportunities. At best, an investor might recover the additional costs he/she made to analyse the data.

Finally, if the market were efficient in the *strong* sense, it would also be impossible to beat the market on the basis of information not available to all market participants. Insider trading, i.e. trading on the basis of privileged information before it becomes available to the general public, would not be profitable. Somehow a strongly efficient market anticipates the price change which the new information would cause.

At the end of his 1970 review of the empirical evidence, Fama concluded that the EMH is exceptionally well supported by the facts: "In short, the evidence in support of the efficient markets model is extensive, and (somewhat uniquely in economics) contradictory evidence is sparse." (Fama, 1970, p. 416) A few exceptions were found to the weak and semi-strong forms, but these were judged to be of minor importance. More serious deviations were detected with respect to the strong form. It turned out that both specialised traders on major security exchanges and corporate insiders are in a position to gain from information of which they have a monopoly. But these deviations were not jugded significant enough to abandon the EMH.

A strikingly different attitude was adopted by Fama in his 1991 sequel of the EMH review. Fama surprisingly pointed out that "market efficiency per se is not testable" (Fama, 1991, p. 1575). The point made by Fama is well-known by methodologists. In any process of empirical verification or falsification the question arises: can we really be sure that the hypothesis we are testing is the one we would like to test, or are we perhaps testing another one? In the case at hand, the joint-hypothesis problem is that a test of the EMH is at the same time a test of a price theory. Since any test must make an assumption on the equilibrium prices which an efficient market would reach, it might well be that a deviation is a signal that the price theory is wrong, not the EMH. Given that the dominant price model, the CAPM, was by the beginning of the 1990s openly criticised (cf. the review by Jagannathan and McGrattan, 1995), it became precarious to draw any firm conclusions from the available empirical evidence.

With that important *caveat*, Fama nevertheless drew some important conclusions with respect to the efficiency of financial markets. The previous category of weak form tests was enlarged to tests for return predictability, on which much empirical work had been done. It turned out that returns are to a certain extent predictable, contrary to what the early research on the weak form seemed to suggest. The predictability is rather small for short-term returns, but quite substantial (up to 40%) for long-term returns (2 to 10 year horizons). The evidence, however, is controversial; part of the debate turns around the existence or not of (irrational) bubbles, on which more below. Some of the 'anomalies' that have been well-documented concern returns on specific days and months. For instance, Monday returns tend to be lower, and returns on days just before a holiday tend to be higher than returns on other days. The January-effect is the term used to describe the fact that returns in January are usually higher than those in other months.

The semi-strong form tests were relabeled event studies, which examine how stock market prices react to firm-specific events such as new issues of stock, changes in dividend policy, modifications of the corporate control structure, and the like. It appears that stock markets generally adjust rapidly (within a day) to such events, and are in this sense quite efficient. There is also evidence, however, that events increase the volatility of returns, which may be due to (irrational) over-reaction to events.

Finally, tests of the strong form, or tests for private information, have confirmed the previous evidence on the profitability of trading by insiders and by stock market operators.

3. Bubbles

One of the signs of a growing criticism of the idea of rational or efficient financial markets is the increased attention to bubbles. Bubbles occur and have been recognised for a very long time: the first two related bubbles have been the Mississippi bubble in Paris and the South Sea bubble in London, both in 1719-1720. Quite a number of people were financially ruined when both of these bubbles burst.

There is no agreement on what a bubble precisely is. It usually indicates the fact that the price of a financial asset rises at a speed which seems too high compared to what the asset is really worth. The mechanism at work resembles a self-fulfilling prophecy: the rise is predominantly fueled by a widespread expectation that the price will continue to rise, which in turn attracts new investors (speculators) to the asset, effectively pushing the price upwards. But eventually doubts about further price rises begin to spread, people want to cash in their gains and the price will sharply decline. In severe cases a panic breaks out, the prices of other assets are affected as well, and the financial market crashes.

Characteristic for a bubble is that during the phase in which it is formed, the main cause for the spectacular increase of the financial asset's price is not the expectation of higher future dividends, but the expectation of the price rise itself. This means that the price of the asset will be increasingly disconnected from its 'fundamentals' (see Box B). But since both future prices and future dividends are expected magnitudes, and therefore uncertain and impossible to observe, the distinction between a price and its fundamentals can be disputed.

One of the themes discussed in the literature on financial bubbles, is whether bubbles are rational. Undoubtedly speculation is one of the main elements contributing to the formation of a bubble, but this does not mean that bubbles are irrational. During the build-up period shrewd speculators have the opportunity of making huge profits. The most difficult point is the timing: it is crucial that one sells the asset before the bubble bursts. Two examples illustrate the difference between a 'rational' speculator and an 'irrational' one (cf. Cohen (1997) for more details). Richard Cantillon, the famous Irish-born economist and friend of John Law, realised at an early stage that the Mississippi-bubble would one day burst, and in 1719 he redrew his capital – with a huge profit – well before the scheme collapsed. He was one who would end up a 'millionnaire' – the very word was coined at that time – while thousand of others lost everything they had. In 1720, Isaac Newton did the same during the South Sea bubble in London, realising a nice profit. Yet when the prices kept increasing, Newton decided to re-invest his capital. When a few months later the bubble burst, he lost everything.

Box B: A bubble formula

Suppose for simplicity that the rate of return is given and constant over time. In equilibrium the price of a risky asset is equal to:

$$p_t = \frac{E[d_{t+1} + p_{t+1}]}{R} \tag{B.1}$$

where p_t and p_{t+1} are the price of the asset at times t and $t+1$, d_{t+1} the dividend paid at time $t+1$, R the given return, and E the expectations operator. After n iterations equation (B.1) can be transformed into:

$$p_t = \sum_{j=1}^{n} \frac{E(d_{t+j})}{R^j} + \frac{E(p_{t+n})}{R^n} \tag{B.2}$$

The general solution of the equation is written as:

$$p_t = \sum_{j=1}^{\infty} \frac{E(d_{t+j})}{R^j} + b_t \tag{B.3}$$

were b_t is a stochastic variable which verifies the equation:

$$b_t = E(b_{t+1})/R \tag{B.4}$$

The first term on the right hand side of equation (B.3) may be called the fundamental value of the asset, while the second term, b_t, is its bubble. A positive bubble will tend to rise over time; it will eventually be too high and burst.

Source: LeRoy & Gilles, 1992.

The story of Isaac Newton illustrates that even the most brilliant minds may find it difficult to resist the temptation to invest when prices seem to rise without limit, as is the case when a bubble is being formed. At times the public appears to be in the grip of a kind of fever and shows herd-like behaviour; a bandwagon effect draws even the most rational people to highly uncertain and risky behaviour.

4. Manias, Panics, and Crashes

Typical for a bubble is that after a build-up phase, which can be characterised as a 'mania' – i.e. a period of 'excessive speculation' – quite suddenly the optimism comes to an end, 'panic' sets in and everyone acts as if running for the exit when a fire breaks out in a theatre. Charles Kindleberger (1989) has written a history of those manias and panics that have led to major financial crises ('crashes'). From the South Sea and Mississippi bubbles in 1720 to the New York Stock Exchange crash in October 1987, he identifies 39 major financial crises. Kindleberger compares and analyses these crises, and inspired by Hyman Minsky's work on financial instability, formulates an economic model of a typical financial crisis.

The rationality issue is an important theme in his book. For Kindleberger there can be little doubt: there is overwhelming historical evidence that financial markets are from time to time irrational. He firmly rejects Milton Friedman's argument that destabilising speculators inevitably lose money and therefore cannot survive. Financial markets can be unstable and irrational (as is the case during manias and panics), but this does not imply that every market participant is at the same time irrational. Kindleberger stresses that the relationship between the irrationality of the market and the (ir)rationality of the market participants is a complex one. He distinguishes six different cases:

(1) *Mob psychology (hysteria)*. Crowd behaviour can at times dominate a market; this will typically involve a high degree of volatility, for instance when the mood of the market changes from optimistic to pessimistic.

(2) *Gradual change from rational to less rational behaviour*. Often periods of speculation start with sound rational investors seizing limited opportunities to make extra-profits, but after a while the main driving force is the hope to realise capital gains, i.e. pure speculation.

(3) *Different groups of participants having different rationality*. Sometimes a distinction is made between 'insiders' and 'outsiders', with the better-informed insiders having the power to gain at the expense of the outsiders, for instance by misleading them. This can result in destabilising market behaviour.

(4) *'The fallacy of composition'*. Every participant acts rationally, but since everybody is doing the same, the system as a whole becomes unstable and eventually collapses. The chain letter is a typical example: everybody could make a profit if the chain continued for ever, but this is not the case. As soon as insufficient new money enters the system, the scheme explodes; those who have arrived at the last stages lose the money they have invested. The Ponzi financial scheme was a kind of chain letter system.

(5) *'Cobweb' reactions.* Even if all market participants have rational expectations about the way in which the market will react to a certain change, they may be mistaken about the right quantity of the reaction. This is especially the case when there is a delay or lag between the stimulus and the response. In agriculture, for instance, the production of beans may have been extremely profitable this year; but if too many farmers decide to cultivate beans next year, it will not be profitable anymore. The resulting dynamics can be destabilising.

(6) *Failures to make the right decisions.* Market participants may base their decisions on a wrong model of the market, may fail to take into account crucial pieces of information, or may decide that some information is irrelevant. The excessive lending by private banks to Third World countries in the 1970s and 1980s seem to have been fueled by such errors of judgement.

Kindleberger arrives at the following conclusion: "On this showing, I conclude that despite the general usefulness of the assumption of rationality, markets can on occasions – infrequent occasions, let me emphasise – act in destabilising ways that are irrational overall, even when each participant in the market is acting rationally." (p. 45)

5. Behavioural Finance

Whereas an economic historian like Kindleberger raises doubts about the rationality of finanancial markets, albeit in a cautious way, others are prepared to go a lot further. Some maintain that irrationality is an integral part of financial markets at any time, not just at those instances in which almost everybody seems to lose their mind and panic sets in. The growing literature on 'behavioural finance' can indeed be seen as an attempt to come to grips with the all too many anomalies observed in financial markets, not by treating them as transitory and exceptional deviations from the rule, but as permanent and empirically verified facts of life. A selective review of results obtained in behavioural finance can be found in De Bondt and Thaler (1995); a more recent survey is by Debels (1998).

The behavioural finance approach is strongly linked to the psychological work of Daniel Kahneman and Amos Tversky, who have done pioneering research on cognitive processes and decision-making.[3] A good example of their work is Kahneman and Tversky (1979), where they start from a critique of the conventional expected utility theory and then develop an alternative account, called 'prospect theory'. Phenomena such as the 'certainty effect' (outcomes that are certain are overweighted relative to outcomes that are probable), the 'reflection effect' (preferences between positive prospects are the reverse of preferences between negative prospects), and the 'isolation effect' (the tendency to focus upon the components that distinguish outcomes) are difficult to reconcile with the theory of expected utility. The alternative theory which they propose seems better equipped to deal with these anomalies. According to prospect theory, individual decision-making under risk involves two phases: first a phase of editing, and then one of evaluation. In the editing phase the offered prospects are submitted to a preliminary analysis, during which several operations are performed (coding, combination, segregation, etc.). In the evaluation phase, the edited prospects are then evaluated and the highest one is chosen.

The world of finance appears to be an extremely fertile ground for the development of Kahneman-Tversky types of theory. By means of experiments and empirical research, behavioural finance theorists have identified a number of characteristics by which typical real-world investors differ from the rational investors with rational expectations featured in traditional finance theory. Many of these characteristics closely resemble the persistent 'cognitive illusions' which according to Kahneman & Tversky are responsible for systematic errors of judgement in individual decision-making under risk. De Bondt and Thaler (1995, pp. 389-391) consider the following behavioural concepts to be most useful to finance:

overconfidence: it often happens that people overestimate the reliability of their knowledge;

non-Bayesian forecasting: probability judgements are sometimes based upon similarity or representativeness;

loss aversion, framing and mental accounting: e.g. people tend to attach more importance to the loss of a given amount of money than to the gain of it, which may lead to the 'disposition effect': many investors are eager to sell assets upon which they can realise

---

[3] Amos Tversky died in 1996; a short assessment of the importance of his work for behavioural finance is by Fuller (1996).

a small profit, but are reluctant to do the same for assets upon which they lose;

fashions and fads: what one person considers to be normal or desirable is influenced by what others think;

regret, responsibility and prudence: many investors have a preference for 'glamour stocks', i.e. stocks of which the price is high in comparison to their fundamental value, or for stocks of well-run companies regardless of the price that has to be paid for them.

In general, there are many cases in which investors seem to overreact to certain types of information.

De Bondt and Thaler (*ibid.*, pp. 392-399) think that these concepts help to explain many anomalies which are observed in financial markets. One such anomaly is the 'trading puzzle': on many financial markets trading volumes are high, whereas in a world full of rational investors trades would be quite exceptional (if somebody has good grounds to sell, then why should anybody else want to buy?). Overconfidence may be the key to understanding the puzzle: many investors seem to believe that they can outwit other market participants. Another anomaly – or rather a range of anomalies – concerns the so-called 'contrarian investment strategies': it sometimes appears to be possible to earn abnormal profits by trading on publicly available information, contrary to what the efficient market hypothesis affirms. An example of a contrarian strategy is to buy stocks with low market-to-book-value. To explain such behaviour one might refer to biased forecasts and misperceptions of risk. A third anomaly is the 'equity premium puzzle': the difference between the returns earned on stock and the risk-free return is much higher than it should be according to financial theory. One of the explanations put forward is that a combination of loss aversion and mental accounting is largely responsible for the gap.

In a recent article, Fama (1998) scrutinises the claims of the behavioural finance literature. He believes its results are not powerful enough to seriously challenge the hypothesis of market efficiency. Overreaction to information appears to be as frequent as underreaction. The anomalies which have been revealed can predominantly be attributed to chance; using appropriate statistical techniques, he thinks it is possible to show that long-term anomalies do not exist.

The phenomenon of noise trading also occupies an important place in the literature on behavioural finance. Fischer Black (1986) has defined noise trading as the opposite of trading based upon information: rational traders make decisions based upon information, but noise traders base their decisions upon noise, i.e. non-information. Not only does the presence of noise traders make financial markets imperfect, but according to Black it also makes them possible. Without noise traders there would be very little trading at all; markets would be quite illiquid. "Noise trading provides the essential missing ingredient. Noise trading is trading on noise as if it were information. People who trade on noise are willing to trade even though from an objective point of view they would be better off not trading. Perhaps they think the noise they are trading on is information. Or perhaps they just like to trade." (Black, 1986, p. 531) Noise trading makes markets more liquid, but the other side of the coin is that prices will be less efficient, since they have more noise in them. "In other words, noise creates the opportunity to trade profitably, but at the same time makes it difficult to trade profitably." (*ibid.*, p. 534).

6. Conclusions

Let me try to bring the different threads of the story together. Starting from the idea that rational financial markets should transmit 'correct' price signals to market participants and should not be completely disconnected from the 'real economy', we have encountered, broadly speaking, three different views on the rationality of financial markets. The first is the one which dominates mainstream finance theory: it more or less coincides with a strong belief in rational expectations and the efficient market hypothesis. Individual agents are considered to be rational, and so are financial markets. With a few exceptions, prices fully reflect the available information. The second view is the one defended by Kindleberger: individuals tend to be rational, but from time to time financial markets turn 'crazy'. A remarkably constant pattern of forces makes markets occasionally go through the series of mania, panic and crash. Finally, the third view comes from behavioural finance theory. The proponents of this theory acknowledge the fact that people do not tend to be rational (in the sense of mainstream finance theory). They therefore have little difficulty in accepting that financial markets are not rational.

It is impossible to say which of these views is the most plausible. Probably empirical evidence alone will not allow the discarding of one or the other of these views. In favour of the second and third position, however, is the fact that they are directly inspired and based upon empirical research, be it of a historical or of a psychological nature. The first approach seems to be motivated primarily by theoretical reasons. In other words, one might say that the efficient market hypothesis has a more prescriptive character, whereas the other two are more descriptive in nature.

Anyhow, it cannot be denied that financial markets, at least now and then, diverge from the ideal of an efficient, rational market. This means that there is room for rules and regulation which enhance the efficiency and stability of financial markets: interventions do not necessarily create inefficiencies and threats to stability. Especially the introduction of rules of conduct with respect to potentially destabilising forms of speculation seems to be appropriate. Ethical theories can certainly make valuable contributions to the formulation of such rules.

References

BLACK, Fischer (1972), 'Capital Market Equilibrium with Restricted Borrowing' in *Journal of Business*, 45(1972)3, pp. 444-455.

BLACK, Fischer (1986), 'Noise' in *Journal of Finance*, 41(1986)3, pp. 529-542.

COHEN, Bernice (1997), *The Edge of Chaos. Financial Booms, Bubbles, Crashes and Chaos*. Chichester, John Wiley & Sons.

CONNOR, Gregory and Robert A. KORAJCZYK (1995), 'The Arbitrage Pricing Theory and Multifactor Models of Asset Returns' in Robert JARROW, Vojislav MAKSIMOVIC and William T. ZIEMBA (eds.), *Finance. Handbooks in Operations Research and Management Science, Vol. 9*. Amsterdam, Elsevier, pp. 87-144.

DEBELS, Thierry (1998), 'Behavioral Finance' in *Maandschrift Economie*, 62(1998)5, pp. 363-388.

DE BONDT, Werner F.M. and Richard H. THALER (1995), 'Financial Decision-making in Markets and Firms: A Behavioral Perspective' in Robert JARROW, Vojislav MAKSIMOVIC & William T. ZIEMBA (eds.), *Finance. Handbooks in Operations Research and Management Science, Vol. 9*. Amsterdam, Elsevier, pp. 385-410.

FAMA, Eugene F. (1970), 'Efficient Capital Markets: A Review of Theory and Empirical Work' in *Journal of Finance*, 25(1970)2, pp. 383-417.

FAMA, Eugene F. (1991), 'Efficient Capital Markets: II' in *Journal of Finance*, 46(1991)5, pp. 1575-1617.

FAMA, Eugene, F. (1998), 'Market Efficiency, Long-term Returns, and Behavioral Finance' in *Journal of Financial Economics*, 49(1998)3, pp. 283-306.

FRIEDMAN, Milton (1953), 'The Case for Flexible Exchange Rates' in *Essays in Positive Economics*. Chicago, University of Chicago Press.

FULLER, Russell J. (1996), 'Amos Tversky, Behavioral Finance, and Nobel Prizes' in *Financial Analysts Journal*, 52(1996)4, pp. 7-8.

HAUSMAN, Daniel M. and Michael S. MCPHERSON (1996), *Economic Analysis and Moral Philosophy*. Cambridge, Cambridge University Press.

HENWOOD, Doug (1997), *Wall Street. How it Works and for Whom*. London & New York, Verso.

JAGANNATHAN, Ravi and Ellen R. MCGRATTAN (1995), 'The CAPM Debate' in *Federal Reserve Bank of Minneapolis Quartely Review*, 19(1995)4, pp. 2-17.

KAHNEMAN, Daniel and Amos TVERSKY (1979), 'Prospect Theory: An Analysis of Decision under Risk' in *Econometrica*, 47(1979)2, pp. 263-291.

KINDLEBERGER, Charles P. (1989) *Manias, Panics, and Crashes. A History of Financial Crises*. New York, Basic Books, revised edition.

LENZNER, Robert (1998), 'Archimedes on Wall Street' in *Forbes Magazine*, 19 October 1998.

LEROY, Stephen F. and Christian GILLES (1992), 'Asset Price Bubbles' in Peter NEWMAN, Murray MILGATE and John EATWELL (eds.), *The New Palgrave Dictionary of Money & Finance*. London, Macmillan, vol. 1 (A-E), pp. 74-76.

LINTNER, John (1965), 'The Valuation of Risk Assets and the Selection of Risky Investments in Stock Portfolios and Capital Budgets' in *Review of Economics and Statistics*, 47(1965)1, pp. 13-37.

MINSKY, Hyman P. (1982), *Can 'It' Happen Again?* Armonk (NY), M.E. Sharpe.

ROSS, Stephen A. (1976), 'The Arbitrage Theory of Capital Asset Pricing' in *Journal of Economic Theory*, 13(1976)3, pp. 341-360.

SHARPE, William F. (1964), 'Capital Asset Prices: A Theory of Market Equilibrium under Conditions of Risk' in *Journal of Finance*, 19(1964)3, pp. 425-442.

SMITH, Adam (1976[1776]), *An Inquiry into the Nature and Causes of the Wealth of Nations*. Edited by Roy Harold CAMPBELL, Andrew S. SKINNER and W.B. TODD, Volume II of the *Glasgow Edition of the Works and Correspondence of Adam Smith*. Oxford, Oxford University Press, 1976.

FINANCIAL REGULATION AND STABILITY
OF THE BANKING SYSTEM

Dirk Heremans

1. Introduction

Recently financial crises in Asia are dramatically reducing welfare in a major part of the world. In Eastern Europe recurring problems in their financial systems are seriously undermining the transition process of their economics. The health of the financial system remains a major concern for economic policy-makers all over the world.

The nature of the financial problems, however, may be changing. In recent decades financial stability was endangered mainly by huge government budget deficits leading to serious government debt crises in the Third World. In the meantime, authorities are learning that deficit financing provides no long-run solutions for their economic problems. Today, as also the Asian crisis demonstrates, it is no longer irresponsible macroeconomic policies of governments but excessive risk taking by financial intermediaries that is the major source of financial instability. Hence, regulation and supervision of banking and financial markets is again becoming the major challenge for public authorities.

Traditionally the financial sector has always been more heavily regulated and supervised compared to other sectors of the economy. However, due to increased competition followed by a deregulation wave, the borders between financial institutions are fading, financial innovations are multiplying off-balance sheet activities, and internationalisation is rendering control by monetary authorities more and more difficult.

As a consequence, the debate concerning the optimal degree of regulation and the policy instruments to be used has been revived in the economic literature. The economic approach of regulatory issues, however, is restricted to efficiency considerations; it does not explicitly focus on broader ethical questions about the social acceptability of market outcomes. Whereas one should acknowledge vague negative feelings among non-economists and also more serious ethical concerns about financial markets, this contribution will focus on the economic efficiency approach of regulation. However, as may follow from recent insights on the operation of financial markets provided by the new information economics, economic efficiency does not necessarily conflict with and may even be desirable from an ethical point of view. According to Schokkaert (1998) financial regulation that deals with problems of systemic risk, protection of small depositors, and guaranteeing equal conditions to all participants, involves important aspects of procedural justice for financial markets. One may even raise the question whether the special protection provided by financial regulation for weaker groups in society, such as for small depositors, does not also involve some aspects of distributive justice.

In any case, instead of the often general and superficial treatment of big financial problems in popular discussions, a fruitful discussion needs more thorough analytical insights into the goals and instruments of financial regulation. Moreover, whatever the motives for regulation, good economic analysis remains necessary to obtain a realistic prediction of the effects, inclusive of the unintended side-effects, of regulatory policies. It points not only to conflicts but also to complementarity between economics and ethics.

For this endeavour, we proceed by first briefly documenting some evolutions in financial regulation over time. It follows that financial stability and regulation has become an urgent concern today presenting a major challenge for public authorities. Next, we analyse the reason for the special regulatory interest in the financial system. Why is financial stability so important? How is it affected by the behaviour of financial intermediaries? What are the macroeconomic consequences of irresponsible financial behaviour and of financial crises? These are the questions to be investigated.

It is followed by an analysis of the regulatory instruments. What is good and what is bad regulation from an economic point of view? How is the efficiency of the different measures of regulation and supervision to be compared? These are the issues to be addressed. Finally, we will look at the problems ahead. What is the respective role for private and public regulatory bodies? How has public regulation to be structured? These are the regulatory challenges ahead.

2. The Evolution in Financial Regulation

Historically, governments have always been involved in the financial system. Their interest was mainly motivated by the political power and revenues conveyed to them by money creation in the payments system. Sovereigns everywhere maintained a government monopoly on minting gold, silver and other coins, eager to reap the 'seignorage' benefits. Excessive emission of money by debasing the currency often resulted in serious inflation and financial crises.

When banks started to issue bank notes, an historical dispute started among economists representing the 'banking view' of free banking on the one hand, and the 'currency school' advocating government control on the other hand. After several episodes of banking crises due to the over-emission of paper money, the controversy was resolved in the 19th century by entrusting a monopoly for the emission of bank notes upon government controlled central banks. When commercial banks started to develop payments systems based on deposit taking, these central banks continued to regulate the money supply by their control of the money base, (D. Heremans and K. Tavernier, 1980). As we are moving towards a cashless society, the imposition of required reserves on banks may become all the more important.

In addition to controlling the money stock, public authorities showed little interest in regulating and supervising the financial system. Some regulation was introduced e.g. the Mac Fadden Act in 1927 in the US severely limiting interstate banking. Also by the National Act of 1916 the supply of insurance by banks had been strictly limited. Regulation, however, was not so much inspired by concerns about the soundness and stability of the banking system, but by the populist concern to limit the concentration of power in financial markets.

The present elaborate regulatory system originated in the aftermath of the Great Depression, due to the crash of the Wall Street Stock Exchange in 1929 and followed by the near-collapse of the financial system all over the world. To limit the contagious spread of bankruptcies in the financial system, mainly structural measures were taken limiting the scope of activities of financial intermediaries. Most prominently in this respect, the Glass-Steagall Act of 1933 in the US introduced a functional segmentation between investment activities on the stock exchange and commercial banking. To avoid runs on banks by depositors, a system of insurance coverage for deposits was developed in the same period in the US.

The extent to which governments did take control of the financial system in the thirties may appear somewhat paradoxical. Did the monetary authorities themselves not contribute to the depth of the crisis by irresponsible monetary policies, i.e. a deflationary monetary policy worsening the credit crunch by commercial banks? Some may argue that stable monetary policies sustained by adequate liquidity provision, i.e. a proper functioning of the lender of last resort function of central banks might have been sufficient to curb financial crises.

Internationalisation, financial innovations, and the overall deregulation wave since the 1970s have led to financial sector liberalisation by removing structural regulatory barriers. Since traditionally unbridled competition was seen as a major threat to the primary goal of stability of the financial system, the financial sector more than other sectors of the economy has been hit by the deregulation wave. Following liberalisation, banking systems have experienced significant problems. According to the International Monetary Fund Study by Lindgren, Garcia and Saal (1996), of the 181 member countries, 133 have experienced significant banking sector problems. Among these, 36 countries suffered from a real financial crisis. A direct connection between financial liberalisation and financial crises is difficult to establish. Financial problems are often due to the lack of establishing adequate internal controls by financial institutions to contain the risk of new or expanded activities and to the failure of authorities to supervise them. This has been especially the problem in developing countries and transition economies. But even the industrialised countries did not escape. According to the IMF study in the period between 1980 and 1992 in the US 1.142 Savings and Loan Associations and 1.395 Banks had to be closed.

Reregulation is taking place at a world-wide level under the auspices of the Bank for International Settlements. The Basel Committee on Banking supervision has introduced default-risk based capital requirements, the so-called Cooke ratio. Recently, additional risk-based capital requirements that take into account off-balance sheet activities and deal with market risk have been devised. These regulatory measures have been extended by the European Union in its Capital Adequacy Directives. Recently, also because of the important macroeconomic consequences of financial crises, the International

Monetary Fund has been forced to pay more attention to these regulatory issues.

Hence, in order to maintain the health of the financial system, governments have developed a whole range of regulatory instruments. They have placed different degrees of emphasis upon the various objectives at different times and have used different regulatory tools to achieve them.

The different regulatory and policy measures are classified in Table 1 according to the following criteria. First, public authorities may limit themselves to *ex post* interventions, offering protection to customers and financial intermediaries in the case of impending insolvency. They may also act in a preventive way by controlling the levels of risk assumed and reducing the probability of insolvency and illiquidity. Second, safety and stability of the financial system may be enhanced by structural limitations of competition and market forces. Instead of these structural measures, more weight is given to market efficiency by resorting to a whole set of prudential measures. Third, regulatory measures may focus on the macroeconomic concerns of systemic risk, or directly aim at microeconomic consumer protection. Still, both are interrelated since the avoidance of consumer risks also limits systemic risks and vice-versa.

Historically, the overriding reason for government intervention has been the desire to avoid systemic risk, mainly by *ex post* rescue operations of financial intermediaries. Preventive measures were mostly of a structural nature by limiting competition. The focus on market efficiency and individual consumer protection by deposit insurance and prudential measures is of a more recent date.

Structural and prudential regulation often involve a whole set of different public regulatory measures which differ from country to country. They are stylised in Table 1 and further commented upon in the next sections.

3. Financial Stability and the Need for Regulation

The major goal of regulation in economic life traditionally consists in protecting uninformed consumers against a variety of market imperfections. In particular financial markets characterised by risk and uncertainty and the fiduciary nature of most financial products may create serious problems of asymmetric information. Deposit holders

Table 1

Protective systems (ex post)		Lender of Last Resort
		Deposit Insurance
Preventive measures (ex ante)		
	Structural	Restrictions on entry and on business activities — product line restrictions — geographic restrictions Regulation of interest rates
	Prudential	Portfolio restrictions and supervision — capital adequacy standards — asset restrictions and diversification rules — liquidity adequacy requirements Disclosure standards or reporting requirements Conduct and conflict rules Inspection and bank examination

and savers lack information about the risks being taken by banks with their funds. Therefore, the goal of banking regulation and supervision is often stated to be the preventing of banks from assuming unacceptably high risks.

However, also typical for the financial sector are the important interconnections among financial institutions involving serious externalities in case of bankruptcy of one intermediary. The characteristics of the financial sector are such that individual problems may easily spill-over and endanger the whole financial system. Failures in the operation of the financial sector not only have consequences for individual investors and savers, but stock market crashes, bank failures and other financial disasters may endanger the health of the whole economy.

Financial operations are characterised by risk and uncertainty. As a result financial decision-making depends heavily upon expectations. It is also characterised by 'herd behaviour'. Market parties adjust their expectations suddenly and collectively, leading to high volatility in financial markets.

Moreover, compared to other sectors of the economy, financial markets are much more interdependent. This is witnessed by very tight interconnections in the interbank market. Events in one financial market or institution may then have important effects on the rest of the financial system. Failure in one market or institution may create a financial panic and end up in a systemic crisis. Due to ever increasing international capital mobility, it may become a worldwide financial crisis.

Banks specifically are faced with a two-sided asymmetric information problem. On the asset side, borrowers may fail on their repayment obligations. Depositors, however, cannot observe these credit risks. The quality of the loan portfolio is private information acquired while evaluating and monitoring borrowers. On the liabilities side, savers and depositors may withdraw their funds on short notice. Banks, however, cannot observe the true liquidity needs of depositors. This is private information.

A true liquidity risk arises when depositors collectively decide to withdraw more funds than the bank has immediately available. It will force the bank to liquidate relatively illiquid assets probably at a loss. A liquidity crisis may then endanger also the solvency of the bank and eventually lead to bankruptcy.

As Dewatripont and Tirole (1994) have observed, the providers of funds are not able to assess the value of the bank's underlying assets. As a result, bad news, whether true or false, may provoke a withdrawal of funds. Moreover, as deposits are repaid in full on a first come first serve basis until the liquid assets are exhausted, depositors have an incentive to act quickly. A 'bank run' may occur when enough savers lose confidence in the soundness of a bank. Moreover, bad news about one bank can snowball and have a contagion effect on other banks. A bank failure could eventually trigger a signal on the solvency of other banks. Even if these banks are financially healthy, the information about the quality of the loan portfolio underlying the deposits is private, so that depositors may also lose confidence and withdraw their funds. These domino-effects lead to a widespread loss of confidence in the banking system and create a 'financial panic'.

Financial market failures and instability eventually leading to a systemic crisis not only affect individual savers and depositors, but the health of the whole economy. Financial crises undermine the efficiency with which resources in the economy are allocated as e.g. companies have difficulty raising capital for investment and job creation. The collapse of financial institutions in general may have important costs of debt deflation on effective aggregate demand in the economy, as is extensively documented by Hubbard (1991).

Because of the importance of banks, it is particularly important to maintain the health of the banking industry. The severity of the Great Depression of the 1930s is often linked to the breakdown of the banking system's ability to provide financial services of risk sharing, liquidity and most importantly of information by providing expertise in project screening and corporate governance. Disturbances in the banking sector have especially severe consequences in developing and transition economies where capital markets are underdeveloped and hence no alternative financing is available. Episodes of financial fragility also hurt the ability of less well-known borrowers to obtain loans i.e. in particular the smaller firms who have no access to capital market financing. Moreover, banks play an essential role in the payments system and in the creation of money. As argued by Mishkin (1997) bank failures could cause large and uncontrollable fluctuations in the quantity of money in circulation and impair sound monetary and exchange rate policies. In the 1980s the US interest rates were reduced, partly to aid the banking system in trouble. It provoked a deep fall in the dollar exchange rate, leading to instability in foreign exchange rates world-wide.

On the fiscal side, substantial amounts of public money have been spent on rescuing ailing banks. In the US the cost of the Savings and Loan industry bail-out is estimated at 130 billion dollars, i.e. 2.4 percent of GDP. The costs for the French government to cover credit losses of only one of its banks, i.e. Credit Lyonnais de France, may well run over 10 billion dollars. Sweden recently spent 4 percent of its GDP on bank support and the Czech Republic even 12 percent.

The case for government intervention then necessarily has to rely upon governance failures. Internal governance of risk taking by banks may fail because of conflicts of interests of owners, bad credit decisions and poor internal oversight by management. Contrary to popular belief due to well publicised cases, it is not necessarily the off-balance sheet activities that are the main danger for instability. Derivatives related losses world-wide amount to some 15 billion dollars, whereas Credit Lyonnais alone suffered losses of 10 billion dollars in ordinary credit activities (Lindgren, Garcia and Saal, 1996).

It appears that well-developed financial markets are usually capable of providing the necessary external governance by market discipline. Financial analysts and Rating Agencies play an important role in this context. In the case of banks, however, external governance by markets may fail due to free-rider problems in the collection of information by small depositors and savers. It follows that the need for government regulation remains essentially of a complementary nature, i.e. to complement internal governance and market discipline.

4. Choice of Regulatory Instruments

The question then arises as to what is good and bad government policy from an economic point of view. Are protective policies in the form of the lender of last resort intervention and deposit insurance provisions not sufficient, or are more extensive regulatory policies and supervision required? What is to be preferred, structural measures limiting unbridled competition or prudential measures and supervision of risk taking?

4.1. *Protective policies*

Central banks can significantly limit the occurrence of systemic crises by their role as a *'Lender of Last Resort'*. Central banks have been set up to control liquidity provision in the economy. They are the ultimate source of credit to which financial institutions can turn during a panic. By providing liquidity as a bankers' bank they can stop the contagious transmission of financial problems among financial intermediaries.

There are, however, several difficulties with the lender of last resort function. First, interventions must be carried out swiftly in a credible way. Credit should only be advanced to solvent financial intermediaries using the good, but illiquid, assets as collateral. They should not be used to bail out insolvent institutions, often at a high cost for taxpayers. Still, it may not be easy in practice to distinguish between problems of liquidity and insolvency.

Second, such policies should not normally focus on individual institutions, but rather on the financial system as a whole. Due to the 'too-big-to-fail' philosophy, the potential systemic dangers of the failure of large intermediaries are often overrated. However, following the IMF study by Lindgren, Garcia and Saal (1996) this philosophy is widely applied. Recently, the Japanese authorities rescued 21 major commercial banks from bankruptcy. In the US, the authorities often resort to merging banks in trouble rather than closing them. The extensive state aid for Credit Lyonnais in France is the exemplar case. The difficult challenge facing the authorities is to ensure that financial intermediaries fail with minimal systemic impact.

Finally, lender of last resort interventions may conflict with monetary policy objectives. In order to avoid a systemic crisis, central banks may extend liquidity and fuel inflationary pressures. Inflation may structurally weaken the financial sector and its capacity to absorb shocks, thereby increasing the probability of a systemic crisis.

In addition, public authorities also intervene by guaranteeing some financial liabilities and by directly protecting investors through 'Deposit Insurance'. Insurance arrangements contain the promise that if a financial institution fails, the investors will be reimbursed for the funds lost. They directly aim at individual investors protection, in particular the small depositors who are unable to determine the quality of the bank's assets. Indirectly they also reduce the threat of a systemic crisis. This is achieved not by bailing out individual financial institutions, but by reducing incentives for bank runs by depositors and by containing the risk of contagion among financial institutions.

Deposit insurance was already introduced in the 1930s in the US in order to stabilise the financial system in the aftermath of the Great Depression. Other countries have since followed, legislating a variety of deposit insurance schemes. Deposit insurance systems differ according to their public or private organisation, compulsory or voluntary participation, fee structure, degree of coverage, funding provisions, etc.

The question arises whether government intervention may not be limited to these protective policies. Why do public authorities resort to more extensive public regulation of the financial system? According to Herring and Litan (1995), further government regulation has to be explained by the potential high costs and moral hazard problems that these protective policies may entail. Certain episodes such as the Savings and Loan Crisis in the last decade in the US teach that moral hazard remains a difficult regulatory concern. Thrift institutions used to finance their long-term mortgage loans by short-term saving deposits. When interest rates boomed in beginning of the 1980s due to very restrictive monetary policies, their short-term funding became too expensive compared to the outstanding low interest rate loans. Lacking an appropriate asset and liability management, they had neglected to cover themselves against these interest rate risks. Many of them sought relief in investing in high-yield, but very risky, junk bonds. When the junk bond market collapsed, more than a thousand Saving and Loan associations had to be closed and others were rescued at very high costs for tax payers.

The extent of these crises may be explained by the existence of safety nets provided by the government. It tempts financial institutions to pursue high risk investment strategies at the expense of the government. Also, when they are covered by deposit insurance, depositors have less incentive to monitor and discipline financial intermediaries. Hence, government safety nets help solve risk problems only by creating other problems. Further government regulation may be in order to counteract these moral hazard effects.

4.2. *Structural regulation*

In order to limit the threat of systemic risks, government intervention in the financial sector traditionally consisted in regulatory measures aimed at limiting competition and at restricting the operation of market forces. Unbridled competition was seen as a major threat to the stability of the financial sector. As listed in Table 1, structural regulation mainly involves restrictions on entry and on business activities, and often includes various measures of interest rate regulation.

It was mainly in the aftermath of the Great Depression, that it was deemed necessary to introduce structural *restrictions* on the scope of *permissible activities* of the different financial institutions. Before the crisis, commercial banks acted as securities market financial institutions as well as depository institutions. They had an incentive to take on more risky activities in financial markets and earn investment banking fees, the risk being shifted in part to the depositors. In order to limit these risky activities and to reduce the risk of contagion within the financial system, these activities became legally separated in many countries. Besides bank investments in industrial firms, their real estate investments and insurance activities often became regulated as well. Not seldom, the ownership of financial institutions and non-financial firms was also separated, and the investments of industrial firms in banks limited. Also *branching restrictions* could be imposed. This was already the case in the US before the Great Depression. Banks were geographically limited and were not allowed to open branches in other states nor to engage in interstate banking.

Since the 1970s the debate over retaining these restrictions has been reopened and limits have faded significantly. It was observed that some countries such as Germany had maintained a system of universal banking, in which banks were allowed to participate heavily in non-financial activities. Did this so-called bank intermediation model not present certain advantages for the economy as the strong economic performances of Germany would indicate? Giving a role to commercial banks in corporate finance may improve information gathering and the monitoring of loans, thereby reducing problems of adverse selection and moral hazard in core banking.

As a result of this recent debate, in its Second Banking Directive of 1989 the European Community adopted the universal bank model extending the scope of activities for financial intermediaries. Also the combination of banking and insurance within the same financial institution is being permitted, mainly in European countries after removing some legal obstacles. The increased affiliation with conglomerates, however, remains a controversial issue. It may stretch the safety net meant only for bank depositors to protect other financial and commercial operations, and induces more risky behaviour. Also the risk of contagion increases as shocks may spread more easily within financial institutions. Finally, domestic branching restrictions may limit the concentration of power and lower the costs of financial services. They, however, increase the exposure of banks to credit risk by reducing their ability to diversify assets. In the meantime, banks have spread world-wide so that it becomes increasingly difficult to maintain these restrictions. The European Community in its banking directives has resolutely opened up the opportunities for European-wide banking through the single banking license. A bank that has been chartered in one member country may freely offer its financial services throughout the whole European Community.

Interest rates are important instruments of monetary policy. Hence, governments traditionally have intervened in the price formation in money and capital markets by regulating interest rates. *Interest rate ceilings* and other pricing rules, however, were also introduced to limit competition between banks and between banks and other financial institutions. Limiting price competition in financial markets would also reduce risk taking and moral hazard problems for financial institutions. Imposing interest rate ceilings such as regulation Q until the 1970s in the US would then lower the cost of funds, enhance profits and reduce the likelihood of bank runs.

Recently, many of these anti-competitive regulatory measures have been removed. They converged benefits to private financial institutions by protecting them against outside competition. Regulators were not seldom captured by those being regulated through lobbying in order to protect their business interests at the expense of the consumer. It was also observed that such regulation did not contribute to financial stability in the long run. It resulted in disintermediation as funds could be more profitably directly invested in and obtained from financial markets. Moreover, many financial innovations were introduced to circumvent these restrictive regulations. In the trade-off between safety, stability and efficiency the present regulatory environment gives more weight to competition and efficiency. Instead of structurally limiting competition and the operation of market forces, regulation is taking more and more the form of prudential measures which may better serve the interest of the customers.

4.3. *Prudential regulation*

Prudential control is exercised first at the market entry stage by *'chartering'*, i.e. the obligation to file an application for a charter. To obtain a license the owners have to supply sufficient equity capital. A minimum of capital is required as a cushion against losses. The chartering of new financial institutions is also subject to a screening of the proposed managers to prevent undesirable people from controlling them. An adverse selection problem arises as financial activities may attract entrepreneurs wishing to engage in speculative activities.

A central instrument of prudential control consists in *capital adequacy* rules. Equity capital provides the necessary cushion against losses, since shareholders may want to increase their activities and the credit risks involved through greater leverage. Capital owners can then improve their return on equity by providing as little capital as necessary. Only in well-capitalised institutions, however, do the shareholders have enough incentive to monitor their financial health. When financial institutions hold a large amount of equity capital, they have more to lose in case of failure, meaning that they will pursue less risky activities.

Capital requirements may take different forms. The current 8 percent risk-asset ratio, i.e. Cooke ratio, imposed by the Basel Committee in 1986 requires banks to hold eight percent in capital against their loan portfolio. The loans are differently weighted according to the credit risks involved. Since 1995 the Basel Committee also recommended that banks hold additional capital to cover market risks, such as foreign exchange exposure, interest rate risk, trading risk, off-balance sheet risks etc. These recommendations have been enacted recently by the European Community in the Capital Adequacy Directives.

As is argued by Herring and Litan (1995, pp. 55-58) sound capital standards are important to offset the moral hazard created by government safety nets for depositors and other creditors. If capital regulation were perfect, no other regulatory interventions would be needed against the danger of moral hazard. Financial intermediaries could then be shut down and creditors reimbursed just before insolvency of the intermediary. In practice, however, regulators face delays in taking appropriate action. Moreover, the measuring of risk and the valuation of assets and capital proves to be difficult. Hence, other regulatory tools are necessary to backstop capital regulation.

Besides structural interventions whereby financial institutions are not allowed to engage in certain activities, such as investments in common stocks by banks, the imposition of quantitative limits on certain asset holdings has more the character of prudential regulation. By 'portfolio diversification rules', such as limiting the amount of loans in particular categories or to individual borrowers, the risk profile of banks can be reduced.

Cash reserve requirements are often imposed as a measure to enhance liquidity adequacy. By providing the necessary liquidity for deposit withdrawals they increase confidence with depositors and reduce the threat of bank runs. In situations of collective withdrawals of deposits, however, they have turned out to be largely insufficient for avoiding a bank panic. Nowadays changes in required reserves have developed to an instrument that is used primarily for controlling the quantity of money and credit creation.

Recent prudential measures foster enhanced *'public disclosure'* of bank financial information in order to reinforce market discipline. Generally, providing appropriate and timely disclosure of financial conditions of companies may help to reduce stock price volatility and excessive speculation. In particular, disclosure of financial conditions of financial institutions not only increases the ability but also gives incentives to investors to monitor the performance and the risk-profile of financial intermediaries.

Recently the Basel Committee issued recommendations regarding the public disclosure of trading and derivatives activities of financial intermediaries. In this respect the standardisation of accounting practices and the obligation of accounting risky assets and derivatives at market value, the so-called mark-to-market practice, are extremely important. Also, by discouraging shareholders and managers from excessive risk taking, public disclosure reduces the threat of systemic crises.

For regulatory measures to have the desired effects, they must of course be enforced. Supervision in this respect is important to reinforce internal governance as well as market discipline. By regular examination and inspection regulators limit moral hazard problems. To this end supervisory structures with independent authorities are set up. Bank examiners also pay periodic on-site visits to the financial intermediaries.

According to the IMF study (1996) regulation and supervision, however, cannot prevent banking problems from occurring. Since markets will not always respond quickly enough to incipient insolvency, bank failures will continue to occur. Therefore the supervision should focus on preventing individual bank failures from becoming a systemic crisis. In fact, the closure of individual banks without systemic repercussions is the best evidence that supervision is indeed functioning.

5. Regulatory Challenges Ahead

Markets are powerful co-ordination mechanisms, yet they do not operate perfectly and cannot do so. Financial markets in particular are seen as imperfect by definition, characterised by asymmetric

information, agency problems and moral hazard. Government intervention, however, does not necessarily provide better co-ordination
and therefore need not replace market mechanisms. In fact, a deli-
cate balance has to be struck between the discipline of the market
and co-ordination by government actions. Moreover, the dynamic
evolution of the financial system constantly presents new challenges
to the regulatory debate. Changing patterns in financial intermediation create the need to adapt regulatory structures. In this evo-
lutionary process there are no definite nor universal recipes to be
found and the balance between market and government may shift
over time.

The need for government intervention as well as the choice of
regulatory instruments depend on the occurrence of systemic crises.
The occurrence of systemic risk may differ among financial intermediaries, implying divergent regulatory needs.

In this respect, the activities of the different financial intermediaries have to be compared according to three criteria: first, the
risks involved that may lead to their failure; second, the interconnections among intermediaries determining the contagion effect;
and finally, their importance for the whole system and the real
economy.

On these counts deposit taking, which is the core of banking, is
found to be especially vulnerable to systemic risk as explained above.
Other financial intermediaries such as investment firms and insurance companies are less subject to liquidity risks; they are generally
less interconnected and are not involved in payments and liquidity
functions. When they fail, the consequences are less dramatic for the
whole financial system and the real economy.

Hence, regulatory requirements are different and accordingly a
system of *institutional regulation* and supervision has developed.
Banks, securities firms, insurance companies are being regulated and
supervised by different regulatory bodies. But institutional regulation becomes difficult to implement when the different financial
intermediaries widen the scope of their activities e.g. when universal
banks engage in securities activities. Maintaining institutional regulation and subjecting universal banks to stricter capital requirements
or providing a safety net also for their securities activities, conflicts
with competitive neutrality of regulation (Heremans, 1993).

Similar issues arise for financial conglomerates. The widely publicised bankruptcies of the Bank of Credit and Commerce International

(BCCI) and the Meridien Bank in the 1990s illustrate the difficulties of controlling financial conglomerates. It proved to be difficult to detect weaknesses in their solvency before they had to close down. This was due to the failure to consolidate the different activities within these conglomerates with off-balance sheet operations, off-shore and foreign subsidiaries. To maintain a level playing field among financial intermediaries together with regulatory efficiency, systems of *functional regulation* are being envisaged. Instead of one regulator controlling all operations, the different activities of financial intermediaries will be subject to distinct regulatory measures and specialised supervisors.

As regulatory structures become more complex, the importance of internal governance and the role of market discipline may increase. The rising tide for market solutions implies an increasing role for self-regulation and private regulatory bodies. Self-regulation will arise when clubs can be formed. Clubs are professional organisations which regulate the behaviour of members. Self-regulation has the advantage of flexibility, but eventually the danger of manipulation by members. In addition, outside private institutions, such as rating agencies, may discipline risk behaviour as the rating of an intermediary affects its funding costs. In the same vein, more flexible regulation is being advocated by Dewatripont and Tirole (1994). The supervisors should not impose rigid regulatory schemes to all intermediaries, but introduce a number of options from which financial institutions should be allowed to make a selection. In this respect, the recent Capital Adequacy Directive explicitly permits that banks develop their own internal risk management systems as an alternative. The role of the authorities then is limited to supervising these private regulatory systems.

Finally, the major challenge, which goes beyond the scope of this contribution, is to find solutions for the increasing difficulties of international governance by national authorities (Van Cayseele and Heremans, 1991). It raises questions as to the best approach to the international co-ordination of regulation and supervision. It may be observed that the difficulties to agree on the international dimension of financial regulation and supervision are enhancing the overall-trend towards greater emphasis on discipline by the market rather than by regulators. One may question however, whether market discipline is sufficient to avoid international financial crises, as recent events in Asia tend to point out. Moreover, once international financial problems are developing the issue becomes of who should take responsibility, and more specifically whether there is a need for an international lender of last resort to tackle an international systemic crisis.

References

DEWATRIPONT, M. and J. TIROLE (1993), *The Prudential Regulation of Banks.* Cambridge (MA)-London, M.I.T. Press, 1993.

HEREMANS, D. and K. TAVERNIER (1980), 'De evolutie van de monetaire denkbeelden in België 1914-1940' in *Cahier Bank- en Financiewezen*, 8-9 September 1980.

HEREMANS, D. (1973), 'Economic Aspects of the Second Banking Directive and of the Proposal for a Directive on Investment Services in the Securities Field' in J. STUYCK (ed.), *Financial and Monetary Integration in the European Community Legal, Institutional and Economic Aspects.* Deventer, Kluwer, pp. 37-55.

HERRING, R.J. and R.E. LITAN (1995), *Financial Regulation in the Global Economy.* Washington (DC), The Brookings Institution.

HUBBARD, R.G. (1991), *Financial Markets and Financial Crises.* Chicago, University of Chicago Press.

HUBBARD, R.G. (1997), *Money in the Financial System and the Economy.* Reading (MA), Addison Wesley Longman, 2nd ed.

LINDGREN, C.J., G. GARCIA and M.I. SAAL (1996), *Bank Soundness and Macroeconomic Policy.* Washington (DC), International Monetary Fund.

MISHKIN, F. (1997), *The Economics of Money, Banking and Financial Markets.* Reading (MA), Addison Wesley Inc., 5th ed.

SCHOKKAERT, E. (1998), 'Ethical Concerns about the Integration of European Financial Markets' in *Tijdschrift voor Economie en Management*, 3(1998).

VAN CAYSEELE, P. and D. HEREMANS (1991), 'Legal Principles of Financial Market Integration in 1992: An Economic Analysis' in *International Review of Law and Economics*, 11(1991)May, pp. 83-100.

ETHICAL RESPONSIBILITIES
IN CENTRAL BANKING

Jef Van Gerwen

Ethical reflection on the role of central banking involves a vast and complex domain of financial and policy issues, relating to all aspects of society, both at the national and international levels. In order to reach some systematic overview of ethically relevant topics, we will examine central banking from three perspectives:

(i) First of all, we will bring to light the underlying values and moral standards of central banking relating to the normal task description of a central bank. The statutes of the European Central Bank will serve as a concrete reference in this respect.

(ii) Secondly, we will examine some typical moral dilemmas or quandaries that are inherent in the decision-making process of central bankers: issues of moral hazard and moral suasion will be discussed here, as well as issues of disclosure and asymmetry of information.

(iii) Thirdly, we will have to reflect on the necessary institutional requirements for a just international financial order. Do we need one global central bank? What kind of global co-operation between central banks would be in the long-term general interest? To what extent do the existing institutions (IMF, BIS) move in the right direction?

1. Ethical Presuppositions of Central Banking

According to a classic Aristotelian conception of ethics, the moral goodness of an activity (practice) can be conceived in analogy to the adequate functioning of a technique: in both cases one asks what is the quality of the end(s) the activity is supposed to realise, and how effective and efficient it is in doing so. Accordingly, we will begin our moral inquiry by asking ourselves what the ends, or objectives, of central banking activities are, and by what means they should be realised.

1.1. *The primary objective: stability*

Stability, in itself, is a multi-dimensional objective. It refers both to the stability of prices within a given financial system, or the absence of inflation (also called 'monetary stability': Crockett, 1996, p. 532), and to the overall stability of the system itself, including the smooth functioning of financial markets and institutions (i.e. 'financial stability', or 'systemic stability'). Central banks have a crucial role to play in the realisation of both types of stability (Lamfalussy, 1994).

1.1.1. Most contemporary commentators will agree that the fight against inflation, and the guaranteeing of stable prices, forms the overriding objective of the central bank's activities. This has not always been the case, as can be discovered when looking at the other objectives of central bank policy (see 1.3.) and at earlier periods of history (before the 1980s), when Keynesian policies justified an important amount of deficit spending by governments and various trade-off's between inflation and other policy objectives, such as a lower level of unemployment or a higher rate of growth. But at least since the fight against inflation has been waged and won in the 1980s, the consensus (including Paul Volcker and Alan Greenspan of the U.S. Federal Reserve, the directors of the Bundesbank, and the statutes of the European Central Bank) is outspoken enough in this respect.

By "price stability" one means the long-term stability of internal prices within a particular country or market (rather than the external stability of prices for export and import). This interpretation is the one prevailing, e.g. in the orientations for the European Central Bank. Practically speaking, most analysts agree that a target rate of acceptable inflation needs to be publicly set by the Central Bank (around 2% a year) as a beacon for policy-making (Fischer, 1994, p. 284). Of course, the price of a currency itself, as indicated through the exchange rate, is a valuable component of price stability as well. But, in the present international situation of floating exchange rates, internal anchors of stability (including inflation targets, stable and low interest rates) are regarded as more reliable indicators of monetary stability than external ones (BIS, 1998, p. 147).

1.1.2. By "systemic stability" one refers to the micro- and macro-prudential functions of central banks with a view of safeguarding the smooth functioning of financial markets and institutions, avoiding systemic risk or breakdown. The micro-prudential function includes supervision and regulatory control of specific financial institutions acting within the national territory over which the central bank carries its responsibility. This function is often delegated, or executed in co-ordination with specific controlling bodies (banking commission, securities and exchange commission, insurance commission). The macro-prudential function of guaranteeing the functioning of the financial system as a whole constitutes a specific core responsibility of the central banks: central banks have to oversee, e.g., the swift and correct functioning of payment and settlement systems. Because of the globalisation of financial markets, this responsibility has to be met through the joint action of central banks, rather than by individual initiatives.

1.1.3. The distinction between price and systemic stability cannot be drawn so neatly in the daily practice of central banking. First of all, price stability within a country may depend heavily on imports and exports, and on exchange rates which are defined abroad by international financial markets. Secondly, price stability may not only include the prices of goods and services (as is reflected by standard approaches) within a single country, but also the prices of financial assets, such as shares and real estate (as is increasingly argued), whose value is much more determined by international fluctuations. As the latter are growing much faster than the former ones, this divergence between the relative values of goods and financial assets becomes a source of instability in itself (*The Economist*, Oct. 4, 1997, p. 89). Central banks may have to intervene in financial markets in order to prevent the development of financial bubbles on stock markets. But it is not clear how they can do so effectively without causing deflation on product markets, and without possibly causing a crash on financial markets. The use of a single tool (namely, raising short-term interest rates) is certainly inappropriate for reaching all these objectives simultaneously. So, here we meet a first fundamental moral dilemma in the world of central banking: for the public good, how should one optimally balance the different dimensions of stability with the limited instruments at one's disposal?

1.2. *The primary moral requirements: independence and accountability*

1.2.1. If price stability is accepted as the primary goal of central banking policies, then independence from external interference by financial institutions as well as governments becomes a major moral requirement. Independence can be understood as a personal virtue (see part 2.2.) as well as an institutional quality. Here we discuss only the latter dimension. Institutional independence of the central bank is enhanced by three types of guarantees:
— constitutional: The central bank is defined as an autonomous institution with regard to the Parliament, the Government, and the private sector of finance.
— political: the selection process of central bank directors and of the president is made independent of government control. Specific policy objectives of the central bank can be decided freely by the directors, as long as they remain within the framework of general objectives as defined by law (e.g. Federal Reserve Act for the U.S., Maastricht Treaty in the case of the European Union).
— functional: The central bank is financially autonomous from government. It possesses its own sources of income, and makes autonomous use of its specific policy instruments (e.g. discount rate, interest rate changes). It should not provide credit or cash advances to the Government (as in Belgium, Germany, Italy, Spain).

In present central bank statutes and policy statements, it is first of all independence from government interference which is being stressed and protected. One should add, of course, that any form of dependence on private interests, such as interference of banks, of non-banking financial institutions, or of private corporations, should equally be avoided. Central bankers have to remain impartial, in order to serve the general interest of their country, and specifically to protect the stability of its currency and prices. Of course, important conflicts of interest may still emerge in a situation where the national interest of a country seems to clash with the global interest of the financial system, or where interpretations of the common good differ widely among actors. How independent is a central banker from national interests, or how does he/she balance the service of national and global interests? We will return to this issue in parts 2 and 4, but there seems to be no easy answer.

1.2.2. This moral condition of independence should only be balanced by the requirement of adequate democratic accountability. The central bank has to report the actual results of its policies to the public and to the Parliament on a regular basis: weekly statements of its financial operations, and quarterly reports should be widely accessible, if possible free of charge. Members of Parliament have a special right to audit and question central bank activities, and should receive swift and adequate information. Central bank representatives should be able to demonstrate how their specific policies meet the general objectives which the law has defined in the fields of monetary and economic policy.

The relationship to the Government remains a tricky issue. In the German Bundesbank, for example, Government representatives are allowed to assist at central bank directors meetings, and have a right to suspend the decisions for a "cooling off" period of two weeks, if they estimate that central policies run against government objectives. (To my knowledge, this possibility of suspension has never been used by a German government up to date, but its sheer existence implies a certain amount of leverage).

Because the central bank may need to act swiftly in times of financial crisis, and because Government Ministers may be supposed to succumb more easily to short-term objectives or partial interests, it seems wise to limit relationships with government to close consultation and continuous information, avoiding any interference on the actual decision-making process.

On the other hand, a central bank which lacks sufficient incentives of policy orientation, and of critical demands for accountability and transparency coming from public authorities, may equally fall short of its responsibilities: "The inherent danger of undefined political accountability was double-edged: it made the central bank more susceptible to falling captive to special interests; at the same time it gave greater leash to elected leaders to scapegoat central bankers to cover up their own undisciplined management of economic policies". (Solomon, 1995, p. 506)

1.2.3. With regard to the statutes of the European Central Bank (ECB), one may notice that its institutional independence is better protected by law than its democratic accountability. More could be done in this respect, precisely in order to correct the evil of "democratic deficit" that seems to hound the institutions of the European Union since their very beginning. This requirement of transparency towards the public presupposes that the governments of the Member States more explicitly indicate to the larger public that price stability is indeed the overriding objective of the ECB. This may be the consensus between insiders; but it has not been clearly communicated to the citizens. Secondly, the ECB cannot function well in a political vacuum. A reform of European institutions in the direction of a federal European government, granting effective controlling powers to the European Parliament in matters of fiscal and monetary policy, seems required in order to fill this vacuum. The present division of labour between the European Council and the Commission will not provide a sufficient framework to resolve this issue.

1.2.4. Finally, a fundamental question remains with regard to the accountability of central bankers acting as a team on the international scene. It is clearly in the general interest that central bankers be able to move swiftly and decisively in order to intervene in a co-ordinated way into the (mal-)functioning of international markets. But such concerted actions imply an increased accountability gap between procedures of national reporting to state authorities, on the one hand (each central bank to its own parliament, government) and the scale of international action, on the other hand (without an effective democratic counterpart: no world government, no global Parliament to represent the public and to evaluate the collective international action of central banks). To a certain extent, central bankers are increasingly functioning in an asymmetric situation, being sanctioned by global markets and by national state authorities. International bodies such as BIS and the IMF may to a certain extent fulfil the role of international public authorities, but they are not the agents of democratic control that will be the counterparts of central bankers for evaluating their international accountability. We will return to this point in part 4.

1.3. *Secondary objectives*

Central Banks may be required to pursue other final goals beside price and systemic stability.

1.3.1. In the case of the U.S Federal Reserve, this is the case for economic growth, full production and employment. As Section 2a of the Federal Reserve Act states, the goal of the Federal Reserve is "to maintain long run growth of the monetary and credit aggregates commensurate with the economy's long run potential to increase production, so as to promote effectively the goals of maximum employment, stable prices and moderate long term interest rates". These final goals are equally spelled out in the Full Employment and Balanced Growth Act of 1978.

1.3.2. In the case of the European Central Bank, one should refer to Art. 3a of the Treaty on the European Union, which defines the general objectives of European economic policy that the ECB is supposed to serve in all its activities:
— a harmonious and balanced development of economic activities
— sustainable and non-inflationary growth, respecting the environment
— economic convergence between Member States
— a high level of employment and of social protection
— the raising of the standard of living and quality of life
— social and economic cohesion
— solidarity between Member States.

All these objectives should be met in the context of an open market, with free competition between financial institutions of Member States, suppressing all sorts of government subsidy of financial institutions (Smits, 1997, p. 193).

1.3.3. As soon as more than one objective is being retained, one has to take into account the occurrence of conflicts between objectives, and of possible trade-offs or compromises. Some commentators have therefore criticised the fact that central banking would have to pursue a plurality of policy objectives, because this would lead to a softening of anti-inflationary policies, and add uncertainty into the markets' estimates of central bank interventions:

> "The Federal Reserve is constitutionally required to pursue both full employment and price stability. That singles it out as an oddball among central banks and makes its job harder, because these goals often conflict. Having two contradictory missions diminishes the Fed's effectiveness as an inflation-fighter. It creates uncertainty in

the markets and sometimes arouses suspicion that the Fed is taking a risk with inflation. Markets are therefore more likely to react badly to news of, say, unexpectedly strong growth. An explicit inflation target would help to strengthen the Fed's credentials and calm inflationary expectations". (*The Economist*, Oct. 7, 1995, reprinted in Farber & Schmit, 1996, p. 115)

One can, however, question the validity of this criticism on several grounds. First of all, under the present policy mix, the U.S. economy seems to succeed in combining low inflation with low unemployment rates. Obviously, the trade-off between inflation and employment is not always as conflicting or contradictory as the criticisms seem to suggest. Neither the present, nor the previous president of the U.S. Federal Reserve seem to consider their obligation toward employment as a major obstacle for their effectiveness in fighting inflation. They will rather mention other policy fields, such as the lack of fiscal policy, the state budget deficit, and too low a savings rate, as sources of concern in this respect (Volcker, 1990).

Secondly, we may suppose that the ECB will be bound to an even more balanced trade-off between the several objectives of the European Union, once it will be in full function. So the Federal Reserve will hardly remain "the oddball among central banks", as the above-mentioned critique has suggested.

Thirdly, one can also question the theoretical presupposition on which the critique rests: "A (second) misunderstanding is the belief that there is a long-term trade-off between inflation and unemployment, and that monetary policy can be used, at the cost of a little more inflation, to make countries grow faster and so reduce unemployment. Anybody who still clings to that belief might well conclude from the current high levels of unemployment that monetary policy is no longer effective in boosting jobs. But the truth is that it never was. A looser monetary policy can stimulate growth only for a short period. In the long term it will feed through into accelerating inflation. That is why many economists say that monetary policy must concentrate on price stability, because it provides the best environment for investment and growth". (*The Economist*, October 7, 1995, reprinted in Farber & Schmit, 1996, p. 101)

1.3.4. Recently, Stanley Fischer, echoing proposals of E. Roll on the Bank of England, has proposed a "charter of a modern central bank", which offers a fine summary of the different points we have been discussing so far (Fischer, 1994, pp. 301-302). This proposal contains the following list of objectives:

(i) The central bank should have a clearly defined mandate, which includes price stability.

(ii) The central bank should publicly announce its intermediate-term policy goals.

(iii) The central bank should be accountable, in two senses: it should be held responsible for meeting its announced goals; and it should be required to explain and justify its policies to the legislature and to the public.

(iv) The government should have the authority to override the Bank's decisions, but the override decision should carry a cost for the government.

(v) The central bank should be given the authority to set interest rates and other monetary policy variables in order to achieve its policy goals.

(vi) The central bank should not be required to finance the government deficit, and should not manage the public debt.

(vii) There cannot be a separate responsibility for setting interest rates and the exchange rate as long as the exchange rate floats.

1.4. *How central banks can reach their objectives*

1.4.1. The major functions of central banks
Without entering into a detailed technical analysis of central banks' daily conduct of operations, we need to gain insight into the major functions and instruments of central bankers before we are able to interpret the ethical aspects of their conduct. This issue cannot be approached in a uniform or static way, since specific functions may differ between institutions of different states, and evolve over time periods. As a first orientation, Nigel Dodd (1996, p. 181) offers a list of seven functions:

(i) issuing money: limited issues of notes and coins, adjusting to seasonal fluctuations in the demand for cash;

(ii) controlling the creation of credit: regulating liquidity through open market operations;

(iii) providing banking services to government: e.g. settling government debt through the private sector, issuing and redeeming Treasury Bills, issuing government stock as registrar of the national debt;

(iv) acting as an external agent to the government: holding and administering bullion and foreign currency reserves and engaging in co-ordinated action with other central banks and international financial institutions;

(v) providing banking services to other banks: holding cash balances of banks in respect of clearing house operations; holding reserve deposits of banks;

(vi) acting as the lender-of-last-resort to the banking system: intervening indirectly through discount houses (overnight balances) or directly with liquid reserves;

(vii) offering overall supervision of the financial system: providing informal guidance reinforcing government directives.

Aside from offering an overview of different functions, one can equally approach the issue from the angle of different types of instruments: regulatory instruments (reserve requirements, interest rate level, credit restrictions), standing offers (discount, refinancing, acceptance of deposits) and open market operations on the one hand (which can all be used in the domains of monetary policy and payments oversight), and banking supervision instruments on the other hand (Smits, 1997, pp. 223-231, 319-327)

In all these overviews, one can recognise the three major axes of classic central bank activities: as a provider of national currency, as an agent of government in matters of monetary policy, and as a provider of services to credit institutions on the financial markets. One could add numerous specifications to this list, since the precise institutional settings of central banks differ between countries, as well as the degree of inter-relatedness between public policy administrations (especially with the Treasury, the ministry of Finance, and the ministry of the Budget) and central bank officials (always maintaining a high degree of independence in principle).

The Annual Report of the Belgian National Bank, for example, mentions several activities which are situated outside the common core functions of the present European System of Central Banks, the forerunner of the ECB. Most of these extra-activities are related to government services, which the Belgian National Bank assumes: providing statistical data, the collection and control of data on corporate accounting and consumer credit. Others are more directly related to the functioning of international financial markets, such as the currency centre, the clearing system for transactions on the primary and secondary securities markets, and the inter-bank payment systems (NBB, 1997, p. 155). If one compares these data to the task list of the European Central Bank (Smits, 1997), one receives yet another picture. A detailed comparative study of differences between several central banks, however, would lead us far beyond the boundaries of the present study. We will limit ourselves, therefore, to the basic orientation provided by the above-mentioned list of functions.

Two more observations, however, should be made in this respect in order to offer a sufficient understanding of central bank functioning: one on the role of a central bank in the context of financial markets (1.4.2.), and another on the historical evolution of central banking (1.4.3.).

1.4.2. Why financial markets need a central bank

In the perception of the larger public, especially in the context of continental Europe, central banks tend to be largely reduced to their role as agents of the state, and (their independence notwithstanding) even as agents of government. It is important to highlight, therefore, the other side of reality, stressing the fact that they fulfil an indispensable role in financial markets as well (Goodhart, 1986). Contrary to some neo-classical monetary theories, the growth rate of the money supply cannot be automatically linked to the growth of the economy (so that economies could function without discretionary agencies in monetary policy, i.e. without a central bank). On the contrary, all free markets need some controlling agents in order to function well; and financial markets are no exception to this "rule".

According to Goodhart, the essential market functions of central banks, even in a fast-changing international context (cfr. 1.4.3.), are the ones of supervision and lender of last resort.

On the one hand, the central bank has to play the role of manager of the "club" of producers of financial services. Stability in the financial system is not only a matter of explicit rules and regulations; it also depends upon an informal culture of reputation and social control. The central bank is the best placed institution to carry out this discretionary job, both because of the inside information it is able to obtain on financial institutions, and because of the pressure it can exert on banks as a provider of essential services to them.

Secondly, the central bank has to provide financial support to defaulting banks in times of potential systemic crisis (lender of last resort). This support is not only justified by the general interest (the avoidance of a major systemic break-down), but also because financial markets are not able to correctly estimate the real value of bank assets. Bank assets, indeed, are often of a non-marketable nature (loans, overdrafts); no secondary markets exist to evaluate and adjust their price. Therefore, the true value of a bank's portfolio is often uncertain, so that market agents cannot evaluate the risk of supporting a bank in need of liquidity in times of financial crisis. The central bank may not be able to arrive at this information either, but at least it is officially entitled to intervene, following its prudential judgement on the seriousness of the case. We will return to the ethical issues surrounding the function of 'the lender of last resort' in part 3. Here we only affirm that such a function is essential for markets, and that a publicly owned central bank cannot be dispensed with, as long as one requires an impartial agent to intervene in the public interest.

1.4.3. The historical evolution of the role of central banks

A mere list of functions does not explain how central banks have had to fulfil their role in a swiftly changing context of reforms in monetary policies, globalisation of markets, and the introduction of new technologies and financial products. With regard to monetary policy, central banks have passed through three different stages since the second World War (Volcker, 1990):

(i) the Bretton Woods era (1944-1971)

(ii) the deregulation of financial markets after Bretton Woods (1972-1984)

(iii) the need for re-regulation because of the emergence of major crises in international financial markets (1985-)

(1) The Bretton Woods system proposed a gold-dollar exchange standard, wherein the dollar could serve as the main international means of payment. It was a system with fixed exchange rates, implying a

close co-operation between central banks, whereby the monetary policies of the U.S.A. necessarily functioned as the central anchor. The remaining reference to gold referred to the earlier era of the fixed gold standard (beginning of the 20th century); but in fact, the dollar served as a paper standard for international exchange, which would not be challenged, as long as the power and economic policies of the USA could not be called into question on the international scene. That situation ended during the 1960s, when the costs (political as well as economic) of the Vietnam war, creeping inflation and a growing amount of "off-shore dollars" led to the final breakdown of the system.

(2) The expansion of international capital markets and the invention of new technologies and products (i.e. derivatives) offered a strong incentive for the liberalisation of international financial markets. The post-Bretton Woods era was characterised by floating exchange rates, offering more autonomy to central banks in order to implement a national monetary policy. Nevertheless, the war on inflation made high interest rates necessary, which again severely limited the freedom of action on the national scene. Indeed, looser monetary policies could only stimulate growth, and create extra-jobs, for a short period before they ended up in accelerating inflation. And central banks could only effectively set short-term interest rates to steer the economy, as long-term interest rates are primarily defined by the bond market. Moreover, the freedom of action of central banks in a deregulated international environment was further weakened by the growing diversity of financial instruments and the diminishing role of banks. Central banks, however, still had some impact on financial markets by their monopoly on issuing currency and by their control on credit creation by banks (shifting the price of reserve deposits of banks). Because the national banks found out that the effect of their traditional tools of intervention was gradually weakening, the need for new forms of international co-operation and regulation was increasingly felt.

(3) The demand for re-regulation of markets was urgently introduced by the response to the debt crisis (first appearance: Mexico, 1982); during the subsequent period, more threats to the stability of international financial markets urged central bankers to intervene in a more co-ordinated fashion: the plummeting price of the Dollar (1985-1987), the U.S. stock market crash of October 1987, the subsequent

debt crises of several developing countries (1986), the Tokyo stock market crises (1990-1992), etc. Typical for this new era of re-regulation is the growing importance of co-ordinated international action among central banks, leading to some global rules and regular exchange of information and informal planning. This co-ordination effort is realised primarily through regular meetings of the central bankers in the so-called 'Group of 10' (G-10) at the Bank of International Settlements (BIS) at Basel, Switzerland.[1]

The G-10 provides the most important, but not the only, example of co-ordinated efforts of central bankers to correct the functioning of international markets. Other platforms are provided by the European Union, and by joint initiatives of central bankers with IOSCO (International Organisation of Securities Commissions) on derivatives and securities settlements.[2] Central bankers are also indirectly involved in other private and public co-ordination efforts (e.g. of the Group of 30, the International Monetary Fund and the World Bank). One also needs to look for platforms that include major economic powers outside the present membership of the G-10, such as the economies of the Asian mainland, and Latin-America. The G-10 remains a unique platform for international initiatives by central bankers, however, because it is, together with the BIS, the only international forum which is completely directed by them, rather than by governments or private financial institutions.

2. The Virtues of Central Bankers

2.1. *Independence and responsibility*

Do the persons who have accepted decision-making responsibility within the central bank have to demonstrate specific moral attitudes

---

[1] The Group of 10 was founded in 1962 to supplement IMF funding to bolster the Bretton Woods monetary system. It included Belgium, Canada, France, Italy, Japan, the Netherlands, Sweden, West-Germany, the United Kingdom and the United States. Later, new members were added, such as Luxembourg, Switzerland, Spain and Saudi Arabia. So the number of 10 no longer indicates the actual number of members. The Basel Committee on Banking Supervision is an important standing committee of the G10 central bankers, meant to follow up the supervision of the international banking system (since autumn 1974). The BIS functions as the central bank of central bankers. Most shares of the BIS are owned by 33 member central banks (= 84% of shares in 1987) (Solomon, 1995, pp. 111-12, 530).

[2] A selected (but rather complete) overview of joint central bank initiatives can be found in the 68th Annual report of BIS, Basel, 1998, pp. 148 and 150.

or virtues? The answer to this question is not so straightforwardly "yes" as one would expect. First of all, there are those who want to maximally reduce the discretionary power of central bankers, limiting their role to that of civil servants, acting within a tight framework of contractual obligations.

2.1.1. As Otmar Issing, member of the Board of the Bundesbank, remarks: "Technically speaking, the 'role' of the central bank is to be determined within the economic policy framework assigned to it and is to be defined by the legislature in the form of a specific central bank mandate. From this point of view the 'responsibilities' of the central bank are divested of their individual identity in this context, and are reduced to performing a technocratic function. This concept has often been refuted for not being a very realistic representation of reality, but it does reflect a widely held and fully understandable basic distrust in view of the fairly extensive discretionary powers of the persons concerned". (Issing, 1995, p. 23)

Here, we seem to enter into an example of the "Rules versus Discretion" debate. However, because the discretionary powers of central bankers are not put into question, but rather their trustworthiness, the effort to limit the freedom of action of central bankers stresses the point of their moral qualities even more strongly. Indeed, all earlier efforts to provide an all-encompassing regulatory framework for central banks, reducing their role to the one of an automatic executioner of pre-defined rules and objectives, have failed, as Issing himself is bound to confirm.[3] As long as the discretionary faculties of bankers are therefore required, their ethical qualities remain equally a relevant issue for reflection and debate. One cannot hide behind the image of the pure technocrat, in order to avoid the ethical question from the start.

2.1.2. There remain, however, other obstacles. Issing highlights a number of them at the end of his reflection on "The Role of the

---

[3] O. Issing mentions the rule-directed approaches of Eucken, Friedman and Simons in his contribution (Issing, 1995). See also the conclusions of Lamfalussy (1981) on this issue. The only argument Lamfalussy does not explicitly refute is the political pressure argument. Central bankers who are perceived to enjoy a lot of discretionary power are more open to political pressure both by politicians and non-elected citizens or special interest groups; but this seems to offer an opportunistic argument in favour of officially fixed objectives, rather than a general argument against discretionary freedom.

Central Bank": "...What criteria should one use to select the right people if ethical considerations are to be included, or, indeed given priority? Again, what is the situation regarding the relationship between individual morals and professional competence? Is it not possible that a trade-off problem might arise here, and, if so, how would it be settled? In the end, however, and above all, the ethics of central bank policy are always bound to relate to a social assessment. But how is the right attitude to be displayed here if not even the mandate involved is clearly formulated? Furthermore, it probably also makes little sense to seek to pass, say, a judgement on the existence of a Phillips trade-off and any possible consequent monetary policy decisions on the ethical plane". (Issing, 1995, p. 24)

These are many different questions, which offer a good illustration of the confusion surrounding the issue of ethics in many professional circles, and of banking in particular (though, I must add, some other insiders demonstrate a keen and well-informed awareness of the specific importance of moral qualities of central bankers, e.g. Volcker, Lamfalussy, Solomon). I will try to offer a brief response to each of them, thereby organising the material for ethical reflection in the subsequent parts of this contribution:

(i) Evidently, one has to distinguish between several levels of moral responsibility when discussing financial policy decisions. An important part of responsibility is defined through institutional channels of governments, corporate boards, international institutes etc.: this is the level of "systemic" justice or injustice, of fair distribution of accountability between corporate players, of a correct distribution of powers within a democratic constitution, etc. But aside from this collective and institutional level, the personal qualities and discretionary powers of the banker also matter. Therefore, it makes sense to direct some specific attention to the personal virtues (or vices) of the persons involved in central banking (see 2.2.).

(ii) As far as personal qualifications are concerned, there is indeed a difference between professional competence and moral qualities of a person. I do not see, however, why a trade-off between both should be accepted. Central Bankers and their staff should be evaluated on both criteria, and meet equally demanding standards of excellence on both counts. This is a necessary requirement, since the office of central banking can only function well as long as the decision-makers retain the confidence of the wider public. This public confidence is built precisely on a combination of competence and moral integrity, not on a trade-off between both.

(iii) The judgement on the existence of a Phillips trade-off (between inflation and unemployment) is not a moral issue but a matter of factual judgement. Economic analysis should inform us to which extent the trade-off is a real possibility, and what are the degrees of liberty for economic agents to move the balance in one or another direction. The policy decision, however, to select a particular mix of monetary, fiscal, and economic policies is not purely a matter of factual analysis, but involves ethical choices, private and public ones: how will I best serve the general interest by selecting one of the alternative policies that are presented as practical alternatives within the trade-off?

In the subsequent points, we will discuss the issue of moral qualities of central bankers, first of all at an individual level, and secondly as a group of insiders. Other issues of political ethics or external relations with financial institutions will be discussed in parts 3 and 4.

2.2. *The virtues of the "right person"*

It is significant that moral qualities of central bankers are discussed in the literature in terms of virtues, rather than rules or utility maximisation. Indeed, virtues are "acquired human qualities the possession and exercise of which tends to enable us to achieve those goods which are internal to practices" (MacIntyre, 1981, p. 178), and banking is a specific practice in the Aristotelian sense of the term. This means that it is not performed solely for the attainment of external rewards (profit), or for the avoidance of external sanctions (defined by legal rules), but that it possesses its own internal standards of excellence, which are oriented towards the service of the common good (or the general interest of society).

In the following overview, we do not distinguish between virtues that should characterise the private life of the person and those that rather qualify his/her professional life. The distinction is not relevant here, because central bankers are to be morally evaluated first of all from an angle of excellence in professional conduct (we are not interested in their private life as such), and secondly, because private vices are evaluated only as such when, and to the degree that, they intervene in the professional conduct of the person. But because central bankers are people to which the highest standards of integrity and trustworthiness apply, this cross-over influence of features of private life upon professional conduct is not unlikely. A person, e.g. who makes himself vulnerable to political pressure because of possible scandals or reprehensible behaviour in his/her private life, is not a person fit for the task of high public office. Here, the adage of "private vices, public virtues" does not apply.

Because they have a leading function both in the world of bankers and financial professionals, on the one hand, and in the world of public office and government, on the other hand, the ethical qualities of central bankers should reflect both the specific virtues of the banking profession and of high public office. With regard to the former, Argandona lists eight central qualities for bankers: professional competence, loyalty to customers, respect of confidentiality, justice, responsibility, prudence, respect for the law, and excellence. Other authors, such as Termes, Basanez & Cortes (all in Argandona, 1995), confirm some of these items, while adding a number of other ones: veracity, austerity, and magnificence. Volcker (1990, 1994) and Lamfalussy (1994), as insiders, put specific accents on the social virtues of central bankers as a group, because of the growing need of international co-operation.

Talking specifically about the virtues required in the practice of central banking, Paul Volcker has described his priorities in the following way:

> "The central bank is inherently and properly a conservative creature, in the sense of the 'cautious sceptic' (...). The lasting qualities – the philosophy if you will – that seem to me the hallmark of central banking are a triumvirate: Continuity, and all that implies for experience and nurturing a long view; Competence, and all that implies for a high degree of professionalism and careful deliberation and communication, and Integrity and all that implies for accountability and simple honesty. Now you may think that I am lost in misty abstractions, and my list is trite. But those are qualities, I would submit, that are regrettably in short supply in governments today. That, I would also suggest, is a main reason why central banks have attained their present prestige and influence whatever the particular institutional relationships". (Volcker e.a., 1994, p. 344)

I will not offer a full description and treatment of each of the above listed virtues, since this would take us too far afield. I simply want to draw attention to some crucial issues:

2.2.1. The moral meaning of professionalism

Otmar Issing was right, of course, to point out that "individual morals" is not identical with "professional competence", and that, evidently, central bankers should at least be eminently qualified in their professional knowledge and skills as bankers. But that is not the main point. As Volcker mentions, "those institutions [central banks] have been an important center for independent policy and professional training, sometimes reaching beyond their immediate operational responsibilities" (Volcker, 1991, p. 7). Professionalism, therefore, does not only include analytical excellence in financial and monetary economics, but also the moral virtues of independence, truthfulness and service to the long-term general interest, that go with it. We should not forget that in Aristotelian ethics, the moral virtues were intimately linked to intellectual virtues, such as excellence in theoretical insight (*"episteme"*), technical skill (*"techne"*) and good value judgement in particular circumstances (*"phronesis"* or prudence). In modern times this connection between intellectual and moral excellence has tended to be neglected, and as a consequence, the inherent moral qualities of scientific and professional practices have been underestimated, or been imposed from outside (through codes of law, or through economic sanctions). At this point, we are reminded of an ancient insight of practical wisdom, namely that important public functions, such as central banking, do presuppose a thorough training in the intellectual virtues.

2.2.2. The crucial role of prudence

Prudence is one of the classic intellectual virtues that is being mentioned by all authors as a central moral quality for bankers. As Aristotle emphasises, prudence includes the art of correctly applying general insights or rules to particular cases: "Prudence is not concerned with universals only; it must also take cognisance of particulars, because it is concerned with conduct, and conduct has its sphere in particular circumstances. (...) For example, suppose that someone knows that light flesh foods are digestible and wholesome, but does not know what kinds are light; he will be less likely to produce health than one who knows that chicken is wholesome" (Aristotle, Nicomachean Ethics, 1141 b8). Prudence is first of all, an intellectual virtue; it should not be reduced to its "moral" connotations of careful consideration, lack of haste, or conservatism. These qualifications are part of the picture, but do not offer the essence of it. The core of prudence is a typical intellectual quality, namely the art of right discernment of the appropriate action in a complex and ever unique context of limited data and uncertainty. It is the central quality for decision-makers, such as managers or judges. In the juridical context, prudence is most often translated by the virtue of equity (*epikeia*): as a judge must correctly apply the law to each particular case, at each time rightly measuring the degree of guilt and appropriate sanction, so should central bankers apply their qualities of discernment and respond with equal care and measure, avoiding all types of neglect or over-reaction. Prudence is an intellectual virtue, which means that it can only be taught in practice. Participants need the necessary theoretical and technical training to be able to interpret the evolving circumstances of financial markets and institutions, but they can only learn to become more prudent by learning from examples, i.e. how their predecessors and colleagues handle specific challenges as they occur. Prudence, therefore, builds on practical experience, but it also transcends it: it becomes evident only when experience is linked to moral integrity. Integrity is defined by the end of the one practising prudent action: the disinterested service of the general interest, rather than some privileged group or individual. This end defines the distinctly moral character of prudent action. The person reaches integrity by remaining loyal to the same end in all circumstances, while swiftly adapting his/her actions according to the different means at his/her disposal. Case 1 presents a further testimony of the importance of prudence already in the early stages of central banking.

CASE 1: ON PRUDENCE IN BANKING

Someone recently referred to the Federal Reserve's recommendations made to bankers in 1863. Nearly all of these recommendations are the reflection of the virtue of prudence or indicate the inadvisability of falling into the opposite vices (…):

1. Do not grant credit that is not guaranteed beyond all reasonable contingency.

2. Only facilitate those transactions which are legitimate and prudent.

3. Insist on all paper being paid for at maturity, whether you need the money or not.

4. Never renew an operation simply because you do not know where to place the money to obtain the same return if the payment is made.
5. Spread your credit instead of putting all into a few hands.
6. Large loans granted to a single firm or an individual, although they may on occasion be licit and necessary, are generally unwise and often unsafe.
7. Every dollar a Bank lends in excess of its capital and reserves, it owes, and its managers are thus under the strictest obligation toward its depositors and toward its shareholders to keep its discounts permanently under control.
8. Never give a discount if you have doubts about its advisability.
9. If you have reason to distrust a customer's integrity, close his account.
10. Aim for a banking business which is direct, honest and legitimate. Do not permit the prospect of large profits to tempt you to do anything that is not permitted.

(Source: Termes, 1995, p. 131)

2.2.3. The virtues of co-operation

In addition to such individual virtues, insiders, such as Volcker and Lamfalussy, clearly stress the social virtues of central bankers: mutual respect, collegiality, collective responsibility. By doing so, they might be referring to the classic role of central banks as club managers, i.e. of the club of bankers at the national level. This role is especially prevalent in countries where the function of banking supervision is not performed by a separate institution (i.e. by a Banking and Finance Commission), but directly executed by the central bank. We will come back to this issue in the next point.

But from the actual context of policy-making, it becomes evident that Volcker and Lamfalussy equally refer to the co-operation between central bankers on the international scene, as is the case in the context of the BIS and the Group of 10. The processes of globalisation, deregulation and growth of financial markets have had as a consequence that no single country, even not the U.S.A., can autonomously define and execute its monetary policy, or avoid threats of a worldwide crisis or system breakdown. Central bankers have therefore been obliged by the circumstances, at least since the 1980s, to co-operate more closely and effectively than ever before. This is not an easy task, since effective international institutions are lacking on the political and juridical levels, and powerful national interests may put substantial pressure on central bankers to move in opposite directions, rather than to defend a common position.

2.3. *The virtues of the club*

Even aside from the issue of co-operation, one has to take into account the morality of groups, and of institutionalised decision-making structures, in the realm of central banking. Modern ethics is always tempted to fall into the trap of methodological individual-ism, limiting the field of morals to the free and intentional actions of individual agents. Of course, individual qualities do matter in defin-ing the virtues and vices of central bankers. But the persons taking responsibility in such an institutional context rarely function as pure individuals. Rather, their training, selection and daily functioning processes are largely determined by a dense network of rules, cus-toms, habitual contacts and influences, that link them to their col-leagues, staff, government representatives and the banking world.

The group ethos manifests itself at least at two occasions: at the regular international meetings of central bankers, and in the contacts with bankers on the national level.

2.3.1. The trust factor at work

In his recent study on the functioning of central bankers, Steven Solomon stresses the importance of the monthly informal meetings of G-10 governors at the BIS headquarters at Basel. He quotes Alexandre Lamfalussy, then acting BIS general manager, saying: "Two full days each month, twenty working days a year, with four full meals, permits an exchange of an enormous amount of knowl-edge. Although voting and concrete decision-making was very rare, consensus somehow formed out of each central banker's explana-tion of the problems he was having and what he wanted to achieve. What occurred was some sort of monetary co-operation by intellec-tual osmosis. How these decisions get made no one really knows". Then Solomon adds: "Kindred professional and personal feelings flourished among central bankers, who often felt that only in Basel were they truly understood.(...) The Basel weekends were almost group therapy sessions that provided not only a quiet testing ground for new ideas and approaches, but also an early warning system when things were beginning to go wrong. More generally, the BIS weekends were what the French would call 'sérieux.' However much money was involved, no agreements were ever signed or understandings ever initialed. The word of each official was sufficient, and there were never any disappointments" (Solomon, 1995, p. 113).

I have quoted this excerpt out of Solomon's "The Confidence Game" at greater length, because it demonstrates an important sociological phenomenon which is relevant for market ethics in general, and financial ethics in particular. When economic systems evolve from a traditional to a modern stage of organisation, one would expect, in connection with economies of scale and new technologies, a new type of rationality to take the upper hand: more impersonal and formal contracts, more automatisation, more room for procedural reason instead of the lengthy processes of personal communication and motivation of substantial reason. As markets emerge, the communication systems of local communities and families disappear, and give way to mechanistic ways of impersonal exchange. This is the process of modernisation as has been described by the classic analysis of Emile Durkheim 'On the Social Division of Labour'.

By blindly following this hypothesis, many analysts fail to observe the persistent need for community-type ("pre-modern") networks in the larger world of impersonal markets. Professionals still seek confidentiality and long-term relationships between a limited number of trustworthy colleagues, in order to be able to share high quality information, without having to fear costly leaks or information abuses. This is called the "club" factor, especially in British literature, where clubs are a well-known feature of social life. The club phenomenon, however, largely transcends the confines of British society, and indicates the need for islands of informal and personal communication precisely in the spearhead sectors of modern economics.

Bankers in general, and central bankers in particular, are no exception to this sociological rule. One can easily understand, then, how a personal network including a limited group of central bankers, representing the most powerful national players on the financial scene, has become a handy platform for preparing effective international co-ordination of monetary policies and regulative efforts, and an important back-up system for gaining personal confidence at home. Indeed, a central banker who can rely on such an international network of colleagues, has acquired an important degree of additional leverage when confronting pressure groups and government representatives at the national level.

2.3.2. The Club Manager.

Goodhart (1986, pp. 12-13; 1988, pp. 57-75) has also offered an interesting analysis of the role of central bankers as managers of the bankers' club at the national level. First of all, he explains the necessity of bankers to form a club as a matter of necessity in view of the information costs that are inherent in dealing with financial institutions (see also 3.1.). Personal contacts with colleagues and a careful collection of inside information are essential assets for bankers for reducing the uncertainty of the markets, while avoiding, or relying too exclusively on, external regulation.

This general function of (soft) self-regulation by the sector is especially relevant for bankers because of two characteristics:

(i) The importance of a good reputation in banking transactions. Banks are extremely sensitive to rumors and popular fears about possible bank failures. Also a failure of one bank may have extensive negative effects on all the other ones, diminishing the general trust of the public. On the other hand, once established, a good reputation becomes a public good that has to be protected against free-riders. Bankers therefore have strong motives to prevent these occurrences by limiting access to the market of banking by forming a club, and by screening candidates to the club.

(ii) The difficulty for outsiders to accurately assess bank assets and risk management. "It is extremely difficult to distinguish between a relatively high rate of return that is offered because of greater efficiency, or one that is offered because the institution is also undertaking a much riskier strategy" (Goodhart, 1986, p. 12). Once the utility of a club of bankers has been accepted, the central bank may find it useful and desirable to enter into the system in order to be informed, and to use the club as a tool of supervision. Banks may welcome the managing role of the central bank in the club, because they prefer an independent and non-competitive body as manager, rather than facing continuous conflicts of interest, when one of the member bankers would be presiding and setting the rules.

One could also formulate some critiques against this club-approach as proposed by Goodhart. First of all, it could well reflect a way of

life which is rapidly fading, in view of the massive changes that
have occurred in financial markets during the 1990s. The relatively
cosy context of banking at the national level has given way to the
"big bang" of international trading, leading to a strongly reduced
role for classic banks, and to a reorganisation of financial institutions
along new lines (mutual funds, combination of insurance, commercial and investment banking, giving more impact to non-banking
institutions, institutional investors and large corporations on financial markets). This evolution leads to the "death of the banker", at
least in the classic form: the classic borders between the sectors of
securities, insurance and banking have faded; one does not see how
an inclusive world-wide club of financial institutions could function
in the future (Chernow, 1997).

Secondly, Goodhart may be representing a type of involvement of
central banking which is typically British, and has become a minority position in the present world of central banking itself. Indeed,
most countries will hold the view that the roles of central banking
and of banking supervision should not be intertwined, and that
supervision should be performed by a separate body (a Banking
Commission): such is the case in Germany, Austria, Belgium, the
Scandinavian countries, Canada, e.g.; it is also foreseen in the
statutes of the European Central Bank (Smits, 1997, pp. 323-326). The
reasons for the trend to separate both functions are of an institutional nature. On the one hand, supervision has to cover a wide area
of non-banking institutions, including securities firms and mutual
funds, so that a specific supervising institution seems appropriate;
on the other hand, governments want to increase their control over
the functioning of supervising institutions, since the tax-payers'
money is increasingly used in the insurance and rescue of financial
institutions. Therefore, if central banks wanted to safeguard their
independence, they had no choice but to cut direct institutional
links with the supervising agency (Goodhart & Schoenmakers, 1995,
pp. 555).

Goodhart's remarks remain valid, nevertheless, first of all, because
the basic need for correcting uncertainty on markets has not been
relieved, so that the demand for club formations of providers of
financial services is as urgent as ever before, albeit on an international scale. If non-banking corporations want to forego all kinds of
intermediation, intervening directly on the markets, they will face

insurmountable problems of transaction costs in managing the necessary information on assets, or run into unacceptable amounts of
uncovered risks (increasing the likelihood of herd behaviour and
speculative bubbles on financial markets). Of course, large institutional investors, such as mutual funds, insurance companies of
corporate pension funds, may attempt to fulfil these information
management functions themselves, also relying on ever greater transparency of market operations. This shift from personal banking
to transactional banking, and to disintermediation, is an important
evolution of which the outcomes are still uncertain (Chernow, 1997,
pp. 78ff).

Moreover, even if one accepts the validity of an institutional separation between banking supervision and the control of monetary
policy (the central bank being limited to the latter role), then one still
needs to grant the central bank some facility for collecting as much
inside information as possible on the world of banking. Relying
only on formal regulation (systemic responsibility, statistical reports,
accounting reports, daily settlement oversight) of markets, central
banks cannot function well; informal supervision (micro-prudential
responsibility), in some way or another, and in close co-ordination
with other supervising agencies, remains a necessary requirement
for the efficacy of central banking operations (Lamfalussy, 1994,
p. 338), even if the institutional roles tend to become separated. In
the case of the ECB, this issue is solved at the national level, where
national central banks (in contact with the Banking Commissions)
remain in charge of supervision, while the ECB retains its independence as the agent of monetary policy implementation. The exact
amount of European supervising co-ordination, however, still remains
a matter of debate (CEPS, 1998, pp. 22-30).

3. Moral Issues in Central Bank Functioning: an Exploration

The ethical requirements for the conduct of central bankers are best
approached by taking into account the triple perspective of financial
markets, the role of banking, and service to the public interest.
Central bankers can be considered to be the custodians of financial
markets and financial institutions on the one hand, intervening with
a mix of regulation, supervision and market operations when correction is needed; on the other hand, they are public functionaries

having to serve the public interest while keeping sufficient independence from governments, political parties and private interest groups. We will take a distinctive look at each of these perspectives, making an attempt to highlight the ethical issues that are involved in each of them; of course, all three aspects are closely linked in daily practice.

3.1. *Correcting the markets*

3.1.1. Why regulate at all?

As Basanez & Cortes remark when offering a "theoretical justification of regulation" (1995, pp. 39-41), regulation is always to be considered as a second best solution to (imperfect) markets. Whenever the conditions of perfect competition cannot be met in real markets, "a choice has to be made between the deficiencies of the unregulated market, and the alternative deficiencies of the regulated market" (1995, p. 40).

Market regulation may be justified in two kinds of situations, one having to do with inefficiency because of a failure of market mechanisms, the other with institutional failures. In practice, however, both sorts of failure often occur in conjunction (see table 1):

Table 1: Market and institutional failures, and types of central bank interventions

Market Failure:	Institutional Failure:
– Loss of contact with fundamentals – Volatility, short-termism – Olygarchy, collusion – Systemic risk, lack of liquidity	– Insufficient capital reserves – Asymmetric information (adverse selection, moral hazard)

Intervention:	Intervention:
– Timely settlement – Circuit breakers – Limits to leverae (margins) – Enhance stability of foreign exchange market	– Minimum capital standard – Deposit insurance – Disclosure requirements – Lender of last resort – Moral suasion, pressure

3.1.2. The role of macro-prudential oversight

Generally speaking, central banks want to guarantee, as much as possible, that nominal prices of financial assets do not deviate from their expected fundamental value. This goal is guaranteed much more by improving the quality and swift distribution of relevant information (= transparency of the markets), than by direct intervention on the markets. If speculative bubbles occur, they will try to avoid price corrections that are too sudden, attempting to provide "a soft landing" of the markets. In times of crisis, central banks will intervene directly on the markets, e.g. by adding liquidity to markets when "knock on" or "contagious" effects threaten to spread from one market into another, thereby pushing solvent institutions into a situation of a lack of liquidity. But even then, because of their (relatively) limited financial means, the effectiveness of interventions will depend more on indirect means of authority and the organisation of co-ordinated actions with a series of financial institutions, possibly including the IMF and other central banks. Central banks may also intervene on the foreign exchange markets in order to support a certain target value of a currency. This course of action may be defended on arguments of national or international interest, in search of greater stability. However, also this type of intervention requires substantial co-ordination and a sufficient back-up of credible economic, monetary and fiscal policies in order to be effective (See, e.g., Baillie & Posterberg, 1997, on the effectiveness of central bank interventions, and Solomon, 1995, pp. 477ff, on the EMS crisis of 1992).

3.1.3. In recent literature, a lot of attention has been given to the ethics of information, including rules of disclosure and dealing with asymmetric information (See, e.g. the contributions of G. Keating, B. Scott-Quinn and G. Pepper in Frowen & McHugh, *Financial Decision-making and Moral Responsibility*, 1995, Ch. 5, 6 and 7).

Asymmetric information is detrimental to the smooth functioning of financial markets. It occurs whenever contracting partners on the market do not make use of the same, sufficient and relevant, information in order to estimate the value of the assets they transact. (This should be distinguished from conflicts of interest, in which e.g. different branches of a same bank are dealing with sensitive information about competing businesses. This information should be blocked from being freely spread throughout the bank by the imposition of "Chinese Walls" or "firewalls" between the branches. Here we are treating information that should be available to all market agents). Asymmetry of information on a market increases uncertainty and transaction costs, because the probability that bad transactions will be made has grown. The role of banks as intermediary agents is precisely meant to diminish the occurrence of asymmetric information on financial markets by acting on behalf of their (less informed) clients. Equally, central banks' primary responsibility is to increase the symmetry of information on markets, both through direct disclosure of relevant information, and through supervision of the quality of information which is provided by financial institutions.

At the same time, a certain inequality of access to information and inequality of treatment are unavoidable in real markets; they may even have positive effects, since maximum disclosure of information on assets does not necessarily lead to optimal fairness of treatment.

In the context of securities markets, Brian Scott-Quinn and Gordon Pepper argue that one should distinguish between information on expected cash flows and the risk of those cash flows, on the one hand, and information on the short-run supply and demand patterns in the market. The first type of information should be made public as soon as possible, whereas full public disclosure of the second type would only result in greater intra-day volatility (Scott-Quinn, in Frowen & Mc Hugh, 1995, p. 91; Pepper, ibid., p. 107). Scott-Quinn equally argues in favour of unequal treatment of transaction orders according to size. 'Normal-market-sized' orders should get better prices than small or exceptionally big orders. The general idea is that dealer-driven markets, if executed in the long-term interest of customers, provide a fairer treatment for all involved than may be offered by more open, market-driven operations.

The arguments of Scott-Quinn and Pepper may have some validity; still, the process towards greater disintermediation and inter-connectedness of financial markets offers little support for the maintenance of separate rules for separate markets, some of them dealer-driven and rather closed, others market-driven and transparent. Central banks may have to opt, on the contrary, for strengthening the institutional backbone of all financial institutions operating on all markets, rather than providing "safe havens" in certain types of markets. The recent regulations regarding swift settlement of securities, foreign exchange and derivatives transactions, as well as those on large-value interbank transfer systems, represent significant initiatives of central banks to improve the correct functioning of markets, avoiding systemic risk (see BIS, 1998, p. 150: "Selected joint central bank initiatives: macro-prudential level")

Consequently, when acting as the custodians of the smooth functioning of markets, central bankers are always facing a basic tension or trade-off: On the one hand, in the name of equity and efficiency of markets, they have to fight favouritism and to stimulate greater transparency of financial transactions, thereby making the markets more impersonal (e.g. encouraging non-negotiable contracts on stock markets, more standardised options and futures on the exchange, less "over the counter" transactions, more internationally uniform standard procedures). On the other hand, they must equally pay attention to the specific historical and relational character of the concretely existing institutions and markets which are built on mutual confidence, inside information and particular customs. No general rule or law can replace the prudential judgement through which each central banker needs to find the optimal balance between transparency and institutionalised trust in each particular case.

3.2. *Correcting bankers*

3.2.1. Inter-mediation and confidence

Central bankers are first of all the "bankers of bankers". Their conduct should serve the purpose of enhancing the quality of the banking services within their territory. Consequently, central bankers have to build on the prevailing ethos of banking, trying to maintain its qualities and to correct its weak points.

Regarding the ethos of banking, one must begin from the recognition that the fundamental social function of banking is one of inter-mediation between savers and investors, or between credit and liability-owners. This service includes substantial transaction costs, as correct information on different savers and investors is hard to collect and to update. Banks, therefore, play an essential complementary role to markets in collecting and correcting this information. Moreover, banks are instrumental in spreading risk among different types of investors and savers, in changing maturities (long-term/short-term debt) and supplying liquidity.

It is essential that banks build up confidence through the provision of these services, so further reducing uncertainty among customers and markets. Confidence can only be obtained through a combination of technical and ethical skills that enhance the dependability, continuity and fairness of financial transactions. This core-function of banking implies two types of ethical qualities: a) enhancing trust and confidence in the relationships to customers through the presence of prudent and dependable judgement on the quality of loans and deposits; b) correct handling of confidential information on different customers and assets.

As financial markets are moving towards a process of disintermediation, involving a greater influence of non-banking actors, and direct access to market-driven transactions by institutional as well as private investors, the role of central banks is also shifting. On the one hand, central banks must continue to control classic banks, defending the interests of clients and small investors against possible breaches of confidence. The regulations regarding minimum capital adequacy standards (1988, 1996) and control of cross-border banking (1975, 1983, 1992, 1996) provide key instruments in this respect. On the other hand, they have to extend supervision to the non-banking sector as well. The 25 Core Principles of Banking Supervision (Basel Committee, 1997) provide a recent framework for such an undertaking: Banks should be licensed before they can act; they should meet appropriate minimum capital adequacy standards; they should have a comprehensive risk management process in place; they should know their customers, excluding criminal clients, and putting their clients' long-term interest as the first priority.

Aside from their responsibilities of regular supervision, central banks have been hailed in the past for their ability to intervene swiftly and efficiently in times of financial crisis, both as lenders of last resort, bailing out illiquid financial institutions in order to prevent the occurrence of systemic failure, and as leaders of financial rescue operations, co-ordinating policies to support failing debtors. While massive interventions may become less frequent in the future, because central banks are increasingly lacking the necessary means and leverage to intervene effectively on international markets (and governments, or international institutions may have to step in to fill this gap), any direct intervention of this kind raises a number of significant moral questions, which will remain relevant also in a changing institutional environment. A first one concerns the moral hazard problem connected to financial rescue operations (3.2.2), a second one regards the use (and abuse) of pressure in order to coerce individual institutional agents to accept a specific policy (3.2.3.).

3.2.2. Moral hazard linked with the lender-of-last-resort function

Moral hazard occurs on markets whenever participants receive an incentive, because of an intervention by some regulating authority, to act against the general interest of all participants on the market. As such, moral hazard is synonymous with taking unfair advantage of created opportunities. The lender of last resort function is a typical function of central banks, destined to restore confidence in financial markets in times of crisis. The central bank offers a public guarantee that it will step in and lend liquidity to illiquid agents in order to prevent a systemic breakdown of markets. In doing so, it intervenes in the free process of markets, preventing certain institutions from going bankrupt immediately. Even if such an action may be justified in view of the potential damage to the economy at large if the institution had failed, it creates several negative effects of inequity and inefficiency (= moral hazard):

(i) The risk of not only rescuing the illiquid, but the non-solvent banks. As Goodhart confirms: "In contrast to what Bagehot defended as the role of Central banks, lending should not only be provided to banks lacking liquidity, but also to insolvent banks, because a neat distinction between insolvency and illiquidity cannot be made in practice. Banks are not only in need of crisis support because of their liabilities, but also because the value of their assets is difficult to evaluate (uncertainty of asset value). Asset value directly relates to the solvency of banks. Therefore, the central bank has to formulate a prudential judgement for each case, depending on at least these two questions: What is the probability of systemic risk in case of immediate bank failure? What is the probability of the institution being supported ever recovering and paying off its debts?" (Goodhart, 1986, pp. 22-24).

(ii) Unequal treatment. Large operators have a better chance of being rescued than small ones, because the probability of systemic risk increases with the failure of a large market agent. (the "too big to fail" syndrome)

(iii) The future effect on management. Those likely to benefit from central bank support in the future tend to systematically underestimate future market risks, thereby undermining market discipline, as well as their own company's management quality.

Classic examples of moral hazard connected to the lender of last resort function have occurred in the United States during the 1980s, in connection with the rescue operations of the Continental Illinois Bank, and of Savings and Loan Associations (see cases below). In Europe, there are comparable cases (on Crédit Lyonnais, see *The Economist*, July 5, 1997, and May 23, 1998). The moral hazard problem is not, however, limited to emergency support for financial institutions. It may extend to the support of private underwriters of shares (as was the case in the British Petroleum privatisation scheme which became caught in the stock markets crisis of October 1987), or even to the massive support of countries unable to pay back their public debt (the crises of Third World debtors of 1982, 1986, and 1994) (see Solomon, 1995, pp. 96-102 (BP); 58, 526 (LDC debt)).

CASE 2: SAVINGS & LOANS ASSOCIATIONS

The S&L bail-out is an example of a financial rescue operation outside the banking sector. Savings and Loans companies formed a network of thrift industry in the U.S. which got into general difficulties at the beginning of the 1980s because, following a change in the regulatory environment, the cost of their variable rate funding had risen above the returns of their largely fixed-term assets (Crockett, p. 549). The U.S. Congress and Government responded to the crisis by offering an expansion of federal deposit guarantees and further deregulation. As a result of this public signal, moral hazard was created: S&L firms engaged in "kamikaze banking" (Volcker), pursuing high-risk lending in sectors where they lacked experience. By 1987, one fourth of the S&L firms had become insolvent, creating an estimated bail-out cost of between $40 and 50 billion.

On the weekend before the stock market crash of 19 October 1987 (= "Black Monday"), one of the firms, S&L Association of California, with assets of $25 billion, was planning to announce its default. This could have triggered a domino effect on the entire network, next to the imminent crisis in the stock markets. No buyer could be found for the failing firm. It was, however, saved temporarily by sharply falling interest rates on the afternoon of Black Monday. The bail-out could be postponed to 1989. Its total burden would come at a cost of $140 billion before interest payments to U.S. government finances (data of 1994). By the end of the 1980s, some 1.142 Savings & Loan Associations had gone bankrupt as a result of maturity mismatching and imprudent lending.

CASE 3: CONTINENTAL ILLINOIS

Continental Illinois (CI), a holding company including Continental Bank, offers a clear example of the "too big to fail" strategy. In the early 1980s, Continental Bank was the seventh largest bank in the U.S., holding $6 billion of the deposit base of 2.300 small banks all over the country. A failure of CI would certainly cause depression over the entire Midwest.

CI came into difficulties a first time in July 1982, when one of the small banks (Penn Square of Oklahoma) to which it had lent more than $1 billion, had become insolvent. A possible bail-out was discussed at that time by the supervising agencies (the Federal Reserve, the Federal Deposit Insurance Corporation and the Comptroller), but rejected for fear of moral hazard. Penn Square went bankrupt, and CI barely survived, having to write off a total $3,3 billion in bad loans ($1,1 billion of Penn Square, $1,2 billion other bad loans, and $1 billion exposure to Third World debtors).

On May 9, 1984 a rumor spread on the markets that CI itself was considering imminent bankruptcy. Because of the earlier event, financial observers took the rumor as a serious disclosure, which triggered a global electronic run on CI deposits.

On May 14, a first rescue operation was launched, when sixteen U.S. banks extended a $4,5 billion thirty day credit line to CI. "The credit line was facilitated by Volcker's comforting wink and nod that the Fed held $17 billion in assets from Continental as collateral to secure its discount window borrowing" (Solomon, 1995, p. 171).

On May 17, the president of the Fed organised a second capital infusion of $2 billion, and at the same time agreed that the FDIC extend the deposit guarantee to all Continental depositors and general creditors (Solomon, p. 535).

Not even this biggest bail-out in US history would help. On July 26, 1984 the US government (through FDIC) would buy out CI, offering $3,5 billion to pay down its Fed discount window borrowings, and $1 billion to acquire effective control of 80% of CI common stock. The bank was thereby effectively nationalised, and the losses "socialised" with tax payers' money.

One should notice that even here, the case of Continental Illinois did not end. In 1986 it acquired First Options of Chicago, a large derivatives firm. During the stock markets crisis of October 1987, First Options also got into trouble. CI had to lend $240 million to its daughter company in order to keep it afloat, whereas such amount of support was forbidden by the "firewall" limits imposed by the Comptroller in order to avoid spreading systemic risk. The Fed finally approved the controversial loan, thereby once more increasing moral hazard by including a non-bank securities firm in its safety net. (Solomon, pp. 76-78). This new problematic exposure by CI had been caused by a lack of co-ordination between the different supervising agencies in the U.S. financial system, *in casu* the Comptroller (which had approved the acquirement of First Options in 1986, but opposed to the loan in 1987) and the Federal Reserve (which followed an opposite course of policy).

All these events would leave an imprint on the US banking sector well into the 1990s. Large banks became convinced that they were too strategic to be allowed to fail. This opportunistic underestimation of market risks was one of the factors leading to a general banking crisis in the US in 1990-91. "Between 1985 and 1990, the Fed had already extended unpublicised discount window loans to over 350 banks that later failed. These loans gave time for depositors to flee. When the banks later failed, the FDIC reimbursed the Fed for the loans". (Solomon, p. 464). This climate eventually led to the crises of the Bank of New England and Citibank in early 1991, which were saved at a heavy costs to the government. In contrast, 125 U.S. banks were closed during 1991, totaling $65 billion in assets.

What can be learned from these examples?

(i) Central bankers, in general, are more reticent to step in with huge financial support than government institutions. They may have to agree on lending to defaulting debtors, as a last resort, in order to cast off major evil, and they also have to act in co-ordination with government agencies in order to avoid less desirable outcomes if these continued acting on their own. But often central bankers and functionaries of the finance or economics departments of governments will tend to disagree on matters of policy implementation, especially regarding prudence and the avoidance of moral hazard.

(ii) Central bankers will try to find ways to offer financial support while limiting moral hazard. During the stock market crisis of 1987, Alan Greenspan refused to inject funds directly into specific security firms, preferring instead to offer extra liquidity through the banking system as a whole (who would in turn provide support to the security sector).

(iii) Safety nets are not a fundamental solution for correcting markets; instead one needs better supervision. Supervision should be globally effective and consolidated in order to produce the necessary results. It should be equipped with sufficient sanctioning power.

(iv) The exact terms of lending of last resort should never be spelled out in advance, in order to maintain discipline among market players. As R. Smits notes concerning ECB: "The absence of any mentioning of the 'lender of last resort' function in the ESCB (European System of Central Banks) statute is not surprising, as the function is normally not spelled out openly in advance in legislation. The 'constructive ambiguity' concerning the availability of lender of last resort support gives the central bank discretion to decide whether to support a credit institution or other financial operator, and in what terms. The 'moral hazard' inherent in such support is a powerful argument against laying down its availability on legal texts. There is no doubt that, for the ESCB, such terms will have to include that adequate collateral be given. " (Smits, 1997, p. 270)

(v) There is no such a thing as a free lunch: if lending of last resort is justified because of systemic risk, then supervisors should monitor the eventual repayment of loans, or withdraw the banking licence at a later moment, causing the bank to default. If debts are not repaid, moral hazard will tend to extend over the entire financial system in the near future. This principle causes no major problem for private companies, which must be allowed to fail (even if this event may have to be postponed for a short period in times of general crisis); but it does cause difficulties for countries, that cannot fail, but are unable to repay their debt. Debt remission is no solution for countries either, insofar as debt has inccurred on private markets. The only solution, there, seems to be a "socialisation" initiative, changing private debt into public debt.

3.2.3. Moral suasion and the use of pressure

According to the classic image of central banking, central bankers should keep a low profile while intervening on markets, or putting pressure on bankers to accept certain changes in the management of their ailing banks. This is not only a matter of style, like the use of understatements and hermetic expressions seems more appropriate to express the prudence of the banker; it also indicates the fear of overplaying one's hand, because the central bank may cause more harm than good by its interventions when it is perceived to act too abruptly. After all, finance is a matter of maintaining confidence among a vast network of parties. Last but not least, moral suasion is meant to offer advice to bankers in such a way that the formal responsibility for taking action rests with the banks, while central bankers make sure that bankers' separate decisions are sufficiently co-ordinated in order to obtain the desirable aggregate result.

Of course, it is easier to "speak with a soft voice when you are carrying a big stick" as a U.S. President once remarked. As long as central banks had a clear and undisputed mandate within the confines of national boundaries, and direct means to control all the financial institutions in their territory (by having some direct impact on the profit margins of their clients, mostly banks or holding companies owning banks), it was easier to convince bankers by the informal "nod and wink" gestures in private communication: the "carrot and stick" mechanism was fully operational behind it. But once the leverage of central banks had been diminished, both because of the effects of globalisation of markets, new financial instruments, the importance of non-bank institutions and the gradual loss of the lender of last resort function, then the old types of moral suasion were not always sufficient in order to provide the required effects (Smits, 1997, p. 320). As a result, central bankers could be tempted to use more heavy-handed arm twisting in order to bring recalcitrant bankers into line.

CASE 3: MORAL SUASION IN THE 1982 DEBT CRISIS

The LDC (Less Developed Countries) debt crisis started on August 13, 1982, when Mexico announced it could not meet repayments which were due on $8 billion of its foreign debt, and would need an emergency loan of $3,5 billion. This potential repayment failure posed a direct threat to a series of U.S. banks, who had offered loans to LDC countries far beyond their own reserves (the top 9 U.S. banks had extended loans for covering non-OPEC LDC debt for 233% of their primary capital). Some Japanese and British banks had done likewise.

Consequently, in order to avoid a world-wide bank crisis, the central bankers of the U.S.A., the U.K., Germany and Switzerland proposed a $1,85 billion loan to Mexico through the BIS, and started organising a co-ordinated initiative including 600 banks in order to temporarily suspend any principal repayments by Mexico for a 3 month period. In order to get the 600 banks to step in line, they worked through an intermediate 13 member bank advisory committee, in which two central bankers, Richardson (U.K.) and Volcker (U.S.), took an active role as crisis managers.

"Each day the amounts due from the Mexican bank branches in New York and London were identified and creditors persuaded to roll over their credits and above all not to sue for repayments. Chairmen of recalcitrant banks were telephoned frequently. Calling upon its moral suasion tradition, Bank of England brass summoned stubborn chairmen to Threadneedle Street (i.e. the seat of the BOE) up to three times to impress upon them that systemic stability required their co-operation. When a foreign bank demanded repayment, the Bank of England and the Fed called their fellow central bankers in the Basel club for assistance" (Lewis Preston, Chairman of J.P. Morgan, quoted in Solomon, 1995, p. 220).

Obviously, by demanding the creditor banks not to sue Mexico for failing its repayments, central banks were stepping far out of the proper line of conduct. The German Bundesbank did not accept to move so far. And even with the Fed's heavy involvement, some American banks demanded repayment nonetheless.

The LDC debt crisis came to another point of urgency in November 1982, after it had become evident that not only Mexico, but also Brazil, Argentina and Yugoslavia could not repay. On November 16, central bankers entered into a co-ordinated effort with the IMF, so that IMF director Jacques de Larosière could effectively make IMF support conditional upon the approval of an (involuntary) lending effort by a bank creditors' cartel of several hundred banks. The IMF offered the political shield to the common effort, making most of the explicit demands on banks. Central Banks would follow up on the IMF's demands, putting tough "moral suasion" on holdouts. At this point, Volcker was pushed into a new moral hazard problem, by virtually guaranteeing the new loans in LDC debt. On the other hand, neither de Larosière nor the central bankers could convince governments, especially the U.S. government, to step in and financially support the lending effort. This lack of political support caused great tensions with European banks and the Bundesbank (who considered the bad loan policies to LDC countries as primarily an American problem, for which they should not be forced to participate).

Again, in putting pressure on bankers to accept offering new loans, central bankers were walking on a thin line between acceptable and unacceptable methods of pressure:

"The central bankers walked bankers through some of the potential implications, systemic and for their individual institutions, of not co-operating. Direct orders to lend, however, were taboo. At least once one of the Fed's phone callers was warned to ease his tone to be sure he was staying on the safe side of the narrow moral hazard line. 'We don't want to be in a position of telling banks what to do', Volcker explains, then confesses: 'I violated it enough to inquire if they were lending or not'" (Solomon, p. 237).

"Central bankers had various means to punish recalcitrants. How? 'By using the heavy eyebrows,' suggests Fed Chief Counsel Mike Bradfield. 'Tell them to cut back on their dividends. Make them dilute their shareholders: all the chairman must say is that a bank is not sufficiently capitalised and the market makes them raise capital. If they're selling below book value, every time they are selling new capital, they are watering down shareholders. That's hard. Actually, you do not have to make the statement, but just be credible enough so people think you might. How hard to push them, that was the issue.'

"'The Fed's ultimate threat,' Walt Wriston (J.P. Morgan) adds, 'was to unleash the latent democratic hostility against banks by publicly singling out a defiant bank for criticism. If you say no, well then, they can let it be known that these greedy bastards destroyed the world financial system. The Fed has played hardball sometimes, and will do it again'.(...) By late January 1983 the bank co-ordinating committee and the Brazilians, with Volcker's knowledge, decided to play hardball: they went public with the names and amounts of the delinquent banks. Each week from February 2, Bankers Trust's computers produced lists of the interbank deposits of some five hundred banks and totals by nationality. De Larosière sent telexes to the delinquent banks and asked their central bankers to twist arms.(...) Bankers, and many central bankers, were furious at the hardball tactics. But they worked. By February 20 1983, interbank deposits with Brazil rose to $7,5 billion". (Solomon, 1995, pp. 239-241)

Eventually, all these efforts of forced lending would not prove sufficient to solve the debt crisis. A political plan of systematic debt relief would have to be implemented in 1987. By their efforts, however, central bankers had bought crucial time, allowing the banks to gradually write off their bad loans, and avoiding the spread of systematic failure during the first year of the crisis.

These events demonstrate several important issues:

(i) On several occasions, central bankers have passed the line of correct use of moral suasion, engaging in undue pressure upon banking decisions. Of course, they could invoke attenuating circumstances for doing so, because the threat of systemic failure was imminent, governments were unwilling – too slow or too badly informed – to step in, and free-riders had to be effectively punished, once the need for a creditors' cartel had been justified by the occasion.

(ii) Abuse of moral suasion is also a symptom of a lack of structural alternatives. First of all, national central bankers, even of the U.S.A. or the U.K., do not have the effective authority or leverage to intervene efficiently on the international scene. A supranational central bank would have played an important role in handling the debt crisis. In the absence of such an organisation, national central bankers were using the existing international organisations of BIS, IMF and the Group of 7 in order to arrive at some effective form of international policy co-ordination. If anything, the debt crisis demonstrated that more supranational structures were necessary in order to avoid the weaknesses of the present ones.

(iii) The practice of moral suasion during this crisis shows why central banks are reticent to give up banking supervision, even if conflicts of interest between monetary policy setting and decisions-making on particular banks may appear. By keeping an effective control on at least a part of the financial institutions, central banks possess an instrument of immediate pressure in times of crisis, whereas they cannot be sure that political supervisors would act with the same insight and speed.

3.3. *Serving the public interest*

Central bankers, not unlike the magistrates of the Courts of Justice, find themselves in a complex relationship to public authorities. Perhaps the closest analogy is with civil servants, who are serving the long-term interests of the State and the people, while dealing with different political coalitions and parties, and retaining a sense of impartiality themselves.

On the one hand, they are non-elected functionaries, who are most often appointed by government (at least the governor of the Central

Bank, often also the other directors). They are supposed to act as agents of government in international bodies, and they are intervening on markets and providing financial services in close co-ordination with the Treasury and the other Ministries of government. On the other hand, they have to remain independent from government and non-governmental pressure, as far as short-term effects of financial interventions (interest rate policies, market interventions, issuing currency) are concerned. According to most commentators (see 1.3.4.: code of Fisher) they should not be required to finance the government deficit, and should not manage the public debt. (One may wonder if this last point is well applied in most countries, e.g. in India, or Belgium, to offer but two examples). Once in office, they should act in close co-operation with government officials, but with independent judgement, and focusing on the pursuit of their own policy objectives, as defined by their statutes and publicly set targets. They should be held accountable for reaching these same objectives, through a regular reporting procedure before the House of Representatives (or a specific Finance Committee of the House).

The relationship with governments is in constant historical evolution, after a period of close control and little freedom of action in the aftermath of World War II, central banks have found more occasion for independent action and influence after the demise of the Bretton Woods era, when deregulation of banking and the rise of international markets required swift interventions and an efficient fight against inflation. The general acceptance of central bank independence during the 1980s came as a result of this trend. But it may well be that the pendulum will swing back to the other end, calling again for a lower profile of central banks, and more political controls, in the near future.

In their dealings with government, central Bank directors or governors are facing several types of dilemmas of a moral nature. I will discuss three of them: truthfulness in disclosure of information, effectiveness of policy mix, and balancing national and international interests.

3.3.1. Lying for the good

A minister of Finance may be required, not only to remain silent about confidential policy matters, but even to explicitly mislead the public by his/her messages, in order to serve the public interest.

Everyone knows that when a government is considering the eventuality of a devaluation of its currency, it will never inform the public in advance of its plans, because such openness would be counter-productive. Morally, a denial of possible devaluation is not considered a lie in this context, since the Minister is not supposed to disclose eventual plans until they have been executed, and this for the public good. Consequently, nobody is supposed to believe the Minister, either, when he announces such denials.

The question rises whether central bankers may be allowed to move as far as politicians in disguising the truth. Most commentators argue they should not, but instead limit their announcements to those data they can honestly affirm as true, rather than adding white lies or deceptive conjectures. Rational spectators may anticipate the untrustworthiness of public announcements; but are they able, in the end, to correctly distinguish between those public messages which should be trusted, and those which should not? Some general blurring of confidence is likely to occur in the end, which may undermine the over-all trustworthiness of the central bank. As Otmar Issing of the Bundesbank remarks: "The theory of rational expectations has curbed belief in the capacity of policy-makers systematically to deceive the general public – generally to be equated with the possibility of exerting an effect in real terms. Moreover, we are indebted to the time inconsistency approach for insights into the tensions to which policy-makers are exposed when they weigh up the advantage to be gained by acting contrary to their earlier announcements regarding their own intentions and the damage which results from such behaviour in the shape of a loss of credibility". (Issing, 1995, p. 20)

Consequently, central bankers need to keep a higher profile than their political counterparts in making public announcements. Their disclosures, when made, should be expected to restore confidence in times of crisis, and command respect, instead of raising the suspicion that they are meant to cover up the real situation. Therefore, central bankers should keep to stricter standards of truth telling in calm periods as well. A governor of the bank, while trying to positively influence the markets or the public by what he/she says, should be prudent only to say what he/she is able and willing to execute, and to stand behind those words in the aftermath (excepting possible errors of judgement, due to lack of data).

3.3.2. Effectiveness

The expectations that governments (or the wider public) put upon central bank officials may be unrealistic, or incompatible, in view of the limited instruments they have at their disposal in order to influence markets.

First of all, in a system of floating exchange rates, one cannot separate the responsibility for setting interest rates and the exchange rate (Fischer, 1994, p. 302). Consequently, if the central bank disposes of the discretionary power to set (short-term) interest rates, government officials should abstain from targeting an exchange rate on their own authority. Of course, a specific exchange rate target may be important for the financial stability of the country, but then it should be pursued as a monetary policy target by the central bank (as has been the case, for example, of Belgium, the Netherlands and France, having pegged their currencies to the D-Mark) rather than causing interference between separate central bank and government policies.

Secondly, monetary policy cannot achieve its ends by using the single tools of currency issuing and interest rate setting. The fiscal policies, as well as the budget and wage policies of the government, have to complement and follow closely the initiatives of the central bank in order to attain the planned targets. Here, central bankers will often complain about the unwillingness of their respective governments to take the supportive policy decisions that are needed, e.g. for cutting the budget deficit, to increase savings and investment, or to reduce taxes on labour. On the other hand, they accept that a number of decisions, even if interfering with monetary policy targets, may have to be taken and are justified by political reasons. Such was the case, for example, with Chancellor Kohl's decision to speed up the process of reunification of Germany by accepting equal value for the East-German currency to the D-Mark. Criticism of government policies will arise above all, when *ad hoc* government decisions are perceived as window dressing, meant to cause an immediate effect on the electorate, rather than helping to fundamentally improve the country's state of economic health (e.g. having a significant effect on the savings rate, public debt, employment rate).

3.3.3. Conflicting interests?

Central bankers may have a different interpretation than government representatives on the best way to balance national and international interests in the search for a global monetary order. Politicians, having to answer regularly to their home electorate and to powerful pressure groups, are predisposed to put the short-term national interests before long-term and broader international concerns, whenever a conflict between both occurs. Central bank administrators, on the other hand, because they enjoy the privilege of a more distanced viewpoint and of more independence from political pressure, should take it as their responsibility to look primarily at the possible contributions their country could make to enhancing systemic stability, and to arrive at a just and stable order of international markets over the long haul. By doing so, they can correct the narrowly nationalistic or opportunistic views of many politicians. I stress 'they can', because central bankers may not always lead the herd toward the acceptance of a more international and enlightened view of their common interest. A good example of this issue might be offered by Paul Volcker's change of attitude toward the strong dollar during the 1980s. For a long time, Volcker took a rather narrow U.S. perspective towards the issue himself, because defeating inflation (with a strong dollar) seemed more important to him than fighting stagnation abroad. Toward the end of the decade (may be too late, after he left office?) he became a more outspoken critic of American consumerism, urging the American people to change their savings and spending trends, in order to reduce the deficit (Solomon, 1995, pp. 275ff).

With these last issues, we have already introduced the question of a trans-national financial and monetary order as a worthwhile moral goal and reference point for responsible conduct.[4] In the following part we want to develop this issue more systematically. Under the present circumstances, it seems impossible to limit the domain of

---

[4] I suggest, at this point, that the same questions of transaction costs and of ethics of information will occur in all types of financial trading. If corporations or individuals want to forego all kinds of inter-mediation, intervening directly on the markets, they will face insurmountable problems of transaction costs in managing the necessary information on assets, or run into unacceptable amounts of uncovered risks (increasing the likelihood of herd behaviour and speculative bubbles on financial markets). Of course, large institutional investors, such as mutual funds, insurance companies or corporate pension funds, may attempt to fulfil these information management functions themselves. This shift from personal banking to transactional banking, or to the suppression of banking as an independent financial institution, is an important evolution which I will touch upon in the fourth part (see also Chernow, *The Death Of The Banker*, 1997, pp. 78ff).

moral responsibility of central bankers to the national arena. Even if the institutional framework may still be lacking, one needs to explicitly introduce the goal of a global order as a necessary frame of reference. This will be the purpose of the next part.

4. The Ethical Argument for a Trans-National Central Bank

In this last part, I want to address the issue of global justice in the international monetary system. This issue should be addressed here, although the solutions to it may appear to many observers as both too complex and too utopian. The issue of global justice in regulating and developing financial markets, however, can no longer be avoided, because:

(i) It touches upon a fundamental problem which has been haunting political and economic ethics at least since the period of the Enlightenment: how to supersede the structure of conflicting and war-prone national states with a just world order?

(ii) The factual globalisation of financial markets creates an urgency to devise a truly trans-national approach to supervision and monetary policy implementation.[5] As we have seen in the previous sections, the actual central banks are not up to this challenge, even when acting within the framework of BIS and IMF. Changes in co-operation are likely to be introduced in an incremental way, following the logic of existing international organisations and power relations between states and blocs of states. Still, any incremental adaptation of institutions or agencies should be based on a fundamental vision of long-term objectives. But what should be the long-term orientations of the International Monetary System?

Ultimately, both pragmatic and fundamental reasons lead us to contemplate a more distant future, addressing our capacity for vision

[5] When using the term 'trans-national', I am referring to an institution in which national states and national interests are no longer the sole members and points of reference, but global objectives and values are pursued regardless of national background (like in a trans-national corporation). At the same time, in an 'inter-national' setting there may be intense co-ordination and co-operation, but still between national states, and following national interests as the ultimate point of reference. 'Supra-national' organisations represent an intermediate term: national states have pooled a substantial amount of authority to the central body, but remain the sole constitutive members of the union.

rather than our analytic and technical skills. We will pursue this line of thought in two ways: first by proposing a critique of the present international situation, and secondly by offering a blue-print for an alternative future orientation.

4.1. *The critique of the dominance by the happy few*

As we know, humanity has needed a long time, and great efforts, before it succeeded in overcoming the violent state of nature by establishing a state of law. First of all, this has been realised on a local scale, in the context of cities, towns, universities and corporations. Later, it was organised on a national scale in constitutional democracies. Today, we are committed to implement the basic rights and freedoms of humanity on a global scale, though we still lack the appropriate institutions.

A parallel can be drawn with regard to the process of emergence of a global monetary order. The creation of national currencies and national banking safeguards offered a fundamental step forward from the anomalies and barriers imposed by the patchwork of local currencies, customs and financial regulations of late-medieval society. During the last two centuries, national institutions have become well established; some international monetary organisations and conventions have been established in the process, but usually under the pressure of economic crises or under the dominance of some world power. This stage of a world-wide financial system under dominance of one key currency as a factual universal exchange standard (first the Pound Sterling, later the U.S. dollar) has not been transformed yet, although world markets have been moving toward a poly-centrical situation, including the Japanese Yen and the Euro) as alternative parallel currencies. However, the question of using national currencies as parallel currencies for international exchange remains: should we not move beyond the level of national currencies, establishing a truly trans-national exchange standard? And what kind of institutions would be required in order to supervise and regulate the functioning of global financial markets?

4.1.1. Robert Triffin's critique

A persistent advocate of such a reform of the International Monetary System has been Robert Triffin, a Belgian financial expert, professor at Yale, and involved in the study of international monetary policy since the 1950s. In this section, I will follow the outline of his critiques and proposals (Triffin, 1991).[6]

Triffin starts by formulating four critical observations on the present international monetary system:

(i) The explosion of international reserve assets and liabilities. This was due, primarily, to the replacement of the Gold Standard (after Bretton Woods) by the Foreign Exchange Standard. The role of gold dropped to 3% of total reserve assets, while the role of Special Drawing Rights of the IMF remained equally limited (between 2 and 3% between 1969 and 1990; the actual amount after the last increase of capital of September 1997 is about $68 billion). The Foreign Exchange Standard (including a huge appreciation of gold at market prices, and increased portions of reserves held in national currencies) grew to more than 90% of total world reserves.

(ii) Regional imbalances between holders of reserves. Not only were the results of mounting gold prices reaped primarily by the rich industrial countries (possessors of the largest gold reserves), and were net capital flows directed from Third World countries to the industrial countries, with an increasing surplus ($144 billion in 1997, $270 billion in 1990); also "...the so-called 'reserve currency countries' – especially the U.S. – have no need to accumulate reserves as long as they can settle their deficits with their own currency; and the other countries have plenty of reasons to accumulate a large portion of their global reserves in interest-earning foreign exchange rather than in sterile – even costly – gold hoards". (Triffin, 1991, p. 8)

(iii) The use of a few national currencies as the major instrument of international monetary reserves becomes the core problem. This situation creates a basic asymmetry in the settlement of balance-of-payment disequilibria: "The deficits of a country may be financed mostly – or even over-financed – by an increase of world foreign exchange reserves, with little or no decline of gross reserves for that country, and therefore, no imperative pressure for the readjustment of inflationary policies" (Triffin, 1991, p. 10).

---

[6] More comments on the ideas and proposals of R. Triffin can be found in the collection of essays which were edited and published in his honour by Steinherr & Weiserbs, *International and Regional Monetary Systems*, 1994.

(iv) "That country" was, first of all the United Kingdom, in the period of the British Empire, and more recently, the United States, both during and after the Bretton Woods agreement. Although the practice of "raising and exporting the dominant country's national debt to finance its foreign affairs" had already been condemned in 1795 by Immanuel Kant,[7] and was equally opposed by many financial experts during this century,[8] no efficient and equitable alternative was ever established. The Gold Standard, e.g., has often been tried as an internationally neutral standard, and found wanting.

4.1.2. Political reasons and counter-arguments in favour of dominance

At the same time, the dominant country, allowing its currency to be used as an international standard, could offer significant political arguments for justifying the imbalance of interests on the monetary scene. A prevalent argument was that the other countries were paying the military and economic price of international peace by participating in the zone of the key currency. In the case of the British Empire, this argument was cast in colonial (and commercial) terms; for the U.S.A., it was presented as a fair burden-sharing after the allied victory over fascism, and as part of a continuous Cold War effort of the Free World against the geo-political threat of communism. Therefore, according to the American viewpoint (shared to a great extent by other Western political leaders during the Cold War), it was only fair that the defeated countries, Germany and Japan, would support the U.S. deficit, which seemed largely caused by

[7] I. Kant, in his essay "Perpetual Peace" (*Zum ewigen Frieden. Ein philosophischer Entwurf*, Köningsberg, 1795), presents a model contract or treaty between nations. The fourth of the preliminary articles states: "No national debts shall be raised by a State to finance its foreign affairs". Kant, of course, was first of all weary of warmongering nation-states. Triffin refers to this text, broadening the interpretation to include all sorts of abuses of foreign-financed deficit spending.

[8] Triffin refers to the Belgian Minister of Finance Léon Delacroix, who favoured the issue of gold bonds instead of the Sterling Exchange Standard, to J. M. Keynes' proposition of "bancor", and to Jacques Rueff, Fritz Machlup and himself in their proposals for the adoption of a single reserve instrument within the IMF. The IMF's reserves and Special Drawing Rights (SDR) were supposed in the earlier Bretton Woods agreement to offer the foundation of such an international currency. But SDR's were never accepted by the major member states (the U.S. having, of course, the dominant role) to play such a prominent role in the international monetary system. (Triffin, 1991, pp. 12-13)

military expenditures that were in the common interest of the non-communist world. Once the rebuilt economies of Germany and Japan were capable of producing large balance-of-payment and trade surpluses, these could partly be turned into U.S. currency assets, in order to support the chronic U.S. balance of payment (and government budget) deficits.

This political justification for the asymmetry of a world system with the dollar as its key currency was, of course, historically limited in several respects:

(i) After the Cold War period seemed over in 1989, the U.S. could not indefinitely continue to justify its preferential treatment in the monetary system by invoking its role as a "global police agent" (though some of this rhetoric is still present, in N.A.T.O. and in the Gulf War coalition).

(ii) The asymmetric system remains inherently unstable, because, even for a country of the size and economic weight of the U.S., an ever-growing degree of indebtedness towards "allied countries" will sooner of later lead to increasing negative estimates regarding the fundamental value of the currency and the state of the economy. This will increasingly be the case when a low rate of internal savings, a high discount rate and a low rate of fiscal income generation proves that Americans themselves are to a large extent to blame for creating the persistent deficits in their current balance of payments. American citizens and corporations should pay themselves the price for their standard of living.

(iii) Moreover, the system is also unstable because the "beneficiary countries (= U.S.) cannot forever stand the handicap of an increasing un-competitiveness of their over-valued currencies in world trade" (Triffin, 1991, p. 8). And the urge of other countries to transfer their surpluses in low saving, low investment economies as the U.S. may equally decrease in the near future. Earlier big lenders to the U.S., such as Japan, Germany, and the OPEC-countries, might look for alternative sources in the future.[9] The important

---

[9] In an article of *The Economist* ("The Vice of Thrift", March 21, 1998) this question is raised: "Can America continue to attract sufficient foreign capital? Some economists reckon that the slump in demand in Asia will push America's current-account deficit to $300 billion in 1999 – higher as a percentage of GDP than its peak in the late 1980s, when the dollar plunged. This is all right as long as America's higher profitability is driving those capital inflows. But it is unlikely that the

fluctuations of the dollar during the 1980s are explained by Triffin as the result of attempts by the U.S.-government to "talk down" the dollar, readjusting its overvaluation and stimulating export trade.

(iv) Last but not least, the system is unstable because of the globalisation of financial markets and the shift of economic and financial power from the territory and institutions of one State toward a more multi-centered, "off-shore", and market-driven network of global finance.

4.1.3. The alternative

For all these reasons, Triffin has been consistently pleading since the late 1950s (e.g., in "Gold and the Dollar Crisis", 1959) for the establishment of a global reference currency to supplant the existing system of parallel use of national currencies. In his view, the International Monetary Fund has to play the key role of guardian and supervisor of the international reserve deposits that would provide the basis for this global reference unit. In the new system:

(i) Countries would transfer to the IMF a fraction of their currency reserves (20% to start, all reserves less a working balance at a later stage). These deposits would bear interest and would be backed by exchange rate guarantees (in order to make them more attractive than any reserve asset in national currency).

(ii) Central banks would be credited to their account with the IMF, the corresponding amounts being debited from the amounts of the issuing countries. The IMF as reserve center would act as a clearing house.

(iii) The system would provide the reserve institution with a lending capacity. Lending would be limited to the rate of non-inflationary growth of the participating countries as a whole, e.g. between 3 and 5% of world reserves. Lending would be conditional (as it is today in the IMF), but with equal conditions for all member States. (De Larosière, 1994, pp. 138-139)

---

return on capital will always remain higher in America than elsewhere. (...) America would be able to sustain its present investment only by increasing its domestic saving".

4.2. *Moving towards a just trans-national monetary order?*

The proposals of Triffin simultaneously impress the reader as being utopian and concrete. They sound utopian because they have never been executed as such, and concrete because they are connected to a particular historical institution, the IMF, and to earlier plans of its reform (of the Group of Twenty, during the 1970s). Several inside experts, such as De Larosière, Aglietta, and Lamfalussy (see Steinherr & Weiserbs, 1994) have offered positive comments on Triffin's proposals. Also, in view of the future, it seems necessary to formulate a bold and new perspective in order to establish a more equitable regulatory framework for global financial markets. Triffin's proposal of pooling the currency reserves of participating states (in principle: all States on the planet, as are present in the United Nations and members of the IMF) in order to regulate the creation of world liquidity is a necessary and fitting step in this direction, because it solves the old problems of the Gold Standard, while moving beyond the stage of national currencies as the only reference in global markets.

In order to complete this proposal, however, two additions seem necessary:

(i) One should not put all the responsibilities and tasks for regulating the international monetary system in the hands of one institution, i.e. the IMF, even with a more equitable form of management (less impact of U.S. government). It seems that some separation of powers is equally required at the trans-national level:
— not one agency, but at least four: (1) a form of effective world government; (2) a world trade organisation; (3) a world central bank; and (4) a supervising agency for financial institutions.
— backed by effective sanctioning power, which probably implies that not only an international system of financial law and jurisprudence, but also international courts or instances of arbitrage should be established.

(ii) We should move gradually but consistently toward this goal, following both trails of installing regional monetary unions (such as the European one) and of increasing the networks of international co-responsibility (such as provided in the BIS, IMF, World Bank), well aware of the fact that these international efforts have to result in due time into the establishment of supra-national regulating authorities.

4.2.1. The division of labour in international monetary relations

In a system which is based on the freedom to create money, which is not completely to be regulated by governments, even not by one powerful trans-national institution, it seems necessary to guarantee the independence of a central bank, which has as its only responsibility to protect the stability of prices on the global market, including the price of the global reference currency. This should therefore be an institution closer to the actual BIS than to the IMF; it should not be involved in financing state deficits, nor in long-term development lending. It should only provide short-term bridge loans in times of emergency, acting as a lender of last resort with regard to countries as well as banks or non-banking financial institutions.

Because all types of institutional agents are mingling and transacting on the same global markets, one can not maintain a separate set of regulating institutions for supervising states and private corporations on the financial markets. So the old distinction between the central banks and BIS dealing primarily with banks, and the IMF dealing with states, has to be left behind. A single world central bank should deal with all global financial agents in times of crisis, acting as a lender of last resort.

On the one hand, this world central bank has to act in close co-ordination with national central banks, which provide it with necessary information and may act as local agencies of the world central bank. On the other hand, it needs to work in close interaction with a global network of supervisors of financial institutions, and with international credit providers (be it for countries, like the World Bank), or private banks and non-banking corporations. This world central bank should be independent from all interference by governments. Its governors should be appointed for ten year terms, and be accountable to the Assembly of the United Nations (supposing that the U.N. would act as a world government). No country could claim preferential treatment by the central bank, nor a controlling power over governors which would be proportionate to its wealth. The governors of the world central bank should take the overall stability of the global financial system as their only over-riding concern, offering equal treatment to all financial agents. Other concerns, justifying differential treatment of poor or wealthy countries or institutions, should be left to the policy priorities of the long-term lending organisations, such as the World Bank. The central bank should limit its interventions to "make available prompt, low conditionality, short-term first line liquidity, to meet unanticipated shocks until more permanent financing or adjustment can be put in place". (Griesgraber, 1994, p. 13)

Moreover, the world central bank could more effectively execute those functions that are already included in present international co-ordination efforts among central banks: intervention on the exchange markets, monetary policy implementation through the shift in interest rates (of the global reference currency!), and smoothing the functioning of the financial systems, intervening as a lender of last resort in times of crisis (in co-ordination with national agents) (Lamfalussy, 1994, p. 35; see also Kindleberger, 1889, p. ix and ch. 9, on international public goods).

Lamfalussy, however, stresses the point that without an effective world government, including world-wide co-ordination of fiscal policies and exchange rate commitments, no central bank monetary policy is likely to succeed when based on the sole tool of fixing interest rates. One cannot shift the interest rate, which is a price of expected risk and uncertainty in money, at will as long as the underlying fundamental uncertainty of a lack of effective global government is not diminished. (Lamfalussy, 1994, pp. 43-45; Vandaele, 1997, p. 7)

4.2.2. Towards a trans-national monetary system

Michel Aglietta, in his essay "The Future of International Monetary Relations", has offered some important observations on the possibility and desirability of a gradual evolution from dominance by one national key currency towards a trans-national system.

First of all, he is convinced the move is necessary, not only for circumstantial (changed political order) but for fundamental (monetary) reasons: "The international monetary problem has a structural, regulatory and an institutional dimension. This does not simply equate to the co-ordination of monetary policies between nations, since money is a means of achieving overall stability, which in turn makes the formulation of coherent economic policies possible. A single currency established by organising a payments area would guarantee the public good of money. On the contrary, the peculiarity of the international monetary problem is brought out by the coexistence of national currencies. This coexistence, however, does not correspond to the general laws of competition, since the currency's definitive feature is its uniqueness. Several 'complete' currencies cannot coexist in equilibrium according to demand and supply. This coexistence between currencies must be organised. This feature makes the international monetary system unique". (Aglietta, 1994, p. 145).

The coexistence Aglietta is referring to, has historically been based on the principles of hierarchy (with one national currency playing the role of key (complete) currency), and on the principle of separation (whereby the use of currencies outside their respective zone or payments area is limited). These methods have become obsolete, because the dollar has gradually lost its key role, taking its place in a tri-polar or poly-centrical monetary system together with the yen and the D-mark (eventually the Euro). The creation of a European Monetary Union has particularly spelled the end of the principle of hierarchy. Furthermore, the principle of separation has become impracticable in the context of global markets.

Therefore, two alternative principles remain available: the principles of co-responsibility and of supra-nationality.

Co-responsibility presupposes the presence of a negotiating forum (as in G7, G10 including BIS) between the various monetary authorities who issue the convertible currencies in demand. Co-responsibility can only function if the present discrepancies in national interests are kept in check by a consensus on global stability, backed up by sufficiently credible guidelines (target zones for exchange rates, growth rates of monetary aggregates, growth of nominal demand) and tools for co-ordinated intervention.

The principle of co-responsibility defines the situation in which we are living today (at least for the rich countries, such as the members of the Group of 10; but these are increasingly joined by a number of "emerging financial centers" in Latin America and Asia, as is the case for the implementation of the Basel Agreement on Adequate capital Standards, and the Principles on Banking Supervision).

Still, the system is inherently weak and hybrid: it is weak because it remains open to a 'prisoner's dilemma' between conflicting state interests, and hybrid because capital mobility on global markets has become too vast and swift in order to allow effective adjustments between several major currencies. One should have to move beyond mere policy co-ordination and introduce structural changes. Aglietta mentions two possible ways of introducing structural change:

(i) Install a new way of sharing international credit between several currencies (e.g. dollar, yen and euro) in a financially integrated world: "If the US Treasury issued part of its annual financial requirements in yen and in European currency, downward pressure on the dollar would diminish as much. Exchange rates could be established with a lower spread between, on the one hand, the American, and on the other, the German and Japanese rates. The US would enjoy lower interest rates and the rest of the world more stable exchange rates. The ever threatening risk of a world recession would recede, and the Third World debt service could be alleviated. It would be an opportunity to reinforce the restructuring of world debt in favour of the yen and European currencies by converting part of the Third Word debt, presently in dollars, when rescheduling programmes take place". (Aglietta, 1994, p. 157)

As such, the controls "should act directly on supply, structuring the currency composition of the world debt so as to minimise the discrepancy between the structure per currency of financial assets supplied and the structure of savers' preferences".

(ii) Although the previous proposal is a step in the right direction, there remains uncertainty about the most preferred liquid asset. Sooner or later, one has to move beyond a poly-centrical system, creating one supra-national fiduciary currency. This global settlement currency would imply centralised control of the world liquidity supply, with "a central supra-national bank for the control of global inflation, and national governments for the monitoring of indebtedness under the constraint of supranational payments currency reserves". (Aglietta, p. 158)

The last proposal of Aglietta, reflecting on earlier ideas of Triffin, is very close indeed to the institutional framework that is being established in the context of the European Monetary Union. This leaves us with the idea, mentioned by several insiders (Triffin, Lamfalussy, Aglietta), but seldom discussed in the larger public, that the project of European Monetary Union could show its ultimate moral meaning as an important regional experiment in establishing a transnational currency and payments union, preparing the stage for a global monetary system. It would be fine if politicians and so-called 'Euro-crats' could present the stakes of Monetary Union in this global perspective to the public.

References

AGLIETTA, M. (1991), 'The Future of International Monetary Relations' in A. STEINHERR and D. WEISERBS (eds.), *Evolution of the International and Regional Monetary Systems*. New York, MacMillan, pp. 144-159.

ARGANDONA, A., BASANEZ, F., CORTES L.,(eds.), (1995), *The Ethical Dimension of Financial Institutions and Markets*. Berlin, Springer Verlag.

BAILLIE, R., POSTERBERG, W. (1997), Why do Central Banks Intervene?, *Journal of International Money and Finance*, vol. 16,no. 6, pp. 909-919.

BASEL COMMITTEE ON BANKING SUPERVISION (1997), *Core Principles of Banking Supervision*. Basel, BIS.

BASEL INSTITUTE OF SETTLEMENTS (BIS) (1998), *68th Annual Report*, Basel, Ch. 8: 'Evolution of Central Banks', pp. 140-160.

BASANEZ, F. (1995), 'Ethics and Regulation in Financial Institutions and Markets' in F. BASANEZ, L. CORTES and A. ARGANDONA (eds.), *The Ethical Dimension of Financial Institutions and Markets*. Berlin, Springer Verlag, pp. 27-65.

CAPIE, F. (1994), *The Future of Central Banking. The Tercentenary Symposion of The Bank of England*. Cambridge, Cambridge University Press.

C.E.P.S. (1998) 'Prudential Supervision in the Context of E.M.U.' Brussel, Centre Of European Policy Studies.

CHERNOW, R. (1997), *The Death of the Banker*. New York, Vintage Books.

CROCKETT, A. (1996), 'The Theory and Practice of Financial Stability' in *The Economist*, 144(1996)4, pp. 531-568.

CUKIERMAN, A. (1996) 'The Economics of Central Banking' Discussion Paper nr. 9631. Tilburg University.

DODD, N. (1996), 'The Politics of International Monetary Integration' in *The Sociology of Money*. Cambridge, Polity Press, pp. 84-104.

ECONOMIST, The (1995), 'Who's in the Driving Seat?' in *A Survey of the World Economy*, (7 October 1995), pp. 2-44.

ECONOMIST, The (1997), 'Banking's Biggest Disaster' (7 July 1997), pp. 75-77.

ECONOMIST, The (1997), 'On the Trail of the Mutant Inflation Monster' (4 October 1997), pp. 89-90.

ECONOMIST, The (1998), 'Crédit Lyonnais. The Bitter End' (23 May 1998).

ECONOMIST, The (1998), 'The Vice of Thrift' (21 March 1998), p. 87-88.

FARBER, A., SCHMIT, M., (1996), Financial Markets: Wild Movements or Controlled Development?', The Millennium Conferences 1996, Brussels, King Baudouin Foundation.

FISCHER, S. (1994), 'Modern Central Banking' in F. Capie (ed.), *The Future of Central Banking*. Cambridge, Cambridge University Press, pp. 262-308.

FROWEN. S and F. McHUGH (1995), *Financial Decision-Making and Moral Responsibility*. New York, St. Martin's Press.

GOLDSTEIN, M. (1997), *The Case for an International Banking Standard*, Institute for International Economics, Washington D.C..

GOODHART, C. (1986), 'Why Do We Need a Central Bank?' Banca d'Italia, Temi di discussione, nr. 57, January 1986.

GOODHART, C. (1988), *The Evolution of Central Banks*. Cambridge (MA), MIT Press.

GOODHART, C. and D. SCHOENMAKER (1995), 'Should the Functions of Monetary Policy and Banking Supervision Be Separated?' Oxford Economic Papers, 47/4 1995, pp. 539-560.

GRIESGRABER, J. (1994), 'Rethinking Bretton Woods' Washington (DC), Conference Report & Recommendations Center of Concern.

ISSING, O. (1995), 'The Role of the Central Bank and Its Responsibility' in S. FROWEN and F. MCHUGH (eds.), *Financial Decision-Making and Moral Responsibility*. New York, St. Martin's Press, Ch. 2, pp. 15-26.

KEATING, G. (1995), 'Ethical Issues in Investment Banking' in S. FROWEN and F. MCHUGH (eds.), *Financial Decision-Making and Moral Responsibility*. New York, St. Martin's Press, Ch. 5, pp. 78-83.

KINDLEBERGER, C. (1988), *The International Economic Order*. New York, Harvester Wheatsheaf.

LAMFALUSSY, A. (1981), 'Observation de règles ou politique discrétionnaire? Essai sur la politique monétaire dans un miliue inflationniste' BIS, Etudes éco-nomiques, nr 3.

LAMFALUSSY, A. (1991), 'International Central Bank Co-operation: What It Can – and Cannot – Achieve' in A. STEINHERR and D. WEISERBS (eds.), *Evolution of the International and Regional Monetary Systems*. New York, MacMillan, 1991, pp. 35-45.

LAMFALUSSY, A. (1994), 'Central Banking in Transition' London, Per Jacobsson Lecture.

LAROSIÈRE, J. de (1991), 'R. Triffin and the Reform of the International Monetary System' in A. STEINHERR and D. WEISERBS (eds.), *Evolution of the International and Regional Monetary Systems*. New York, MacMillan, 1991, ch. 9.

MACINTYRE, A. (1981), *After Virtue. A Study in Moral Theory*. South Bend (IN), Notre Dame University Press.

MAYSTADT, P. (1996), 'Quel rôle pour le Fonds monétaire international à l'aube du XXIème siècle?' Conference at the Société Royale d'Economie politique de Belgique, 15 October 1996.

MYERS, R.J. (1987), *The Political Morality Of The IMF. Ethics and Foreign Policy* (Carnegie Council on Ethics and International Affairs, 3). New Brunswick, Transaction Books.

N.B.B. Verslag 1997, Nationale Bank van Belgie, 23 February 1998.

ROUMELIOTIS, P. (1993), 'Rapport de la commission économique, monétaire et de la politique industrielle sur la coopération monétaire internationale dans le cadre de la réduction des restrictions sur les marchés des capitaux' Parlement Européen, A3-O293/93, 2 December 1993.

SCOTT-QUINN, B. (1995), 'Ethics and Regulation in Securities Market-Making' in S. FROWEN and F. MCHUGH (eds.), *Financial Decision-Making and Moral Responsibility*. New York, St. Martin's Press, Ch. 6, pp. 87-102.

SOLOMON, S. (1995), *The Confidence Game*. New York, Simon & Schuster.

SMITS, R. (1997), *The European Central Bank. Institutional Aspects*, Doctoral Dissertation.University of Amsterdam, Dordrecht, Kluwer.

STEINHERR, A. and D. WEISERBS (1991), *Evolution of the International and Regional Monetary Systems*. MacMillan, New York.

STRANGE, S. (1995), 'From Bretton Woods to the Casino Economy' in S. Corbridge, R. Martin and N. Thrift (eds.),*Money, Power and Space*. Oxford, Blackwell, pp. 49-62.

TERMES, R. (1995), 'Ethics in Financial Institutions' in A. Argandona et al. (eds.), *The Ethical Dimension of Financial Institutions and Markets*. Berlin, Springer Verlag,pp. 119-135.

TRIFFIN, R. (1987), 'The Paper Exchange Standard: 1971-19??' in Princeton Essays in International Finance, n. 169, December 1991.

TRIFFIN, R. (1991), 'The I.M.S. and the E.M.S.' Bulletin de l'IRES, U.C.L., n. 158, December 1991.

VANDAELE, J. (1997), 'Vrijheid is onvermijdelijk, maar niet te snel' an interview with A. Lamfalussy in *De Morgen*, 8 November 1997, p. 7.

VOLCKER, P. (1990), 'The Triumph of Central Banking?' Per Jacobsson Lecture.

VOLCKER, P. et.al. (1994), 'The Philosophy of Central Banking' in F. Capie *The Future of Central Banking*. Cambridge, Cambridge University Press, pp. 342-359.

DERIVATIVES:
POWER WITHOUT ACCOUNTABILITY

Luc Van Liedekerke & Danny Cassimon

In his *Politics* (Politica, 1259 a3-a23), Aristotle relates the following story about Thales of Milete. One day Thales, who happened to be an excellent weather forecaster, decided to rent all the olive presses in the region because he saw that there was an excellent harvest coming. He offered a small fee to the owners of the olive presses in return for the right to be the first one to use the press at the time of harvest. Harvest came and was indeed abundant, meaning that everyone wanted to rent an olive press, but because Thales held the right to use them first, nobody could actually get one, except by buying this right from Thales at a far higher price. Aristotle uses this story as anecdotal evidence to contradict the saying that good philosophers are necessarily bad businesspeople. We shall leave that problem unanswered and use the story as an excellent early example of a derivative contract, more exactly of a call option, that ends up bringing in good money. In the example Thales places a bet: he bets that the harvest will be plentiful and he is willing to pay a premium for this bet (the fees he gives to the owners) because he believes to possess superior information on future weather conditions. His risk is limited (the fees), the possible return is unlimited. This is the essential story behind any option used for speculative purposes. The crucial elements are: limited risk, unlimited gains and the belief to have superior information. Speculation is the goal.

The instrument he uses to place his bet has some attractive properties: he does not need to buy all the olive presses, he only buys a right to use them first. By providing a limited amount of money – the fees – he is able to mobilise a much bigger amount of money – the combined value of the olive presses. This property which lies at the center of derivatives, is called their leverage capability. It means that a small amount of money (the premium in financial jargon) can move around a very large amount of money (the underlying), making derivatives ideal for speculative purposes.

A second story, this time not by Aristotle, concentrates on the poor farmer who is not so good at weather forecasting. He/she will be lucky or unlucky, depending on the will of the gods. To stop this constant cycle of happiness and misery, the farmer decides to sell his/her future harvest well before the actual time of harvesting. By doing this the farmer limits his/her risk and has an income that might be lower than the possible income, but that is at least certain (that is if the buyer pays the price). This is a typical forward operation, invoked to hedge risk and shows us the other side of derivatives markets. Essential elements here are: an unwanted risk that is passed on to another party in return for cash or a different risk (the risk not to be paid). Hedging is the goal.

Usually, the one who buys the harvest will be wealthy enough to withstand a bad harvest, and in this sense he/she is better placed to bear the risk of the all-too-fickle weather gods. In this sense we can say that derivatives act as an insurance mechanism that allows people to stabilise their cash flows. This attractive property of derivatives, together with their somewhat more disputed speculative character, turn out to be two sides of the same coin.

Historically, derivatives originated in the agricultural markets, with the establishment of contracts for the future delivery of produce (e.g., the farmer who sells next year's olives). Derivatives based on physical produce remain crucial and important markets covering everything from orange juice to crude oil. In the 1970s, however, purely financial derivatives became important when futures markets in Chicago started trading contracts with US treasury bills and bonds (short- and long-term promissory notes of the US government) as its basic product. A combination of financial deregulation, technological development and a better understanding of the products involved ensured the fast geographical spread of derivatives, turning them into the financial success story of the 1990s. By now, according to one study (IMF, 1997, p. 121) derivative contracts engage about as much money as the entire market value of all bonds, equities and bank assets in North America, Japan and the 15 countries of the European Union combined. This in itself is already sufficient reason to take a closer look at the derivatives revolution. Derivatives have linked international financial markets and ensured that price movements circle the globe in a matter of minutes rather than days. In this sense, then, we can say that they influence the economic policy of governments. Derivatives have also obscured the transparency of financial markets, and this at a time when regulators have turned away from explicit regulation and toward the self-disciplinary nature of the market. It is clear that when markets are not transparent, self-discipline becomes a dangerous instrument for regulation.

These and other problems will be discussed in the present text. But before entering these problems, we shall first introduce some terminology. What are derivatives precisely (1) and who uses them and for what reason (2). Next we discuss the most important risks involved in derivative markets (3) and present figures illustrating the growth and the size of the derivatives market (4). Finally, we discuss some of the regulatory problems involved (5). Throughout the text we illustrate the functioning and disfunctioning of derivative markets with cases. These cases will also teach us more about the challenges that regulators face. Readers familiar with derivatives can easily skip the first three sections and begin with (4).

1. Demystifying Derivatives

A derivative is a contract between two parties (the buyer and the seller) to buy or sell an asset – say IBM shares, oil, Treasury bills, dollars – at a specified price on a specified date. The common feature of all derivative contracts is that the price is negotiated today when the contract is agreed upon, while the settlement and delivery of the contract is somewhere in the future. As such, the crucial determinant of the value of the derivative contract will be the relation between the price that was specified in the contract and what the asset is worth (i.e. its market price) at the time of the settlement of the derivative contract.

A basic classification of the different types of derivatives can be made on the basis of three characteristics:

(i) Is the derivative of the forward- or option-type?

(ii) Is it exchange-traded or traded 'over-the-counter'(OTC)?

(iii) Does it deal with a one-time or regular-interval exposure?

1.1. *Forward-type versus option-type contracts*

In a forward-type contract, the buyer of the derivative contract has the contractual obligation to fulfill the commitment at settlement, i.e. to buy or sell a specified asset at the before-negotiated price, even if this price is unfavourable to him/her, compared to the current market price of the asset. This also holds for the seller of the contract.

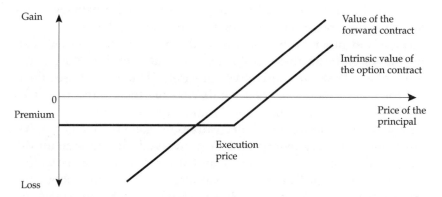

Figure 1: Speculative side of Forward and (call) Option contract

As a consequence, from a speculative perspective (see figure 1), buying (and selling) such a derivative contract enables someone to profit from an advantageous change in price, but at the same time, exposes them to the disadvantageous scenario. From a hedging perspective (see figure 2), whatever the future market price evolution, at the expense of realising an ('opportunity') loss when not hedging would have given a better result because the market price at settlement is better than the contract price. The loss or gain from the contract moves linearly with the market price evolution.

In an option-type contract, however, the buyer has the right (the 'option'), but not the obligation, to execute the derivative contract at the time of settlement, i.e. choose freely whether or not to buy (a call option) or to sell (a put option) the asset at the contract price. The counterparty, i.e. the seller of the option contract, has to accommodate the choice of the buyer. For that right, the buyer pays a specified, non-refundable fee to the seller of the contract up-front (i.e. when the contract is negotiated); this is called the 'premium'. Of course, the decision of the buyer whether or not to execute the contract will depend on the price relation between the negotiated contract price and current market price of the underlying asset. When the contract price is more interesting, he/she will execute the option contract, if not, he/she has the freedom not to honour the derivative contract, but buys or sells the asset directly in the ('spot') market, at the more interesting current market price.

As such, and unlike the forward-type, from a speculative perspective (figure 1), buying an option-type contract effectively enables one to profit from an advantageous change in price, without at the same time being exposed to the disadvantageous scenario (because of the freedom not to execute the contract in the disadvantageous scenario): the maximum one can lose is the paid premium. From a hedging point of view (figure 2), buying an option-type contract effectively enables one to lock into a certain minimum income or maximum cost, while at the same time continue to profit (to some extent, i.e. after taking into account the paid premium) from the advantageous scenario. Consequently, the pay-off schedule of an option-type derivative will be non-linear.

Both contracts are symmetric insofar as what one party gains, the other party loses. As such, derivative contracts can be seen as zero-sum games, at least for the two parties involved.

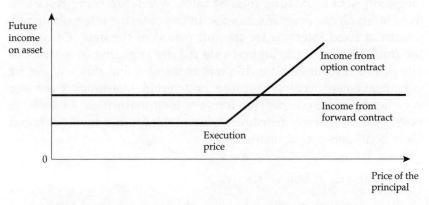

Figure 2: Hedging side of Forward and (put) Option contract

1.2. *Exchange-traded versus 'over-the-counter'*

In essence, derivatives can be traded in two different ways, over-the-counter (OTC) or at an exchange. Over-the-counter derivatives are freely negotiated between two parties. The terms of the contract – in terms of maturity date, contract price, notional – can be customised to the specific needs of the users ('tailor-made'). Since the contract is tailor-made, it is difficult to resell it before maturity (i.e. there is no active 'secondary market'). As such, the holder of the contract is exposed to 'counterparty risk', i.e. the risk that the other party will be unable to meet its obligations at maturity. For non-financial end-users, this counterparty is typically a bank.

In exchange-traded derivatives, the counterparty in the contract is the clearing house of an exchange, matching supply and demand for a given contract. As such, in order to provide liquidity, the terms of the contract need to be standardised. This enables the creation of a liquid secondary market, where the value of a specific derivative contract is determined daily, and positions can be unwound on a daily basis before maturity. The fact that the counterparty is the clearing house rather than an individual market participant reduces counterparty risk considerably.

1.3. *One-time versus fixed-interval exposure*

The exposure to risk can be a one-time event, but can also be incurred at fixed intervals. Consider, for example, a company with long-term debt at floating interest rates, which are being reset at a fixed interval, say every six months. In this case, the interest rate risk returns at fixed intervals for the full period of the debt. Of course, the firm can hedge the interest rate risk by engaging in a series of one-period instruments for different maturities, but this will not be very convenient, mainly because one-period instruments are not very liquid or very expensive for very long maturities. As such, in essence, multi-period instruments are nothing other than packaged ('bundled') one-period instruments.

1.4. *A taxonomy of basic derivatives*

On the basis of these characteristics, the basic types of derivatives, being forwards, futures, swaps and options, can be classified as in Table 1.

Table 1: Basic types of financial derivatives

| | Forward-type | | Option-type | |
	Exchange	OTC	Exchange	OTC
One-time exposure	Future	Forward	Option	OTC-Option
Multiple exposure		Swap		Cap, Floor, Collar

Forwards, futures and swaps are the most common forward-type derivatives. A *forward* is the most basic type of derivative, whereby users of it promise to buy or sell a specified asset at a specified price for delivery at some future maturity. Insofar as it is an OTC-instrument, terms are freely negotiated, but there is no secondary market and settlement is at maturity. Until then, no cash changes hands. A *swap* is nothing other than a bundle of forwards and shares all the basic features. The exchange-traded alternative to a forward is a *futures* contract. This is nothing other than a standardised forward with an active secondary market. Here trading occurs anonymously with the clearing house as a counterparty; the value of the contract is determined daily and contracts are 'marked to market', i.e. cash (a 'margin payment') is paid in by the user to cover any value losses on the contract, and is also paid out (on an account of the user at the clearing house) to the user when the value of the contract increases, on a daily basis. This last specific feature of futures contracts greatly reduces counterparty risk.

An *option* contract gives the buyer of the contract the right, but not the obligation, to buy (a 'call' option) or to sell (a 'put' option) an asset at a specified price (the 'exercise' or 'strike' price). The seller of the option contract (the 'writer' of a contract) has to accommodate the buyer when this he/she decides to execute the contract). For this freedom of choice, the buyer pays a non-refundable fee (the 'premium') to the writer up-front. While forwards are settled when they mature, options are settled when they are exercised, which may occur until maturity ('American' option) or only at maturity ('European' option).

Options are available both on exchanges and OTC. Again, the OTC-market offers greater opportunity for tailoring, while the exchange market offers daily valuation, anonymous trading with the clearing house, and an active secondary market. Even exchange-traded options are typically not marked to market, so, apart from the premium payment, no further money changes hands until exercise.

Caps and *floors* are to option contracts what swaps are to forward contracts: a cap is simply a package of call options and a floor is a package of put options. For example, if a company issues long-term floating rate debt, with the interest paid and the rate reset every six months, a cap ensures that its total interest costs do not exceed a target maximum level, while still enabling lower interest rates to be taken advantage of. A floor would lock in a minimal rate of return on a long-term floating rate investment, with an opportunity for higher returns when interest rates rise. A *collar* is a combination of both: e.g. simultaneously buying a cap and selling a floor reduces the up-front cost of the transaction (the premium) in exchange for giving up part of the upside potential.

These basic building blocks offer an unlimited potential for combination. The more complex instruments that are created on the basis of such building blocks are often referred to as 'exotics' and are simultaneously shunned and admired for their unique capability of making and losing money by using them.

1.5. *Underlying assets*

The assets underlying a derivatives contract can be a whole range of things, such as shares, bonds, commodities, currency, interest rates, indices. The market is inventive enough to find an ever-growing number of assets that form the basis for derivative contracts. A recent and very successful innovation is the creation of an OTC market for credit derivatives. One example of a forward-type credit derivative is the loan portfolio swap, whereby two financial institutions (typically with a loan portfolio that is heavily concentrated towards one (different) type of loans or borrower segment) swap the income of a part of their loan portfolio. As a result, the income flow from the loan portfolio of both institutions is more diversified after the swap. An example of an option-type of credit derivative is a default put whereby the buyer of the contract has the option to sell a portfolio of bonds at a specified price (in exchange for a premium). As such, he/she is hedged against a decrease in value of his/her bond portfolio (e.g. due to financial difficulties of the debtors involved). To the extent that financial intermediaries themselves are using these derivatives, they shift the risk of their core business, i.e. financing, to other intermediaries (Scholtens, 1997). In this sense we can say that derivatives are really changing the structure of financial markets. We shall return to this subject at the end.

1.6. *Why hedge?*

The value-added of hedging looks trivial at first sight: to the extent that a number of financial variables that influence cash flow (possibly negatively) show large unexplained variability, covering against them by hedging is a valuable thing a priori. On second thought, however, this intuitive statement that hedging (always) creates value is heavily challenged, especially from the perspective of traditional finance theory. In general, it can be argued that hedging does not systematically create value since, on average, the profits of hedging and its (opportunity) costs balance out; sometimes you win, sometimes you lose, since *ex post* cash flow could have been higher without the hedge. To the extent that one includes the transaction costs of carrying out hedging operations, it might actually even lower value.

For firms, the traditional corporate finance theorem (i.e. the Miller-Modigliani theorem) takes this argument one step further. This theorem states that firms only create value by making good investments, i.e. those that increase (future) cash flow; whether those investments are financed through debt, equity or retained earnings is irrelevant. If methods of finance and the character of financial risks is not treated differently by investors with respect to the required rate of return they ask for their investment, managing these risks by hedging is pointless. Moreover, if investors want to avoid the financial risks attached to holding shares in a specific firm, they can reduce this risk by diversifying their portfolio of shares, investing also in other firms. The conclusion is then: firms need not manage their financial risks, investors can do it for themselves.

In recent years, this 'traditional' theorem has been challenged and it has been demonstrated that hedging can indeed create value for a limited, specific number of reasons. One is that risk management can reduce taxes (cutting the average tax bill because derivatives can reduce profits in good years and raise them in bad years); another reason might be that some investors may not want, or be able, to hold diversified portfolios (for instance, because the firm is privately-held, and not traded publicly). But most prominently, risk management can add value because it can reduce the 'cost of financial distress'. In *sensu stricto*, this refers to the probability of severe financial problems and even bankruptcy because of a sharp cash flow downturn: a risk management programme that eliminates this risk of bankruptcy does increase the agent's value position.

More importantly, *sensu lato*, this notion of financial distress refers to the inability to execute the value-enhancing investment options an agent has because of financial constraints, be it the lack of internal resources and/or an external credit constraint, as a result of an (unhedged) lower than expected cash flow outcome. As such, hedging cash flows (and, as such, locking into a certain or minimum annual cash flow) can ensure that an agent (individual, firm, country) has enough internally-generated resources to finance the desired volume of investment projects that enhance the agent's value in future (Froot e.a., 1993), or can overcome an external credit constraint. A typical example of value-enhancement through derivatives as to ascertain that sufficient resources are available to finance investment is presented by the case of Mexico at the end of the 1980s (see Case 1).

CASE 1: MEXICO'S OIL HEDGING STRATEGY

In late 1990 and the first half of 1991, Mexico executed a financial risk management program to protect its crude oil export earnings (roughly 1.3 million barrels a day) against oil price risks. The strategy consisted of buying oil put options at different strike prices (to guarantee a minimum price), selling oil futures and using short-term (up to one year maturity) oil swaps (to guarantee a specified price) to hedge against a decrease in oil prices in world markets. By using these derivatives, the country effectively insured a minimum price for a part of its main exports over the near future. In addition, it established a special contingency fund to protect against a trend of declining oil prices.

This overall strategy ensured that Mexico received at least US $17 dollar a barrel, the price used as the basis for its 1991 budget. This reassured the international financial community (with the IMF on top) and investors that, *regardless of oil price movements*, the economic program and the budget would be sustained. Since oil prices fell significantly in early 1991, the strategy was successful *ex post* as the oil revenue was higher under the hedging program than without it. But even more importantly in this context, it created value *ex-ante* by sending a strong signal of economic adjustment capability and willingness to the international financial community, which paved the way to get a Brady-type external debt reduction deal in 1991, and, as a consequence of this Brady-deal and adjustment stance, regain voluntary access to international capital markets.

Source: Claessens (1993), p.36.

A clear example of an external financing constraint that was lifted using derivatives is the case of the Mexican copper producer Mexicana de Cobre (see Case 2).

CASE 2: MEXICANA DE COBRE

In 1989, Mexicana de Cobre (MdC), a copper mining subsidiary of Grupo Mexico, needed US $210 million to refinance debt that was assumed when the company went public and was acquired by Grupo Mexico in 1988. At that time, no Mexican firm was able to borrow on the international financial markets because of the debt crisis. The New York branch of investment bank Paribas nevertheless managed to arrange the loan with a syndicate of international investors, based on setting up a financing scheme including the use of derivatives.

The basic problem was that in order to accommodate investors, the coppor-price and the payment risk had to be reduced. To deal with the payments risk, a long-term contract with a coppor user, SOGEM, and an escrow account were established, whereby SOGEM agreed to monthly purchases of a certain amount of copper anodes; the revenue was sufficient to cover the loan repayments, albeit at world market prices. The revenues of the deal were to be placed in an escrow account at Paribas, so the proceeds could only be used for repaying the loan (and not used by MdC for other purposes). In order to deal with the coppor price risk (because the supply contract was at variable world prices), Paribas entered into a commodity swap with copper being the underlying asset (a 'copper swap') with MdC through its London branch, whereby MdC agreed to pay (out of the escrow account) Paribas an amount based on the floating copper price it received under the SOGEM deal and Paribas agreed to pay (into the escrow account) MdC an amount based on a fixed price for the copper for the full term of the loan. The combination meant that the necessary funds to pay back the loan would be available in the escrow account, regardless of copper sales or world copper price changes. This scheme, together with MdC's history of excellent operating performance and Mexico's favourable economic reform policy, made possible the first voluntary lending to the Mexican private sector in hard currency since 1982, despite the Mexican sovereign debt crisis which was not yet fully resolved.

Source: Claessens (1993).

2. Who Uses Derivatives and Why?

The participants in derivatives activity can be divided into two groups: end-users and dealers. End-users consist of corporations, governmental entities, institutional investors, and financial institutions.

Dealers consist mainly of banks and securities firms, with a few insurance companies and highly-rated corporations (mainly energy firms) having joined the ranks.

2.1. End-users

Derivatives are used by end-users to lower funding costs, enhance yields, diversify sources of funding, hedge and express market views through position taking. We shall further discuss the first three targets.

Lowering funding costs: Before large private or public organisations, including governments, issue new bonds the swap opportunities are considered very carefully. A standard example is a firm issuing bonds in a market that is cheap for the corporation at hand, and then swapping the proceeds immediately to the currency needed for financing the investment. It has been estimated that from 1985 to 1989 about 70% of all new issuances where swap driven. Arbitrage gains of 0.5% where not uncommon in these days and implied huge savings for the issuer. Governments use currency and interest rate swaps extensively when managing their public debt. For example, during the 1987-1990 period and because its foreign debt was too expensive, the Finish government entered into approximately 50 swaps. This allowed the treasury to transform about 30% of all its foreign debt into local debt. In 1989 Yen denominated foreign debt accounted for 23% of all foreign debt, one year later only 5% was still Yen denominated. With the Yen rising fast, this operation implied considerable economies for the Finnish citizen.

Hedging risk: Volatile interest rates may affect the value of the firm's assets as well as its liabilities. Corporate treasurers take this increasingly into account when designing a firm's hedging strategy. Derivatives allow them to adjust the interest rate sensitivity of the firm's debt so that it more closely matches the interest rate sensitivity of the asset side of the balance sheet. This protects the firm's net worth from interest rate risk.

Financial risks often originate from the activity of the corporation itself. For example, the micro-chip producer Intel is often paid in local currency but has few expenses in local currencies. On top of that, it takes considerable time before an order is executed and paid, while in the meantime the price, expressed in local currency, remains fixed. Both factors combined generate a huge currency risk that is natural to the firm's operations. The way out is extensive use of option and forward contracts to control the currency risk.

Stabilising and increasing yields: Institutional investors are heavily involved in the use of derivatives. Such an investor might for instance be interested in reaping the high yields of a foreign stock market but fear the foreign exchange risk. A family of swaps, called quanto swaps, have been designed to meet this demand and allow investors to diversify further without incurring currency risk. Derivatives also allow institutional investors to combine investments with different risk and return characteristics, resulting in a portfolio with a more or less fixed return.

2.2. Dealers

The explosive development of derivatives markets has radically changed the position of dealers. Early in the evolution of OTC markets, financial institutions acted for the most part as brokers finding counterparties for their customer and receiving a fee in return for this service. Acting as a broker, the institutions took no position and hence were not exposed to risk. But soon this brokerage role evolved and financial institutions started to offer contracts them-selves, thereby invoking risk. But contracts were still in relatively small numbers. The next step in the evolution was the 'warehousing' of derivatives transactions. Customers could now choose between a set of contracts, permanently on offer. Today dealers use the port-folio approach in which every new contract is added to the portfolio and the net risk of the entire portfolio is managed. The focus of risk management thereby changes from individual contracts to portfolio exposure. This allows dealers to accommodate an ever-increasing number and types of transactions.

Banks have become the dominant derivatives players, but they hold no monopoly. Securities firms, insurance companies and highly-rated corporations (especially in the energy sector) are all involved as dealers in the market. Income is generated through dealer activity as well as through taking up certain positions yourself. Often big dealers will join and form a clearing house that offers derivatives on an exchange market. Income is here generated through the bid-ask spread between contracts. Dealers undoubtedly use derivatives for the same reason as end-users, but ultimately their goal is different: they enter the market to generate income. It is in this respect remarkable to see that interest income of America's seven largest banks has decreased steadily while trading income and 'fee income' is rising. At the same time, the exposure to OTC derivatives has increased dramatically.

The existence of derivatives is usually justified by pointing to the many advantages these instruments offer to end-users, advantages that were pointed out above. But at the same time we should mention the fact that the bulk of OTC trading is inter-bank trading (cfr figures 3 and 4). It would of course be nonsense to believe that these purely financial transactions serve no purpose whatsoever. They ensure the liquidity of derivatives markets and liquidity is to a financial market what oil is to an engine, remove the oil and the engine stops.

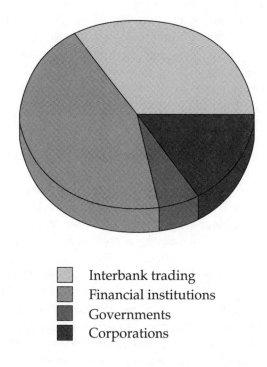

    Interbank trading
    Financial institutions
    Governments
    Corporations

Figure 3: Users of new interest rate swaps in 1987

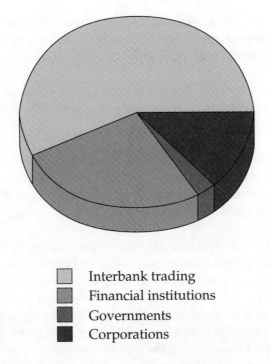

Interbank trading
Financial institutions
Governments
Corporations

Figure 4: Users of new interest rate swaps in 1995

3. The Risks of Derivatives

The risks to end-users and dealers involved in derivatives can be broadly categorised as market, credit, operational and legal risk. These risks are of the same types that banks and securities firms have faced in their more traditional roles. We shall hereafter introduce the different types of risk and illustrate the problem at hand with cases.

3.1. *Market risk*

The market risk of derivatives, like that of any other financial instrument, depends upon their price behaviour when market conditions change. Market risk is usually further broken down into six different forms of risk. We shall not introduce all of them here, but concentrate instead upon just two forms: absolute price (or delta) risk and convexity (or gamma) risk.[1]

Absolute price (delta) risk: This is the exposure to a change in the value of a derivative contract corresponding to a given change in the price of the underlying asset.

Convexity (gamma) risk: This is the risk that arises when the relationship between the price of an underlying asset and the value of the related derivative is not linear. The greater the non-linearity (i.e. convexity), the greater the risk.

The dominant risk for forward based derivatives is the absolute price risk. The gamma risk is usually very small. This makes managing this type of derivative and hedging against adverse market conditions rather simple. Nevertheless, in the case of Barings it was precisely such a forward contract, more specifically a futures contract on Japanese stock indexes, that was not properly hedged and caused the spectacular fall of the parent company.

For option contracts there is no simple linear relation between the price of the underlying product and the option price. Stated differently, the gamma risk is substantial and this makes options risky in terms of pricing and hedging. The foundations of option pricing were laid in the 1970s by Black and Scholes, whose formula defines five components of an option price. It is clear that this theoretical breakthrough – which provided its inventors a Nobel Prize – helped to develop derivatives markets. At the same time, there remain substantial pricing uncertainties. A typical problem is that Black and Scholes use a wrong specification of the volatility of the underlying product. So called fat tail distributions make the pricing of long-term options an especially devilish task. Financial institutions that offer long-term options are well aware of this and their prices will therefore contain three elements: (a) the price as determined by a theoretical model like Black and Scholes, (b) a fee for providing the brokerage and trading services and (c) a fee to compensate for uncertainty

---

[1] The other risk forms are: volatility (or vega) risk, time decay (or theta) risk, basis or correlation risk and discount (or rho) risk. For more information on this, consult any good introductory book on financial economics.

about the theoretical model. This means that option pricing always contains a grey area. Nobody really knows what the exact price and thus the exact risk connected to an option is. In a hotly contested market, it is not impossible that traders start to nibble at this grey area, thereby endangering their position and that of the market. At the level of the market, this pricing uncertainty reflects itself in uncertainty about the proper level of margins.[2]

CASE 3: MARKET RISK IN THE BOND MARKET

When in March 1994 the Bundesbank announced that the key measure of supply, M3, had grown by a freak 20 percent in one month, this message was sufficient to send a shockwave through out financial markets. On the trading floor of Liffe, the London futures exchange, dealers were overwhelmed by orders. Prices crashed. By mid-morning, the London clearing houses responsible for settling futures trades had called for members to put up,£500 million of fresh collateral to cover their position – the largest call in the market's history. On that same day, trading on Liffe hit an all-time high of £300 billion – roughly equivalent to half of the UK's annual gross domestic product. For British citizens the immediate effect of this crisis was that all fixed rate mortgages were suddenly withdrawn and replaced a few days later by much less generous offers.

The bond market crisis of the spring of 1994 was a worldwide crisis driven by a sudden swing in the direction of interest rates. This sudden shift caused considerable damage, also among corporate traders. Citicorp reported huge losses caused by swap trading on its own behalf rather than for clients, and Procter & Gamble took a $175 million hit on just one swap transaction.

Source: Ruth Kelly (1995), p. 213-214.

3.2. Credit risk

Credit risk is the risk that a loss will be incurred if a counterparty defaults on a derivatives contract. The loss due to default is seldom or never the notional principal value of the contract, but rather the cost for replacing the old contract with a new one at the new market

---

[2] On this see for instance Gordon Gemmill, Margins and the safety of clearing houses, *Journal of Banking and Finance*, 18, 1994, pp. 979-996.

conditions. Therefore, upon determining the credit-risk associated with a contract, one should ask two things: (a) what would it cost to replace the contract today, which determines the *current exposure* and (b) what would it cost to replace the contract in the future, which determines the *potential exposure*.

It is clear that there is a big difference between both types of exposure. It is rather simple to determine the present exposure. All one needs is present market prices about similar contracts. However, in order to determine the potential exposure, one needs to know future market prices and these can only be estimated. Market participants use historical prices and eventually Monte Carlo experiments (rolling the dice) to determine future prices. This gives two measures of potential exposure: an average exposure which determines the expected loss at default and a worst-case-scenario exposure which determines maximal loss. In the end, the basic rule with respect to credit risk in derivatives markets is the same as in all other markets: diversify, make sure that exposure is not too concentrated with one client, sector or country.

3.3. *Legal and settlement risk*

Few financial transactions are settled on a same-day basis. In the US equity markets for instance, the difference between the date that the contract was struck and the settlement date is five days. As a result, one party could suffer considerable losses when the price would move extensively over this five day period and might refuse to honour the deal or even be unable to do so. *Settlement risk* is part of most economic deals, because transactions usually take some time before they are executed. When it comes to financial markets, however, the size of the contracts involved is often so huge that the settlement risk must be deemed considerable. This is certainly the case for contracts which involve the exchange of the underlying (for example, currency swaps in contrast to interest rate swaps). Apart from the size of contracts, we must also mention the enormous growth of derivatives market in volume as well as in number of contracts. Both factors increase settlement risk further. A possible way out consists in the bundling of contracts – so-called 'netting' – into a master agreement. The settlement risk associated with each contract separately is now brought together into one contract. Private organisations like ISDA strongly promote the use of master agreements and have introduced a basic contract among their members that is fast becoming a market standard. Signing a contract, however, is not the end of the line; the contract must also be enforceable. And here we turn to *legal risk* i.e. the risk of loss because a contract cannot be enforced. Given the fact that derivative markets function on a global scale and bring together partners operating under different jurisdictions, we must deem the legal risk considerable. In fact, master agreements can and have at times only further obscured the legal picture.

CASE 4: HAMMERSMITH AND FULHAM BROUGH COUNCIL: A LEGAL RISK
    FAILURE

Hammersmith and Fulham Brough Council is an English local council that engaged in swap and option contracts for a combined value of $10 billion. When interest rates suddenly started to rise, these contracts implied a $1 billion loss, a debt the council could not possibly pay. Banks sought debt repayment through legal means, but the court judged that Hammersmith and Fulham had exceeded their authority by engaging in this type of contract in the first place. The contracts were therefore declared illegal and debt repayment became impossible. In this way, the dramatic position of a public authority was completely shifted towards private institutions.

CASE 5: THE MARKET THAT DISAPPEARED: NORTH SEA BRENT CRUDE OIL
    (SETTLEMENT AND LEGAL RISK)

Brent Blend is the market name for a certain type of North Sea crude oil. For this type of oil there is a well-functioning forward (i.e. OTC) market. All trading is bilateral, there is no clearing house or margin payments, and contracts are standardised. The contract size is 500.000 barrels (roughly one tanker) with delivery at Sullom Voe, the site of a tanker loading platform in the Shetland Islands. Buyers are responsible for providing tankers to transport the crude oil, which is shipped to refineries in Europe and North America. Only ten percent of all contracts result in actual delivery, the rest is settled financially. As such, this forward market is primarily a financial market.

Contracts follow each other up in what is called a daisy chain. At one end of the chain, we find a company that produces crude oil from North Sea fields, at the other end is a firm that wishes to take physical delivery. In between are purely financial operators. These daisy chains span, on average, a two or three month period. Contracts stipulate no pricing margins that influence the validity of the contract. In other words, once you enter into a contract all risks associated with price movements are yours. Another important feature of the contract is the 'fifteen-day rule'. This rule states that sellers must give buyers fifteen days notice in order to allow sufficient time for a tanker to be sent to Sullom Voe.

During the first months of 1986, the price of Brent Blend shifted dramatically from $30 a barrel in the beginning of January to only $10 by the end of March. Those who bought at the end of 1985 or the start of 1986 saw themselves confronted with huge losses. In order to escape default, many buyers refused to accept delivery of goods on grounds that the fifteen day rule had not been observed. Furthermore, many companies were situated in legal paradises like the Bermudas or the Cayman Islands. This made any legal action against defaulters very difficult. The *Wall Street Journal* reported that about 200 contracts were in dispute. This endangered the entire chain of bilateral commitments. A chain of bilateral deals is by its very nature vulnerable to default. If any link breaks, companies further down the chain will likely be obliged to default on their delivery obligations as well. In the end the entire market almost came to a halt, but did not disappear altogether. Large market participants were willing to accept short-term losses in order to keep the market going. It was not however until July 1987 before business returned to normal.

This dramatic episode did not change the micro-structure of the market; standardised contracts and daisy chains remained. It did, however, change the faces of buyers and sellers. Small trading companies who played an intermediate role in searching out deals and handing them down the chain were almost completely wiped out. Large Wall Street based investment banks replaced them and effectively took over the market. The anonymous victims of this short but powerful price movement were individual traders that disappeared without notice.

Source: R.J.Weiner (1994), pp. 955-977.

3.4. *Operational risk*

Operational risk is the risk of losses occurring as a result of inadequate systems and control, human error or management failure. Again this is a type of risk that is present in the economy at large. However, the complexity of derivatives have at times proved difficult to manage for business organisations. Some of the most spectacular accidents in derivative markets have to do with a failing internal control system. Consequently, private as well as public organisations have issued a series of recommendations to all organisations involved in derivative dealings. We mention the most important ones.

(i) Oversight by senior management of derivatives activity. This also implies that senior management can grasp what is going on, which is not self-evident given the complexity of the instruments involved.

(ii) Documentation on policies and procedures listing approved activities and establishing limits and exceptions, credit controls and management reports.

(iii) Independent risk management function that provides senior management validation of results and utilisations of limits.

(iv) Independent internal audits which verify adherence to the firm's policies and procedures.

(v) A system of independent checks and balances throughout the transaction process.

(vi) A back office with the technology and systems for handling confirmations, documentation, payments and accounting.

In another text on derivatives in this book, the authors testify how the managers of Belgian state debt engaged in derivatives contracts and more or less neglected all the above recommendations, which resulted in a dramatic failure. We shall hereafter focus attention on the Barings case, undoubtedly the most spectacular accident in derivatives markets that was largely caused by the failure of internal control mechanisms.

CASE 6: THE BARINGS DISASTER

On February 27, 1995, Barings plc, the oldest merchant banking group in the United Kingdom, was placed in 'administration' by the Bank of England. Barings was reported to have experienced losses of about $1.4 billion, exceeding the entire equity capital of the firm – estimated to be $860 million at the time – from trading in very large unhedged positions in futures contracts on the Nikkei 225 index. This spectacular case, in which one trader – Nick Leeson – sinks an entire company through one speculative act, raises two types of questions: (1) how effective is internal control? (2) how effective are local control authorities?

(i) Internal control and risk management
The absence of adequate internal audit and management-control systems is undoubtedly the direct cause for the Barings failure. Losses occurred in exchange traded markets where positions are marked-to-market and margin payments are a daily affair. This implies that over the entire contract period (about two months) it was possible to check the value of outstanding contracts each day. Nevertheless, losses accumulated and this was due to the fact that the person who engaged into the contracts was at the same time responsible for daily margin payments. This was a crucial mistake. The separation of the responsibility for payments and settlements from trading functions and independent trade verification are important elements of an effective risk-management system. Research into the disaster has revealed that management at Barings was well aware of this problem and internal reports on the matter had been circulating for about three years, but no action was taken.

But even if we take this control failure into account, it seems highly unlikely that nobody knew about what was going on. Why did nobody react? Even a belated reaction, two or three days before the final collapse could have saved the company. At a time when regulators like BIS and SEC turn more and more to internal risk-management to guarantee systemic safety, it is at the least worrying that a sophisticated merchant bank like Barings allowed risky operations to go on undetected or uncurbed for two months.

(ii) Local market authorities
Three futures exchanges were involved in the fatal contracts: the OSE (Osaka Securities Exchange), the TIFFE (Tokyo International Financial Futures Exchange) and SIMEX (Singapore International Money Exchange). SIMEX has a large trader-reporting system whereby accounts with more than 100 Nikkei 225 index futures contracts are reported to the surveillance authorities. The extent of the tradings position taken on by Barings was thus well known to SIMEX and probably some other market participants, but was not considered problematic. Barings' operation in Singapore frequently carried large positions, which were offset by opposite positions on the Osaka and Tokyo exchanges, in an attempt to profit from the small differences between the prices of like contracts. Only this time there were no offsetting opposite positions. SIMEX continued to demand daily margins, even when these became exorbitant. This continued until Friday,

February 24, when it became clear that Barings was no longer capable of meeting its margin requirements. Suddenly SIMEX was confronted with some large uncovered contracts, and some clearing members and customers expressed concern about the ability of SIMEX to continue to guarantee settlement of payments. This could have entailed the collapse of the entire futures market. However, monetary authorities in Singapore reacted swiftly and issued a press release agreeing to stand behind the SIMEX clearing house. On Monday, February 27, all of Barings' accounts on the three exchanges were suspended and the positions of the insolvent bank were as quickly as possible unwound to limit spreading uncertainty.

Regulators can learn from this episode that the controlling power of local market authorities in a global financial market is very limited. If SIMEX and OSE had exchanged information on the total position of Barings, losses would have been curbed far sooner and the collapse would not have taken place. Without systematic exchange of information, the local controller is a blind-folded player.

The Barings disaster did not stop with the Nick Leeson affair. Customers of the bank had about, $2.5 billion in deposits. Following the rules of the British Deposit Guarantee Fund, only, $35 million had to be refunded. Luckily enough, the bank was taken over and depositors rescued.

Source: IMF (1995), pp. 162-164.

3.5. Growth figures for exchange and OTC traded derivatives

Finding figures on organised derivatives exchanges is relatively easy; figures on the OTC market, by contrast, are scarce and partial. Only private industry groups offer OTC market data. This is about to change as the BIS has begun, belatedly, an initiative whereby leading market participants will report statistics on OTC market activity on a regular basis (BIS, 1997, p. 175).

The most popular measure for market activity is the notional principal value outstanding at a certain point in time (usually end of year data). This measure calculates the total value of all derivative contracts when taking into account the value of the principal (the underlying) involved. The notional principal measure provides an excellent idea about the total amount of money engaged by derivative contracts. Table 2 provides notional principal figures for the OTC market until the first half of 1997, Table 3 for market exchanged derivatives.

Table 2: Notional Principle Value outstanding of OTC traded interest rate and currency swaps and interest rate options

(in billions of US$)

	1987	1988	1989	1990	1991	1992	1993	1994	1995	1996	june 1997
Interest rate Swaps	683	1,010	1,503	2,311	3,065	3,851	6,177	8,816	12,811	19,171	22,115
Currency Swaps	183	320	449	577	807	860	900	915	1,197	1,560	1,585
Interest rate options	0	327	537	561	577	634	1,398	1,573	3,704	4,723	5,033
Total	866	1,657	2,489	3,449	4,449	5,345	8,476	11,304	17,712	25,454	28,733

source: IMF, International Capital Markets, August 1997, p. 18 and ISDA internet site

Table 3: Notional Principle Value Outstanding of the most important *Market traded* derivatives

(in billions of US$)

	1987	1988	1989	1990	1991	1992	1993	1994	1995	1996
Interest rate futures	488	895	1,201	1,454	2,157	2,913	4,959	5,778	5,863	5,931
Interest rate options	123	279	388	599	1,073	1,385	2,362	2,624	2,742	3,278
Currency futures	15	12	16	17	18	26	35	40	38	50
Currency options	59	48	50	56	63	71	76	56	43	46
Stock market Index Futures	18	27	41	69	76	80	110	127	172	199
Stock market Index options	28	43	71	94	133	159	230	238	329	390
Total	729	1,305	1,767	2,290	3,519	4,634	7,771	8,862	9,188	9,885
North America	578	952	1,156	1,268	2,152	2,695	4,359	4,819	4,850	4,840
Europe	13	178	251	461	710	1,114	1,778	1,832	2,242	2,832
Asia-Pacific	138	175	360	560	657	823	1,606	2,172	1,990	2

source: IMF, International Capital Markets, August 1997, p. 17

The most striking aspect of these figures is the spectacular growth of both markets. Over the past decade the average annual growth of outstanding notional principal for the market traded activity was 32 percent, for the OTC market it was 45 percent. These are historically unprecedented growth rates for any financial market and an indication that the development of derivatives is more than a cyclical phenomenon, it is a real structural change which confronts us with a new type of financial system.

Secondly, we see that growth in the regulated market has more or less stagnated. This is however not the case for the OTC market (see Table 4). It continues to grow and overtakes the exchange traded activity by far. At the end of 96 the OTC market was about 2.5 times the organised exchange market. OTC markets are fast becoming the cornerstone of global derivative markets. There are several reasons for this success, we single out two of them. First, the flexible, personalised nature of the OTC market gives them a natural advantage in terms of arranging suitable packages of products for customers. Secondly, the OTC markets have an important regulatory advantage over the exchange traded markets. In the US, still by far the largest derivatives market, activity on organised exchanges is regulated by the Commodities Futures Trading Commission, which has however no authority when it comes to OTC traded products. This discrepancy might be considered worrying, especially when we take into account the size of the OTC market.

Table 4: Notional Principle Value outstanding of *new* OTC traded interest rate and currency swaps and interest rate options.

(in billions of US$)

	1987	1988	1989	1990	1991	1992	1993	1994	1995	1996	june 1997
Interest rate swaps	388	568	834	1,264	1,622	2,823	4,105	6,241	8,699	13,678	10,792
Currency swaps	86	124	178	213	328	302	295	379	455	759	463
Interest rate options	..	..	335	292	383	592	1,117	1,513	2,015	3,337	2,567
Total	474	692	1,347	1,769	2,333	3,717	5,517	8,033	11,169	17,774	13,822

source: IMF, International Capital Markets, August 1997, p. 259 and ISDA internet site

The figures on the OTC market provided in Tables 2 and 4 originate from the International Swaps and Derivatives Association (ISDA). This private industry group has by far the most comprehensive data available, and the figures are used by IMF and BIS alike. But ISDA is just one association and does not provide us with the full picture. In order to rectify this situation, the BIS launched its own survey of OTC market activity in the spring of 1995. The results were amazing. At the end of march 1995 the notional amount outstanding was estimated at $40.6 trillion (see Table 5). Taking into account that even this survey did not reach all OTC participants, BIS put the final figure for the OTC market at $47.5 trillion, far above the $17.7 trillion reported by ISDA. In addition to these OTC activities, the respondents revealed that they were engaged in a further $16.6 trillion of exchange-traded derivatives. This puts the total figure for the global derivatives market at $64 trillion. To put this figure into perspective, the aggregate market value of all bonds, equities and bank assets in North America, Japan and the 15 countries of the European Union totaled $68.4 trillion, which is only about 7 percent larger than the size of the derivatives market. If we were to extrapolate the figure for the OTC market at the ISDA observed growth rates, it is not impossible that the notional principal outstanding in the OTC market alone approaches the $100 trillion at the end of 98. This figure is so huge, and the power that this money exerts so enormous that we must deem it a small miracle that such a market can get around unregulated and without even a proper idea about its size and activity.

Before sounding too alarming, let us quickly point out that the notional principal value measure is a crude measure that teaches us something about market activity, but nothing about the risk exposures associated with derivatives. A far better measure for this is the net replacement cost for a portfolio of derivatives contracts. The measure determines what it would cost to replace an existing contract by a new one at a certain point in time. This cost is a fraction of the notion principal value of the contract. The gross market value of outstanding contracts, reported in table 5, gives us a far better idea about the real exposure associated with derivatives. As can be seen, this exposure differs considerably by type of instrument. Interest rate swaps for instance entail the swapping of interest risk but not of the underlying principal, and are therefore rather inexpensive (about 2 percent of the notion principal value of the contract). Currency swaps on the other hand, imply the swapping of the principal and thus entail far bigger risks. The replacement value of a contract here can climb to around 18 percent of the notion principal value. At the end of March 1995, the BIS study puts the overall average gross market value over all types of derivative at 4 percent of notional amounts outstanding. If we combine this with the previous extrapolation on the notion principal value outstanding in the OTC market (end 1998), the real risk exposure would stand at around $4 trillion. Not the massive amount mentioned above, but still a very considerable amount of money. Furthermore, this figure could raise dramatically at times of crisis, when renewal of contracts becomes very expensive or even impossible, leaving the participants with the full notion principal value at risk.

Table 5: The OTC derivatives market at end-March 1995

(in billions of US$)

Market risk category and instrument type	Notional amounts oustanding	Gross market value	Gross market value as percentage of notional amount
Foreign exchange related instruments	13,095	1,048	8
Interest rate related instruments	26,645	647	2
Equity and stock indices	579	50	9
Commodities	318	28	9
Total	40,637	1,773	4

source: BIS, annual report, 1996, p. 159

3.6. *Structural changes in the derivatives market*

The undoubtedly most impressive structural change is the *growth* phenomenon described above. Some of these jumps have cyclical roots. The first half of 1994 noted a sharp rise in interest rate related products. This reflected the crisis in the bond market which forced market participants to hedge their positions. But the growth is too sustained to be mainly cyclical. It is fuelled by a technological revolution that allows for around the clock and around the globe trading; it is also fuelled by a better theoretical understanding of the pricing of derivative contracts; but most of all it is fuelled by an increased understanding of the unique capabilities which derivatives offer. They allow one to take leveraged positions, and with long-term hedging, risk can be packaged and adapted to one's portfolio position. It is clear that with the advance of emerging economies, this growth phenomenon is not at an end. More and more people will use these instruments simply because the advantages are real and clear-cut.

A second phenomenon in derivatives market is *commodisation*. Derivatives have developed from a 'high margin – low volume' product into a 'low margin – high volume' product. Products have become standardised. Some have argued that the reason for this is the highly publicised losses by financial and non-financial enterprises (Orange County, Procter and Gamble, Barings, Metalgesellschaft). And it is indeed the case that in the aftermath of such drama's demand for exotic, highly leveraged products collapsed and a shift towards simpler products like currency and interest rate swaps could be observed. But at the same time, we should note that most of these spectacular losses are not at all associated with exotic derivatives, but rather with standard products whose risks were relatively well known. It is not so much the product, as the way it was used which generated the excessive risk.

Commodisation not only implies the return to relatively simple products but also the standardisation of what was previously considered exotic. Digital and barrier structures, derivative products which link the pay-off to whether a certain underlying asset price reaches some trigger level, have become mainstream products because they facilitate the trading of volatility of asset prices itself. Finally, commodisation has not prevented the successful entry of new products. Credit derivatives have been a spectacular success, allowing banks to trade their credit exposure directly. We shall have more to say on this later.

A third structural change is *consolidation*. By the end of 1996 US commercial banks had $20 trillion notional principal of derivatives on their account books. Just 8 banks accounted for 94% of this amount, and the top 25 banks for 98%. The US situation is not unique, but mirrored around the globe. OTC derivatives activity becomes increasingly concentrated among the handful of institutions that can truly claim to be global institutions. This globalisation of derivative markets is also apparent in the exchange-traded segment of the market. The major US derivatives exchanges have established close links among themselves and with foreign markets. In Europe the competition and drive towards cooperation among exchange markets is particularly fervent because of the EMU project. It is very likely that the introduction of the Euro will force the until now still nationally organised European markets to become partners on a global scale or simply close down.

The final change is that the OTC market has become the cornerstone of global derivative markets. The flexibility of the market and its regulatory advantages were already mentioned as two explanatory factors. Besides this, we should also mention that the OTC market has matured and adopted positive aspects of exchange markets. In 1996 eleven of the major players in the swaps market established a swaps collateral depository, which standardises and automates the process of managing collateral, payment netting, trade valuation, administration and global reporting to other dealers involved in OTC Operations. This is certainly a positive evolution which brings OTC and exchange markets closer together.

4. Power Without Accountability

In this last part we develop a more normative approach to our topic. The central theme will be 'power without accountability'. Derivatives are not right or wrong, they are simply powerful. And power needs to be monitored and controlled. We argue that there is room for improvement with respect to monitoring and controlling, and this on the individual level as well as on the levels of the firm and of the system. This improvement should centre around the idea of accountability. To clarify this somewhat further we make a distinction between liability, responsibility and accountability. Let *liability* refer to a strictly legal interpretation of accountability. At the other end, we find *responsibility*, which has a much deeper, ethical content. When someone is held responsible for something there is a often a sense of culpability involved. Accountability should be situated somewhere in between these two. When someone is held accountable, that person has a certain responsibility for what he/she is doing, though it could be hard to place the blame entirely upon that person, or make him/her repay the damage. The distinction is undoubtedly somewhat loose, but we can try to sharpen things a little bit by way of an example. Take for instance the Nick Leeson affair. It would be counterproductive to blame the entire Barings failure upon this single person; still, Nick Leeson should be held accountable for his acts and this in a stronger sense than purely legally. What he did was also wrong in a moral sense. Accountable people are aware of the fact that what they do involves them in a deep personal sense and not just at a safe distance. At the same time, we cannot expect from a trader that he/she is constantly fully aware of the far reaching potential consequences of each trading act. This would immobilise the trader. An accountable trader knows that his/her acts can be potentially dangerous for other persons, but exactly how dangerous need not be part of his/her knowledge. It is sufficient that he/she realise that something is at stake. Likewise, an accountable company should be aware of the potential impact it has on its surroundings. A culture of accountability is careful in its operations; it breeds safety and security. We shall argue hereafter that at the personal, the company and the systemic levels there is hardly a culture of accountability, but rather a culture of unaccountable striving for fast fortune.

4.1. *The rogue trader*

Reverend Justin Welby, a former trader who turned his eyes to God, reports how he bought an US $1.5 billion option in just a few minutes over the phone (not even very large transaction). The premium for this option was US $40 million. This is a leverage of about 40 times the contract price. Each one cent move in the $/£ exchange rate altered the value of the contract by about US $7 million. This example illustrates the gearing capacity of derivatives and it is this gearing that causes the likeness of gambling, where the odds have a similar effect. The derivatives trader clearly plays with high stakes, while at the same time not putting any of his/her money at risk. It invokes an albeit exaggerated sense of power: the power to move markets and economic systems by a single phone call or from behind your desktop. It is this feeling that is embodied in Tom Wolfe's book *Bonfire of the Vanities* where the bond traders are called 'masters of the universe' and have a sense of omnipotence. This image carries much of the marketing behind the mutual funds business where successful individual traders acquire a mystical status (cfr. Soros and Boesky). They are the new alchemists converting your savings account into a goldmine. These are dangerous and unrealistic pictures that promote a culture of unaccountability. The geared nature of derivatives increases this culture of risk taking. The tragic element is that it always involves other people's money, and sometimes even their economic existence. The real effects of a gamble turned sour are rendered invisible to the fund managers by the veil of financial markets, but not in the homes of those who were lured into the gamble or who lost their job because of a company failure (cf. hereafter the case of Metalgeselschaft).

The salaries offered to these young people are at times so exorbitant that it is difficult to look upon such remuneration as compensation for labour, seeming more like buying the entire person with all the energy and time at his/her disposal. The transfer of star-performers in fund management is very much like the transfer of stars in soccer and basketball. In a certain sense, they should be considered modern slaves. And like the slave, once they stop performing, they become redundant and can be sacked without notice.[3] When they drop out, sometimes after just a short time period, many of these young people find it particularly difficult to reestablish contact with the real world.

The star of fund managers glows for just a short time-period, and then disappears into the darkness of infinite anonymity, some of their more tragic decisions however are felt over considerably longer time periods. The entire culture of financial whiz-kids must drive the young people who populate the City and other financial centres into risk-taking behaviour which they would never dare to undertake when left on their own. This has detrimental effects for society at large, as well as for the individual person involved.

Stories about rogue traders, individuals gone on a rampage, are all too familiar. Theirs are not single, unfortunate accidents, but must be considered the inevitable outcome of a culture that breeds unaccountability. The amazing part is not that they happen, but rather that they do not happen more often.

Regulators blame the individuals involved or the missing control systems within companies. But we must also mention the company culture and the implicit or explicit value system that rule financial markets. It is possible to change this culture, to breed accountability, to show traders that their acts do have consequences that reach beyond the Reuters screens.

CASE 7: THE ROGUE TRADER

On June 13, 1996, Sumitomo, one of Japan's five big trading companies revealed that Mr. Yasuo Hamanka, head of their copper trading department and an acknowledged master in his field, had lost $1.8 billion through futures and options trading on the London Metal Exchange (the real figure is estimated to be $2.6 billion). For more than ten years Hamanka had succeeded in covering up mounting losses from his employer. Like Nick Leeson at Barings, Yasuo Hamanka ran his own back office, responsible for settling the trades, on top of that he was also able to borrow from other banks without authorisation from anyone else. This allowed him to take huge positions in the

---

[3] After the 1987 stock market crash, one Wall Street company sacked almost a third of its staff without any advance notice. At 5 pm the unfortunate were informed that their presence was no longer required.

copper market, a relatively small market. By artificially limiting the supply of copper, he tried to squeeze the market and force prices up. This succeeded, but not enough. In the end British and American regulators started a full scale investigation into the functioning of the copper market and found out about the manipulation.

Already in 1991, Sumitomo was informed about strange dealings by Hamanka. A second warning came in 1994. When in the beginning of 1996 a full scale investigation into the functioning of the copper market was started, Sumitomo was again informed but failed to conduct a proper internal investigation. It would take several months and pressure from the British on the Japanese finance ministry, before Sumitomo finally came to terms with the affair and uncovered to true story.

(Source: *The Economist*, June 22, 1996.)

4.2. *Avoiding catastrophe: a case for integrated risk management at the company level*

A risk management strategy for a company has to be developed at the 'integrated' level, taking into account all risks and exposures at the same time. This is very complex, since different risks are correlated with each other and there may be 'natural' hedges. A natural hedge refers to the possibility that a certain exposure to risk on one side of the agent's balance sheet, say a future claim in foreign currency, is neutralised by a compensating position on the other side of the balance sheet, say a future liability in the same currency, to the extent that the timing and amount of the payments are the same. Hedging this already hedged position will result in not hedging at all, but create an additional risky position instead. A simple example of this is the Lufthansa case (as in Case 8), where an already hedged individual transaction, on an overall basis, results in not only an unnecessary (transaction) cost, but also adds to risk instead of curing it, because of an unspotted natural hedge.

CASE 8: UNNECESSARY HEDGING BY LUFTHANSA

In the autumn of 1984, Lufthansa signed a contract to buy US $3 billion of aircraft from Boeing. In order to hedge itself from a strong and even strengthening dollar, the firm decided to hedge this exposure by acquiring a forward contract for US $1.5 billion. Lufthansa, however, did not take into account that the firm's cash flow was in effect largely dollar-denominated. As such, when the dollar would strengthen, Lufthansa's cash flows would also increase. What happened was that the dollar weakened in 1985, falling by around 30% from its peak. This resulted not only in decreasing cash flows (as measured in the firm's home currency, the Deutschmark), but due to the derivative used, a large foreign exchange loss on the dollar forward transaction. As such, a position (the purchase of aircraft in dollars) that was in fact not exposed because also income was dollar-denominated, was turned into a exposed position due to the forward transaction.

Source: *The Economist* (1996), pp.16-17.

In the traditional view of risk management, the central goal of hedging is to minimise variance of future net cash flows. This would imply hedging of the forward-type. A pure forward transaction, however, eliminates the opportunity to potentially benefit from the upside potential. This opportunity might prove to be important, especially when one introduces the possibility that the agent believes to have superior understanding of certain risks, i.e. that they possess some comparative information advantage to exploit. As such, the ultimate goal of risk management could then be restated as to *eliminate costly lower-tail outcomes, designed to reduce the expected costs of financial distress, while at the same time preserving as much as possible the company's ability to exploit any comparative advantage in risk-bearing it may have.*[4]

However, it is not always very clear whether this presumed comparative advantage is real, and moreover, that what is effectively observed is a policy of more or less *conscious* decisions to bear significant exposures to market risk. Sometimes this presumed information advantage, with the hope of earning abnormal returns, comes with the cost of the elimination of costly-lower tail outcomes. Both issues are clearly illustrated by the Metallesellschaft case (see Case 3).

---

[4] In financial jargon, the aim of risk management can be reformulated as "the purchase of 'well-out-of-the-money put options' that eliminate the downside while preserving as much of the upside as can be justified by the principle of comparative advantage" (Stulz,1996, p.8).

CASE 9: 'HEDGING' AT METALLGESELSCHAFT

In late 1993, MGRM, the U.S. oil marketing subsidiary of the German multi-national Metallgesellschaft, contracted to sell 154 million barrels of oil through fixed price contracts ranging over a period of ten years. MGRM decided to hedge this long-term exposure to oil price increases, albeit in a non-straightforward way: instead of hedging with off-setting positions of matching maturities over the long run, it chose to take positions in short-term derivative contracts such as futures and short-term swaps, only hedging short-term with the intention of 'rolling' the entire hedging package forward each time the short-term contracts expired. It can be shown that, although complicated, the hedge was not necessarily incorrect: the firms's choice of short-term contracts can be explained in some part by the lack of liquid markets for longer-term hedging vehicles (e.g. for oil futures only up to 12 months); furthermore, it was demonstrated that, ignoring any 'complications' such as basis risk and the daily marked-to-market requirements for futures, over the 10-year period, each rolled-over futures contract would have eventually corresponded to an equivalent quantity of oil delivered to customers.

Still, even if this was indeed the case, it is clear that the hedge was not devised with the aim of minimising the variance of their net position in oil during the life of the contracts. This is because the 'complications' do matter here: the team that devised the hedge presumably took the position they did because they thought they could benefit from their specialised information and market knowledge, betting in fact on the persistence of the long-run tendency of oil spot prices to be higher than the futures prices (in 'futures' language: a situation of 'backwardation'); in more technical terms, that they would be able to turn 'basis risk' (see section 2) into their favour, because then the futures contracts could be rolled-over at a cheaper futures price.

When spot oil prices fell considerably in 1993, this had two consequences:

(i) The firm lost on its futures positions and gained on its cash positions (i.e. the present value of its long-term delivery contracts). But because the futures positions were marked-to-market while the delivery contracts were not, MGRM's financial statements showed large losses, which were in fact largely 'paper' losses when viewed over the long-term horizon of the delivery contracts;

(ii) Compounding this problem of large paper losses, however, was that the situation of backwardation of oil prices also disappeared, which added real losses to the paper ones because the short-term hedge now had to be 'rolled over' at higher futures prices: basis risk materialised, but disfavourably to the company.

Confronted with the reports on mounting losses, both 'paper' and real, the chief management of Metallgesellschaft decided to liquidate the hedge. This was due, in part, to their lack of understanding the 'paper' nature of certain losses. This decision, however, had the unfortunate consequence of also turning these 'paper' losses into real ones, leaving MGRM also exposed to rising prices on the fixed-price contract.

In order to avoid failure, Metalgesellschaft was forced to ask banks for a \$2.1 billion capital injection. At the same time, a large restructuring operation took place in which the company reduced its work force by 17%. An operation that started from presumed superior knowledge, finally turned sour not so much for those who began the operation as for the blue collar worker who had nothing to do with it.

Source: Culp and Miller (1995), Stulz (1996).

The case of Metallgeselschaft illustrates again how powerful derivatives are and how dangerous it is to play with so-called information advantages. Still, apart from the 'don't play with fire' lesson, there are other more important conclusions to be drawn.

The involvement of senior management: Derivatives should be used in a manner consistent with the overall risk management and capital policies approved by senior management. Therefore, the policies governing derivatives use should be clearly defined, including the purposes for which these transactions are undertaken. Senior management should approve procedures and controls for implementing these policies, and management at all levels should enforce them.

All this presupposes that senior management knows what is going on with respect to derivatives and really understands the risks involved. Unfortunately, this is not always the case as indicated by the Metalgeselschaft example.

The involvement of other affected parties: Derivatives branches of a firm are usually marginal in terms of the number of people working in it. The impact of this financial management, however, is not marginal. We have accordingly argued that senior management should be deeply involved in its operation. But not only management should be involved; whenever operations are undertaken that put 17% of the work force at risk, there is a strong argument that the work force should also be informed about what is going on, and even be allowed to veto a policy considered too risky. Derivatives are a shady part of the functioning of firms on which little information will be found in annual reports. Still, it is their powerful nature which forces us to reconsider this policy. Good, reliable figures plus a clear statement on the nature of the financial policy of the firm and the eventual control systems with respect to derivatives branches should be provided to all those that have a stake in the company.

Insurance before risk: From an ethical point of view, integrated risk management at the company level should be based on a strategy of 'minimum insurance-cum-open upside potential', with minimum insurance as the primary objective. The reason is very simple, the potential social costs of not giving priority to the insurance side are simply too large. In the case of Orange County, another well publicised case of a betting strategy that turned sour, the final effect was a cost cutting restructuring of the County budget with, among other things, a lay-off of 16% of the work force (around 3000 labourers) and a reduction of $18 million from the assistance budget for low-income families. It would be counterproductive to bar companies from any speculative operation. The information advantage can at times be a real one and reward the company for one of its essential tasks: knowing its field. But the minimum insurance objective should always take priority.

4.3. *Systemic risk*

In one of its reports, the BIS defines systemic risk as: "the risk that a disruption (at a firm, in a market segment, to a settlement system, etc.) causes widespread difficulties at other firms, in other market segments or in the financial system as a whole."(BIS, 1992, p. 35) The definition is very general and indicates that systemic risk surrounds our economic system. Nevertheless, some authors have argued that the derivatives revolution has in more than one sense increased systemic risk in the financial system. The main arguments for this position are given below.

Volume: As indicated in part four, the volume of derivative markets, especially OTC markets, continues to grow at a fast pace. The weight they have in the total financial system therefore increases year after year. Yet the OTC markets remain unregulated. This must be cause for concern.

Concentration: In 1991 ISDA announced that the top eight dealers in interest and currency swaps controlled about 58% of the entire market. Since then, the figure has only risen. The derivatives market is certainly not the only concentrated capital market; the bond market is probably even more concentrated. But given the fact that much of the activity in derivatives occurs unregulated, this must again be reason for concern. The possible impact of the disappearance of a big market participant might be considerable and simply unaffordable for the financial system (the too big to fail phenomenon). This in its turn increases the moral hazard problem.

Lack of liquidity: OTC products – the bulk of all financial products – are customer specific. This is the key to their success, but at the same time makes it difficult to resell an OTC product; in other words, they are illiquid. When market conditions turn the wrong way, such illiquid products can generate serious losses. The portfolio approach offers a solution. It has allowed market participants to move from risk associated with specific contracts to risk components of the entire portfolio. Usually there is enough liquidity in markets to manage these risk components. At times of crisis, however, market liquidity can suddenly collapse and leave market participants with the old product risk. A dramatic example of this is the 1986-87 case of perpetual floating-rate notes. These financial products were considered highly liquid market instruments and therefore ideal for managing net risk positions. And then suddenly they were no longer liquid, prices collapsed, and in the end the entire market disappeared. It has never been clear how much money was lost, but the amounts were considerable and the cause was a far too optimistic belief in market liquidity.

Market linkages: The flexibility of derivatives is undoubtedly one of main factors in the advent of global financial markets. The linkages between different financial markets, in terms of different instruments as well as in terms of different physical locations, has certainly increased the efficiency of financial markets, if only because of the increased arbitrage opportunities. But at the same time fostering these linkages has also made it possible for shocks to be transmitted faster and farther than was possible before. The collapse of one market is a potential threat for all markets. The Asian crisis has convincingly demonstrated the importance of contagion effects and the role of derivatives markets in these.

Unregulated market participants: Many participants in financial markets escape regulation either by situating themselves in unregulated off-shore financial centres or by circumventing existing regulation. Undoubtedly the most famous unregulated market participants are the so-called *Hedge Funds*, which, contrary to what their name suggests, do not engage in hedging but mainly in speculative activities. Hedge funds are very actively involved in derivatives markets. The leverage property of derivatives allows for aggressive position taking, which can set a financial flood into motion. In the case of the 1992-93 ERM crisis, it is clear that hedge funds have played a major role, and this in its turn has raised concerns about their impact. It should be noted that hedge funds, even when taking into account the leverage capabilities of derivatives, remain small market players, certainly when compared for instance with institutional investors like pension funds. Still, because of their active market role, they might be looked upon as leading indicators of future market evolutions. Combine this with herding behaviour and you have a recipe for financial crises. According to some observers, this is precisely what happened with the French Franc in 1993.

Lack of transparency and increased credit risk: Many transactions taking place in the derivatives market, and especially the OTC market, remain off-balance. Given the extent of the OTC market, this implies that it becomes very difficult to evaluate the exposure of counterparties. The solution seems simple enough: increase transparency, but as we shall see below this is not a simple task.

Changing the nature of credit relations: One of the most recent successes in derivatives markets have been credit derivatives. The idea is simple: if a bank believes it is overexposed to some big borrower, it can use a credit swap and exchange the initial credit risk for another. If the borrower defaults, it is not borrower's bank, but the one who accepted the credit swap, that will carry the damage. A simple instrument with an enormous potential. The advantages to the bank as well as to the borrower can be huge. The bank can manage its portfolio better and offer the borrower better conditions. But at the same time, the widespread use of such instruments could alter the nature of credit relations altogether. And it is not clear whether this would be for the better or the worse. To see why, we must consider the basic economic functions of banks. It has been argued by economists that one of the central tasks of banks is to act as a delegated monitor. It would be very hard and inefficient if each individual saver were to monitor the creditor in order to make sure that it does not default on its obligations. A bank not only pools the savings of individuals, but is also better placed to monitor the behaviour of borrowers. But when the bank can pass on the credit risk to another, the incentive to monitor might become much smaller. Whatever the net result, it is clear that credit derivatives are another nail in the coffin of old-fashioned relationship banking.

4.4. *Transparency and accountability: the heart of self-regulation*

Reports on derivatives markets from private (G30, ISDA) as well as official financial regulators (BIS, IMF etc.) are often ambiguous. On the one hand, they downplay the risks connected to these instruments: they are just another invention in a fast evolving business, the risks involved are not new, derivatives markets function reasonably well, they are excellent hedging instruments and do not threaten systemic stability. Conclusion: no need to worry, let alone to increase regulation. But on the other hand, new risks are exhibited and a wave of best practices advice is often given, underscored by a questionarie pointing out that these best practices are at this point not common practice.[5] It is interesting in this respect to follow the annual reports of the BIS, undoubtedly one of the most important regulators involved. In their annual report of 1995, officials at the BIS state: "the official view remains that existing regulations, complemented by further efforts to improve internal controls, external transparency and market functioning, should be sufficient to contain systemic risks" (BIS, 1995, p. 183). In the 1996 report, the same point of view is held up, in fact: "growing public recognition of the economic benefits of derivatives markets, a better understanding of such instruments and more prudent use of them meant that calls for

[5] Take for instance the G30 report, *Derivatives: Practices and Principles*, July 1993.

regulatory action in the area of derivatives markets abated" (BIS, 1996, p. 154). In the 1997 report, however, there are suddenly reasons for concern, and we quote here at length:

> The foregoing review of developments in the international financial markets last year has highlighted the continuing rapid growth of collateralised lending and OTC derivatives business. The resulting broadening spectrum of actors in the wholesale markets and the intermingling of exposures are raising a number of questions concerning the nature and role of core market participants, the increasing acceptance of lower rated underlying instruments and counterparties, the potential impact on the financial system of the failure of one or more large participants, and the adequacy of firm's present management structure. These developments underline the need for adjustments to the existing regulatory framework. At the current stage of the financial cycle, characterised by ample liquidity and investor's pursuit of higher yields, the potential for more varied and subtle types of risk that are not adequately captured by models of risk assessment procedures cannot be ignored. This puts a premium on greater prudence and accountability on the part of individual market participants. (BIS, 1997, p. 139)

For anyone familiar with the cautious and rather dull official language of BIS reports, the above quotation spells doom.

CASE 10: STRUCTURED NOTES, MEXICAN BANKS AND THE PESO-CRISIS

Structured notes are investment vehicles that can vastly leverage the initial capital invested. Nevertheless, in value accounting systems they can be booked as normal (non-leveraged) investments and in the currency denominated in the prospectus. They are thus an easy method to circumvent prudential regulations on currency positions or market risk associated with open positions. During 1994, Mexican financial institutions took large positions in structured notes with investment houses in New York. These notes were currency bets, that went unnoticed to the Mexican regulators and allowed banks to take advantage of the positive interest rate spreads between peso and dollar money markets. When the Mexican peso devalued in December 1994, Mexican banks were forced to sell pesos and buy dollars, thereby greatly enhancing the crisis and driving the Mexican economy into ruins. In the end, Mexican banks misjudged their market risk position and this error, or should we say unaccountable attitude, translated itself into a macroeconomic disaster that spread rapidly across the Mexican border.

Derivatives like structured notes reallocate the market risk in the financial system. Unfortunately, existing accounting practices are unable to reveal this reallocation and leave regulators with a blind spot. In this way derivatives affect macro-economic stability.

Source: David Folkerts Landau and Peter M Garber (1997), pp. 290-313.

By now we can say that there is a fairly large consensus among economists that the emergence of a bewildering array of OTC traded derivatives has obstructed the transparency of financial markets, and that this may lead to serious financial crises (Case 10 provides an example). Five reasons are put forward:
— OTC products are off-balance and few know the exact derivatives position of any company. Given the extent with which these products are used, it is impossible to judge the capital at risk position of any company when information on possible large derivative positions is lacking.
— Accounting rules are slow to adapt to the new products and are very likely to lag behind even in the future. This hollows out the effectiveness of celebrated international rules like the Cooke norm.
— Companies report their results on an annual or semi-annual basis. But given the fact that the value of derivative contracts can change dramatically with even the smallest price changes in the market, such frequency is insufficient to present a clear view of the financial position of the firm.
— OTC contracts often involve several parties, operating under different jurisdictions. In order to judge the value of such an international contract, worldwide information regarding prices and judicial rules is needed.
— Derivatives in general alter the spreading of risk in capital markets. Lack of information implies that it has become almost impossible for official regulators to have a clear view on the market position. This is especially a problem in times of crisis and prevents effective crisis management by the regulators.
Private as well as official regulators recognise the above problems and agree that a regulative answer is needed. The standard approach is to enhance the frequency and depth of financial reporting in order to give regulators as well as market participants the possibility a clearer picture of the net capital position of a market participant. Rendering markets transparent again and using the self-regulating

capacities of the market to prevent any major disaster, seems to be the strategy behind this approach. The case of self-regulation has been supported by private groups (ISDA, Group of Thirty) and official bodies (G10) alike. It fits well and is often argued through an ideology of self-regulating markets, which has supported, and still supports, the deregulation movement in financial markets. But it is probably more realistic to say that self-regulation is at this point the only option left. Globalised and liquid financial markets, with their highly diversified accounting practices, have left nationally organised regulators on the defence. In the end, the only option is to ensure that the individual financial players all have the right information and good risk management systems.

Increasing information streams is undoubtedly an important aspect of the problem, and any proposition that helps to enhance transparency (and reduce the asymmetric information problem) should be supported. But it is unclear whether transparency alone will do the trick. There is for instance an ongoing debate between private organisations and official regulators about what type of information is needed and it is very unlikely that this debate is going to stop soon. The reason is very simple: in an industry where there is a permanent battle over information, and in which small information advantages move fortunes, it is unlikely that a consensus on what to reveal by whom will emerge very soon.

But even if we were to reach a consensus, and even if we were to devise good risk management models, there is still this other aspect, which is according to us the most important one: what is the attitude of market participants? How do they use their risk management models? As the above BIS quotation suggests, in the end it all depends upon the accountable attitude of market participants. And here there are indications that the virtue of prudence is sometimes completely neglected. As an example, consider another recent financial debacle: the collapse of LTCM.

CASE 11: LTCM AND THE RISK ATTITUDE OF BANKS

Long-Term Capital Management (LTCM) is a hedge fund that had John Meriwether among its founders, a legendary former head of Solomon Brothers' bond-arbitrage unit, as well as Robert Merton and Myron Scholes, who shared the 1997 Nobel price for economics for their contributions to the understanding of financial risk. Formed in

1994, the Hedge Fund had been successful for several years in a row, with average annual returns of 40 percent. But in the summer of 1998, things went seriously wrong. Market prices moved in the wrong direction and in just a few weeks the $4.3 billion in equity capital were almost wiped out. On September the 24th, Alan Greenspan himself summoned the bosses of leading banks to a meeting in New York. They were kept in the room until 3:00 a.m. the following morning, until they had hammered out an injection of $3.65 billion to keep LTCM alive. This arm-twisting attitude of the Fed revealed that there were serious worries that if LTCM had gone bankrupt, others could have followed and resulted in a major financial crisis.

In the aftermath of the crisis, it became clear that the major participants in LTCM were big banks (UBS, JP Morgan, Deutsche…) who had lent at an incredibly generous rate, giving a debt to equity ratio of fifty to one! Nobody with such a debt burden should be able to convince a bank to continue to give money. However, the stratospheric returns of the previous years convinced banks to continue to support the hedge fund, as if such returns themselves did not reveal the risky investment strategy of LTCM. But what is even more worrying is that big banks themselves used the same investment strategies as LTCM. This was probably the most important reason for the Fed's intervention: if LTCM had failed, it would have left some major banks badly exposed. Some reports say that banks had an exposure of over $3 trillion in the same types of arbitrage strategies that caused the downturn of LTCM. Another adverse move in prices could have caused the downfall of a major market player, and serious trouble for the markets in general. In the end, the problem rests with the risk-management strategies of banks. These strategies are supposed to stop any major crisis, but the above example points out that a bank's attitude of unaccountability with respect to risk, provokes rather than prevents disaster.

Source: *The Economist*, October 1998, several issues.

Conclusion

Occasionally infamous, increasingly ubiquitous, derivatives have transformed financial markets and continue to do so. We can and do not want to deny their existence, the benefits they have brought are real and the basis of their success. But we must point out the dangers as well.

Financial markets are like nuclear energy plants. They generate a lot of power that can be used for many beneficial tasks. At the same time, however, there is always this risk, this doom that something might go wrong with possible disastrous effects. When he describes the 1987 stock market crash, Reverend Justin Welby turns to this nuclear metaphor.

"The events of October 1987 are often referred to as the melt-down of the markets. My clear memory is of the whole executive board of directors standing in my office gazing in awe at a Topic Screen (showing FTSE prices) as waves of red chased across the screen. The use of nuclear metaphors was apt. A system that seemed safe had assumed a life of its own." (Welby, 1997, p. 92)

Financial crises, like nuclear disasters, come quick and with a far spreading fall-out which causes damage over a considerable time period.

Derivatives are powerful instruments, which demand rigourous checks and balances at the level of the individual firm, at the level of the financial market, at the systemic level and at the political level. It would be criminal negligence not to control them.

References

BIS (1992), *Recent Developments in Interbank Relations*, Bank for International Settlements.

BIS (1995), 65th Annual Report, Basel, Bank for International Settlements.

BIS (1996), 66th Annual Report, Basel, Bank for International Settlements.

BIS (1997), 67th Annual Report, Basel, Bank for International Settlements.

BIS (1998), 68th Annual Report, Basel, Bank for International Settlements.

CLAESSENS, S. (1993), Risk Management for Developing Countries, World Bank Technical Paper n° 235.

CULP, Christopher and Merton MILLER (1995), 'Hedging in the Theory of Corporate Finance: A Reply to our Critics' in *Journal of Applied Corporate Finance*, 8(Spring 1995), pp.121-127.

ECONOMIST, The (1996), 'Too Hot to Handle. A Survey of Corporate Risk Management' (10 February 1996), 25p.

Folkerts-Landau, DAVID and PETER M GARBER (1997), Derivative Markets and Financial System Soundness, in: Charles Enoch and John H. Green (eds.), *Banking Soundness and Monetary Policy: issues and experiences in the global economy*, IMF, 1997, pp. 290-313.

FROOT, K., D. SCHARFSTEIN and J. STEIN (1993), 'Risk Management: Coordinating Corporate Investment and Financing Policies' in *Journal of Finance*, XLVIII(1993)5, pp.1629-1658.

GEMMIL, Gordon (1994), 'Margins and the Safety of Clearing Houses' in *Journal of Banking and Finance*, 18(1994), pp. 979-996.

GROUP OF THIRTY (1993), *Derivatives: Practices and Principles*. Washington (DC), Group of Thirty.

GROUP OF THIRTY (1997), *Global Institutions, National Supervision and Systemic Risk*. Washington (DC), Group of Thirty.

IMF (1995), 'International Capital Markets: Developments, Prospects and Key Policy Issues', August(1995), 250p.

IMF (1997), 'International Capital Markets: Developments, Prospects and Key Policy Issues', November (1997), 270p.

ISDA, Internet site, http://www.isda.org/

KELLY, Ruth (1995), 'Derivatives: A Growing Threat to the International Financial System' in Jonathan Michie and John Grieve Smith (eds.), *Managing the Global Economy*. Oxford, Oxford University Press, pp. 212-240.

STULZ, René (1996), 'Rethinking Risk Management' in *Journal of Applied Corporate Finance*, 9(1996)Fall, pp.8-24.

WELBY, Justin (1997), 'The Ethics of Derivatives and Risk Management' in *Ethical Perspectives*, July (1997), pp. 84-94.

WEINER, R.J. (1994), Default, Market Microstructure, and Changing Trade Patterns in Forward Markets: A Case Study of North-Sea Oil, *Journal of Banking and Finance*, 18 (1994), pp. 955-977.

FINANCIAL ETHICS
ON THE USE OF DERIVATIVES
IN SOVEREIGN DEBT MANAGEMENT

The Case of the Belgian 'Maystadt-swaps'

Jef van Gerwen & Danny Cassimon

1. Introduction

On 2 October 1996, during the debate in the Belgian House of Representatives on the Federal Budget for 1997, Herman De Croo, a member of the opposition and chairman of the Flemish Liberal-Democrats (VLD), accused the Belgian Federal Minister of Finance, Philippe Maystadt, of bad governance: "In its debt management policy, this government is speculating with the Belgian Franc, without informing the House; at the moment, losses are due to amount to about 44.3 billion BEF".

This accusation came as a complete surprise to the other members of the House, as well as to the members of the government. At that moment, Mr. Maystadt himself was out of the country, chairing a meeting of the Interim Committee at the International Monetary Fund (IMF) in Washington, DC. He was called back urgently to justify his federal debt management policy. After a brief, but fierce, debate wherein the complex, technical arguments by far surpassed the comprehension of the average observer (and most of the members of Parliament), a vote of no-confidence was cast on the Minister's policy, and rejected by the majority. It was argued that the losses would not be as high as mentioned at first by Mr. De Croo, and would have no significant impact on the budget. With this statement, the majority settled the case for the time being, although it was clear that the issue would be debated in greater detail in the Finance Committee of the House. In August 1996, however, the public attention was immediately diverted towards other, more emotional dossiers, such as the Dutroux affair, the Agusta and Dassault affairs (dealing with corruption of political parties, and several ministers), and the Rwanda-Committee (investigating the death of ten Belgian soldiers on a UN-mission). In this stream of emotional public events, and special parliamentary committees of investigation, a highly technical dossier on sovereign debt management policy was quickly forgotten.

This, however, does not seem justified. Losses on financial operations in the range of several billions of Belgian francs, possibly as a result of speculative behaviour, are significant enough. They are even more so, when they are incurred by an actor who is a not a private investor, but a public authority, who may be assumed to respect a specific deontology. Moreover, this issue emerged at a moment when more people began to worry about the increased use of derivative financial products, and the risks involved, mainly as a result of a series of catastrophes, both in private firms (Barings, Metallgesellschaft, Gibson Greetings), as well as semi-public entities (e.g. Orange County). Apart from the individual risks, one wonders whether the massive use of derivatives is not increasing the risk of a major breakdown in the international financial system (the so-called 'systemic risk'). Is more regulation needed here? And what happens when governments, who are supposed to control and regulate the system, are themselves starting to act as investors, and possibly as speculators? Can a Finance Minister at the same time be active as an investor on the market, and, in the international organisations such as the EU or the IMF, as a regulator or controller of the same market? With this contribution, we come back to the original debate in the House on the 'Maystadt-swaps', in order to place the issue within a broader political and ethical framework.

2. An Attempt to Reconstruct the Facts

As is the case in other countries, the Belgian government is covering part of its financial needs by borrowing externally in foreign currency. As a part of its debt management policy, the Treasury is using common financial derivative techniques such as swaps, including so-called currency swaps, interest rate swaps, as well as cross-currency swaps.

A swap is generally defined as an exchange operation, by which two parties within a specified time period, at regular intervals, exchange payments. These exchanged payments can be of a dual nature: either they are exchanges in different currencies (labeled as currency swaps, e.g. exchanging a payment in US-dollars with one in DEM), in different interest rates (labeled as interest rate swaps, e.g. exchanging a fixed interest rate payment for a variable interest rate payment), or a combination of the two (cross-currency swap). Depending on the type of swap, one will only exchange interest payments on the underlying loans, or also the underlying loan principal itself.

The rationale for using swaps is based on the principle of comparative advantages, enabling both parties in the swap to lower their financing costs on the underlying loans; at the same time, they can be useful for hedging.

Using comparative advantages by swaps can be briefly explained as follows: a party can have more advantageous borrowing conditions in one segment of the international capital markets than in another one (say in US dollars versus DEM), while another party can be in the opposite situation. Both, however, prefer to borrow in the segment (here, in the currency) with the disadvantageous conditions, e.g. for hedging reasons. As such, both can gain by borrowing in their relatively cheap market, while immediately swapping the proceeds of the borrowing amongst them. By doing so, both parties can borrow in their preferred, but relatively costly, market segment at terms that are close to the borrowing conditions of their cheap market segment. They share the total profit determined by the terms of the swap.[1]

By using these techniques, the Treasury indeed manages to reduce the financing cost of external borrowing. At the same time, these instruments can be used for hedging, since the swaps change the currency or interest rate structure of the debt involved.

2.1. *The initial operations, denoted as 'arbitrage swaps'*

Apart from these conventional swap techniques, between 1989 and 1992, the Belgian Treasury engaged in a series of operations,

---

[1] Similar to the Hechkser-Ohlin theorem of relative comparative advantage in international trade, it is not necessary that each party in the swap has an absolute comparative advantage in one market. The fact that the difference in lending conditions is bigger in one market than in the other one is sufficient for mutually advantageous swaps to exist.

apparently named (by the Treasury itself) 'arbitrage swaps'. Basically, the Treasury tried to create liabilities in strong currencies (at relatively low interest rates), such as the Swiss franc and the DEM, while having assets in weak currencies (at relatively high interest rates), such as the Italian lira, the Spanish peseta and the British pound.[2] By doing so, it was hoping that the net gain on interest rates (higher interest income received than paid) would not be dissipated by changes in the value of the (weak) currencies, so that the financing cost of debt could be further reduced.

Although these latter operations can be labeled as 'swaps' in the broad sense, they can not be considered as 'arbitrage' operations in the strict, financial sense of that term. Arbitrage refers to taking positions leading to a certain and well-known profit, without any type of risk involved. One type of arbitrage is the so-called 'covered interest rate arbitrage', leading to the theorem of covered interest rate parity, which states that, at each point in time, the observed forward premium (the percentage difference between the current spot and forward bilateral exchange rates) should equal the interest rate differential between both currencies.[3]

To the extent that no hedging element (such as a currency forward operation) entered in the arbitrage swap operations of the Treasury, these operations should rather be labeled 'uncovered interest rate parity', stating that, *ex ante*, market expectations of changes in the nominal bilateral exchange rate between two currencies are reflected in the difference between interest rates, earned on investing in the two currencies: in order to make up for the value change of the weakening currency, agents require a higher interest rate on investing in that currency. As such, arbitrage swaps can result in a gain when the depreciation of the weak currencies, as implied by the difference in interest rates, does not (fully) materialise during the horizon of the operation. They can result in substantial losses when the weak

[2] In the 'Annual Reports on Sovereign Debt' ('Staatsschuld. Jaarverslag'), these operations can be found under the heading: 'debt in foreign currency', starting from the 1990 Report. The 1995 Report states: "On 31 December 1995 the total amount of arbitrage swaps outstanding amounted to 58.6 billion BEF, with the following composition: against 54.7% CHF, 41.2% DEM, 2.7% BEF and 1.4% DFL, stood 37.4 FRF, 37.4 ITL, 19.7 UKP and 5.5% SKR." ('Staatsschuld. Jaarverslag 1995', p. 72, our translation).

[3] More precisely: $F/S = (1+r_h) / (1+r_f)$ where F is the current forward rate, S the current spot rate, r_h the home currency interest rate and r_f the foreign currency interest rate (expressed in direct notation).

currencies unexpectedly depreciate much more than indicated by the interest rate differential: currency risk is not hedged here, also explaining why counter-parties for these 'swaps' could easily be found.

Apart from the speculative element, the arbitrage swap operations seem to have had a cosmetic, but clearly political, 'budgetary-technical' advantage: the Belgian budgetary accounting system calls for interest payments transactions and exchange rate valuation changes to be booked under different headings of the budget. As such, the higher interest payments earned on the 'weak' currencies caused an immediate positive effect on the budget (deficit), more precisely, on the current account balance (title I of the budget), while (potential) losses due to exchange rate changes could be somewhat concealed in a different section of the budget.

Between 1989 and 1992, the notional amount of the arbitrage swap operations of the Treasury increased gradually, from 52.6 billion BEF in 1990 to 36 swaps and a notional amount of 97 billion BEF in April 1992.

During that period, at first sight, the exchange rate risk appeared to be small, since most of the currencies apparently used in the swaps were linked to each other in the 'currency snake' of the European Monetary System (EMS), allowing only for limited fluctuations, with European Central Banks (and governments) committed to taking a firm stance on exchange rate stability, with a view on future European unification. As such, betting on higher net interest income than currency losses, at first looked like a strategy without much risk.

All seemed quiet at the exchange rate front, until the Pound left the EMS in September 1992 (while rapidly depreciating afterwards), and the Italian lira and Spanish peseta devalued soon after. As a consequence, the higher risk premium (coming from anticipated depreciation, reflected in the interest rates) and the likely gain on interest rates was overcompensated by the exchange rate depreciation of the weak currencies: against about 10 billion BEF in net interest gain from the 1989-1992 period, stood currency losses of about 44.3 billion BEF (measured at the time of the De Croo statement, on 2 October 1996; according to a later statement by the Minister of Finance, the Treasury itself used an even higher estimate of potential loss at that time, namely, 53.8 billion[4]) The exact final

----

[4] *Financieel Economische Tijd*, 23 January 1998.

outcome cannot be calculated yet, first of all, because some of the operations have not yet matured, so that future currency changes will still influence the result, and secondly, because the Treasury, trying to limit its losses, engaged in new operations during 1992.

2.2. *Trying to make up for the initial losses*

The initial reaction of the Treasury to the first signs of a likely devaluation of the Italian lira appears to have been a move to hedge its exposure by engaging in a new series of (arbitrage) swaps in the order to spread the risks over more currencies (including operations in the Swedish crown and the French franc) and by regrouping the maturity dates of existing swaps into the period of 1998-2002. To achieve this result, 21 new swaps were contracted in June 1992, for an underlying amount of 19 billion BEF.

In the second half of 1992, however, it became clear that not only the Italian lira, but also the Swedish crown, the French franc and the Spanish peseta were endangered, meaning that the diversification efforts would only result in postponing losses, without really limiting them. When confronted with this new situation, the Treasury decided to limit further losses by using other hedging devices, and among others, to engage in a combination of options operations.

Options are another type of financial derivative product, having a number of characteristics different from swaps. An option is a contract between parties giving the buyer the right, but not the obligation, to buy (call option) or sell (put option) a specified amount of a financial asset at a predetermined price (the strike price), and this during a specified future period (= American option), or at a specific moment in the future (= European option). For that right, the buyer pays a non-refundable up-front fee (the premium) to its counterparty, the seller (or writer). The writer cashes in the premium, and has an obligation to honour the contract when the buyer decides to execute the option.

Contrary to forwards and swaps, the pay-off profile of an option is non-linear. The maximum a buyer of an option contract can lose is the premium; however, the buyer can gain a great deal. The counterparty in the option, i.e. the seller (or 'writer') cashes in the premium; he/she must honour the obligation whenever the buyer decides to execute the contract. His/her gain is limited to the premium and his/her losses can be considerable.

The Treasury basically combined buying (five) currency put options with a short maturity and selling (five) long-term put options.

The purpose of buying put currency options as a hedging device is clear: it gives the owner the right to sell (in this case the weak) currency at a minimum price, the strike price, and as such, to limit losses when the weak currency indeed depreciates, while at the same time still allowing spot transactions when the feared weakening does not materialise.

At the same time, five other options were sold, obviously in order to cover the cost of paid premiums on the bought options. These options which the Treasury sold appear to be of the knock-out type. A knock-out option belongs to the third-generation options (so-called 'exotic options'), within the class of 'barrier options'. When the barrier is reached, the contract stops existing and all contractual obligations (for the writer) are wiped out.

More specifically, the instrument most likely included a cap barrier: if the particular currency further appreciated to the barrier level, the contract was canceled, and the Treasury could cash in the premium without any other contractual obligations left on the option contract. However, if the currency involved would instead substantially (i.e. taking into account the premium received) depreciate, the option contract would result in a substantial loss (see figure 1).

One of the knock-out options was a so-called 'power' knock-out (on dollars). Although this concept appears to be unknown in financial derivative textbooks, reference to other cited instruments in textbooks (such as power swaps), enables us to assume the likely effect: the possible occurrence of a more than proportional loss (e.g. the squared difference between the spot and exercise price). As such, for a naked option, the likely pay-off profile of a written power knock-out put can be sketched as in figure 1.

Apparently, the feared scenario of a falling dollar exchange rate materialised, resulting in additional losses incurred on the sold power knock-out option.

2.3. *Who was involved in the decision-making?*

Until now, we have tried to reconstruct the debt operations of the Treasury, without specifying the persons involved in these operations. Evidently, the people steering and executing the debt management policy are public servants: members of the administration of

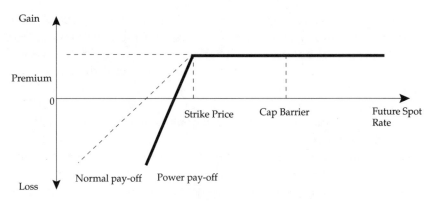

Figure 1: Likely pay-off profile of a
naked written power knock-out put option

the Treasury and members of the cabinet staff of the Minister of
Finance. Some, like staff personnel, are appointed by the Minister,
meaning that the Minister has to take political responsibility for their
actions. In the House of Parliament, Minister Maystadt has stated
that he had never been informed about the above-mentioned initiatives during the operations. Only the broad policy framework and
the general results were known to him. Only in September 1993, so
he declared, was he briefed specifically about the disappointing
results of the swap and options operations by Jean Basecq, who was
then inspector-general of the Treasury.

Mr. Basecq appears to have been solely responsible for the daily
foreign currency debt management operations in derivative products. This implies that one and the same person was running both
the front and the back office, a position comparable to the one of
Nick Leeson in the Singapore Office of Barings. No wonder that the
Annual Report of the Treasury of 1992 stated the necessity of restructuring the swap operations office, including the establishment of an
effective control unit, which would supervise also the operations in
Euro Medium-Term Notes, which were at that moment carried out
in another unit.[5]

---

[5] 'Staatsschuld. Jaarverslag 1992', p. 52. ('Annual Report on Sovereign Debt'). The
comments on the external debt management policy in the Reports between 1990 and
1995 excel in their use of elliptic and hermetic language. Those knowing the facts
from other sources are to a certain extent able to interpret the text; but, relying solely
on the Annual Reports themselves, no conclusions can be drawn regarding the
magnitude of the losses, or the sequence of policy decisions at any particular time.

The broader policy decisions on external debt management appear to have been made in the so-called 'Market Committee' of the Treasury, at that time comprising (among others) Olivier Lefebvre, then financial advisor of the Minister, and Grégoire Brouhns, a former Head of staff of the Minister and from 1990 the Administrator-general of the Treasury. Jean Basecq reported directly to the Market Committee, and through the Committee, to the Minister and to the Controller of Government Accounts (Cour des comptes, Rekenhof).[6]

In practice, it appears rather unlikely that a single public servant was able to decide on transactions valued in billions without informing the Minister. During a recent visit to the Treasury, the Finance Committee of the House learned that the decision on the 'power knock-out' was taken by Olivier Lefebvre, Jean Basecq and "someone from the debt management unit of the Treasury".[7]

At least three additional features are worth mentioning with respect to the absence of good governance in the Belgian debt management:

(i) It was not until 1992 that the Treasury started to install the necessary computer infrastructure in order to run 'Asset-Liability Management' models to monitor the consequences and risks of its debt management policy. A note of the Controller of Accounts states that the software supporting such models was not yet fully operational by April 1996. This means that the Treasury was completely dependent on the information delivered to it by its counter-parties in the derivative contracts, and that it was not able to assess the risks involved independently.

(ii) Only in 1994 did the Minister of Finance take effective measures to guarantee internal control of the foreign currency operations of

---

[6] This information is included in a note of the Finance Ministry to the Controller of Government Accounts, drawn up by Jean Basecq, on 15 October 1993: "Des opérations de swaps, d'options et d'arbitrage entrepris par le Trésor" (*De Morgen*, 10 October 1996, p. 17; *Trends*, 24 October 1996, p. 24-25). Olivier Lefebvre later became Chief of Staff of Minister Maystadt (on September 1, 1993) and is now president of the Brussels Exchange (since 1996); Jean Basecq died on 20 January 1996, ending his career of civil servant as Director-General of the Treasury; Grégoire Brouhns was promoted to Administrator-General of the Ministry of Finance.

[7] Quote from the *Financieel-Economische Tijd*, 13 November 1996, which also identified the third person as "possibly Baudouin Richard, a former employee of JP Morgan".

the Treasury (e.g. by installing separate front and back offices). They became operational in 1995.

(iii) Both the Controller of Government Accounts and the Minister himself have always avoided informing Parliament before they were forced to do so by the 1996 initiative of the opposition, arguing that "they did not want to risk undermining the confidence in the Belgian Franc". On several occasions, the Controller tried to pressure the Minister to inform Parliament. On 27 April 1996, the president of the Controller explicitly asked the Minister to brief the president of the House of Representatives, Raymond Langendries, in order to give a systematic account of the results of the arbitrage swap operations since 1990. At the moment when Mr. De Croo disclosed some of this information to Parliament, on October 2 of the same year, the Minister had not yet taken any initiative to this effect.

2.4. *Silently rewinding the operations*

Since the beginning of 1994, the Treasury seems to be more active in rewinding and restructuring the former positions, whenever the financial markets situations allow it to do so.

First of all, the Treasury has restructured the power knock-out contract, in order to restrict its likely losses. This restructuration is a costly operation in itself, having cost the Treasury almost 5 billion francs up to now. To this effect, a provision (composed of up-front reserves) has been made of about 20 billion francs, kept outside the regular budget (off balance) and outside the country, probably on London accounts of intermediaries. In March 1998, the power knock-out expired, resulting in an effective loss of about 5 billion BEF. At the same time, both as a result of a positive market evolution and of the risk reduction strategy, the potential loss on capital was reduced from 46.2 billion in October 1996 to 15.9 billion in December 1997.

In October 1996, it became known that the Treasury was also negotiating with the counter-party of the power knock-out option contract, trying to obtain an arbitrage settlement. It defended the argument that it had received insufficient information on the speculative nature and the possible risks of this type of instrument.[8]

---

[8] *Financieel-Economische Tijd*, 29 October 1996. The identity of the counter-parties of the Treasury was not revealed at the time of the debate, although rumors at that time included investment banks such as Morgan Stanley (according to FET), Merrill

In January 1998, the arbitrage committee decided the case in favour of the Treasury; this will probably lead to an out-of-court settlement between parties later in 1998, whereby Merrill Lynch will pay a certain sum to compensate the Treasury. The Treasury is asking 11 billion BEF, but the payment will likely be much more limited (between 3 and 4 billion BEF). Additionally, as a result of the favourable decision of the arbitrage committee on the power knock-out, the Minister decided to extend the arbitrage procedure to other similar derivatives transactions.

3. Analysing the Moral Issues

3.1. *Speculation?*

Once the facts became known to the wider public in 1996, most commentators focused on the speculative character of the operations. How could one possibly allow the Treasury to speculate on the international markets with the taxpayer's money?

But before jumping to conclusions, one must define what is meant by speculation. In a broad sense, every participant in financial markets, even the most prudent one, is a speculator, because he/she is willing to buy or sell financial products according to his/her subjective estimates of the expected evolution of prices. Speculation in a stricter sense, however, implies that an agent actively seeks to profit from future changes in the price of an asset (and is willing to take some risk to this effect) without actively contributing in any way to the value change of the same asset.

Most observers agree that the Belgian Treasury has been involved in speculation in the latter sense as well, since it has borrowed foreign currencies in order to profit from prevalent differences in interest rates between those currencies, and was willing to accept the exchange rate risk without due hedging, in order to maximise its expected profits.

The Minister of Finance has responded to the accusation of speculative conduct that the arbitrage swaps could not be regarded as

Lynch, and the Swiss bank consortia UBS and SBC. It was not until the Treasury publicly announced the successful arbitrage settlement on the knock-out power option (in March 1998) that the identity of some of the counter-parties was revealed: Merrill Lynch confirmed in July 1998 to be involved in a negotiation with the Belgian Treasury on a payment of damages.

speculation, because the effective profits were used as a subsidy in order to decrease the interest payments of existing loans in foreign currency, and not to realise any direct result in the public budget.

That argument, however well-intentioned, misses the point: the speculative character of a transaction is not determined by the destination given to the realised profit, but rather by the starting position of the agent (does the agent hedge an existing position, or does he/she engage in a new field of risky transactions?) and by the type of means involved (especially the degree of uncovered risk-taking).

But even if we accept that the Treasury has been involved in speculation, the question remains: why should it not be allowed to do so? What type of financial risk management is appropriate for a government service, dealing with the tax money of its citizens, rather than with the risk-bearing capital of private investors? This is the real issue, to which we will turn in a moment.

3.2. *Inside information?*

A second critique, which has been voiced mainly by Jean-Paul Michel in the *Wall Street Journal* of 18 October 1996, focused on the issue of abuse of inside information by the Treasury, especially between May and September 1992. In order to reschedule in due time a series of outstanding swaps, e.g. in Italian lira, the civil servants of the Treasury would have used internal information about the upcoming devaluation of the lira, before it was available to the wider public.

Abuse of inside information is indeed a morally reprehensible practice, which is in fact prohibited by law in several countries, including Belgium. It seems possible, also, that a Minister of Finance may regularly be confronted with potential conflicts of interest in this regard, because he/she enjoys some privileged access to information about the monetary policies of Member States in the Union, while he/she is at the same time responsible for the market positions which the Treasury is taking in relation to the currencies of those same States. Such a conflict of interests might well offer some justification for the course which the Minister followed, namely, of preferring not to be informed by his staff on the daily market positions of the Treasury, but only to define the main orientations of the active debt management policy.

Nonetheless, if one looks at the above mentioned facts, one does not find indications of abuse of inside information, but rather of the opposite: the agents involved seem to have neglected crucial information about the weakening position of a number of currencies, even when it was publicly available. Eddy Plettinck, an economic advisor working at the Gemeentekrediet (Bank for Municipal Credit), stressed the fact that the depreciation of the lira in 1992 was quite predictable: "Between 1988 and 1992 inflation in Italy amounted to 30%, whereas it remained limited to 15% in Germany. This difference in purchasing power parity within a system of fixed exchange rates could only lead to a 15 % devaluation of the lira against the mark".[9] As such, it was a mere matter of time before the interest rate differences on which the Belgian Treasury had placed its bet would be translated into exchange rate fluctuations.

3.3. *A deontology of public management?*

With the following third critique, we touch upon the heart of the matter: did the Minister and his functionaries not act wrongfully, by allowing the use of financial products which may be well adapted for the management of risk capital of private investors, but not for the public finances of the State, which are destined to serve different ends (even when we are talking about public debt)?

We think we have to answer this question affirmatively. First of all, also within the private sector of investment funds, stricter rules of risk management are applied to those who control capital funds with a long-term orientation (such as pension funds, savings etc.) than to those who do not (in Dutch: "bestemmingsvermogens" versus "gebruiksvermogens").[10]

For the latter type, the maximal short-term growth of the capital fund may become a primary criterion, whereas for the former type, the certainty of obtaining a specific level of guaranteed value at a specific future date will prevail. Directors of long-term funds will therefore be required to take less risks, and to count more on fixed rent assets; they will follow additional rules of prudence and precaution. Investors of public finance should follow the model of private investors of long-term funds, rather than the model of short-term risk takers. This is also true because, in the short-term perspective,

---

[9] Quoted in 'CEPESS-Kronieken: de financiële toestand', October 1996, p. 10. (CEPESS is the study service of the Christian Democratic Party).

[10] The distinction is explained by Henk Van Luijk in: *Om redelijk gewin. Oefeningen in bedrijfsethiek*, 1993, p. 103-107.

they would increasingly be tempted to avoid taking responsibility for all the effects of their policy decisions, taking credit for the premiums obtained, and having moved out of office before the final results are in (putting off the payment of bad risk for their successors).

At the lower levels of public finance (municipal and provincial administrations) the prudential rules of finance management are very strict, indeed. One can summarise them using the following rules of thumb:

(i)   one should never spend money that one does not own;

(ii) one should immediately invest the money one does not need as well as possible;

(iii) investments and loans should be executed with the lowest possible risk;

(iv) the Treasurer is held personally accountable for possible errors of management.[11]

These would be draconian rules, if one applied them without further qualification to the management of Belgian debt at the national level. Certainly, the Treasury needs some extra manoeuvring room in order to re-finance and to reschedule its expiring loans, and even to swap loans in foreign currencies, in order to reduce the total interest burden of the debt in the long run. But, on the other hand, some similar rules of prudential judgment should also be respected at the federal level. We will mention three of them.

3.3.1. First of all, the Treasury should only be allowed to borrow, particularly in foreign currencies, when the benefit of such transactions can be realised with a limited, controllable and necessary risk. Therefore, it should borrow in Belgian francs rather than in foreign currencies, and with a fixed interest rate rather than with a floating one. Moreover, it should borrow in order to diminish the overall risk of outstanding debt rather than to enter new extra-risks. This course of action is also the one being followed by the Treasury since 1994. At the start of 1996, the public debt in foreign currency had decreased to 10% of the total debt (in March 1998, even to less than 8%); the proportion of short-term debt (maturing in less than 1 year)

---

[11] Guy Tegenbos in *De Standaard*, 4 October 1996, p. 3.

had decreased from 35% to 21%, whereas fixed rent borrowings had increased from 66% tot 77%. All these are positive indications of a safety-first policy on behalf of the Treasury. Moreover, an analysis of recent Annual Reports shows that the Minister of Finance has reached better results in debt reduction by using safe methods of debt management (new types of state loan issues, breaking with the bank monopoly among the buyers of state loans, rescheduling of terms on outstanding debt, etc.) rather than with its 'arbitrage swap' policy. After all, high risk derivatives were not necessary to reach the goal of a yearly debt reduction of 70 billion francs, which the Minister rightfully claims as his major success.

3.3.2. Secondly, prudent management implies that the systems of internal control are well adapted to the type of financial instruments one uses. Regarding this point, the Ministry of Finance has often put the cart before the horse. It started to use a variety of derivative products since the end of the 1980s, without installing the necessary technical infrastructure. Civil servants were depending on second-hand information, graphics and personal intuition, rather than on currently updated data bases. Computer data bases were only introduced in 1992, when the different administrative services dealing with swaps within the Treasury were integrated and the necessary computer simulation programs to estimate the optimum price/risk ratio of possible public debt arrangements (a 'benchmark debt portfolio') only at the beginning of 1997. This means that the Treasury depended largely on the estimates provided by the same intermediaries with which it needed to do business in derivative products: an unacceptable relationship of dependency for a national public service with regard to foreign private banks.

Moreover, the evolution of derivative transactions should be continuously monitored and controlled by an independent back office. In the private sector, such controls are executed on a daily basis; likewise, any bank must inform the Commission for Banking and Finance (the independent control body in Belgium, comparable to the Securities Exchange Commission) before starting to trade in a specific type of derivative product. While the Treasury is not legally bound by this type of control mechanism, which are limited to the private sector, it would nevertheless act wisely if it were to implement at least the same level of internal control as is required by private banks which are trading actively on derivative markets. Obviously, things only changed when it was too late.

3.3.3. Thirdly, the rules of democratic control require that the Treasury ought to regularly and correctly inform the members of Parliament, not only about general policy orientations, but also about actual financial results. Such external control was, if possible, even more poorly handled than the internal one.

From the public record as described above, we already know that the responsible civil servant, Jean Basecq, only informed the Minister of Finance about the effects of the 1992 swap and option transactions in the Autumn of 1993. This lapse of time seems rather appalling, if one starts from the supposition that a Minister is in principle accountable for the activities of the civil servants acting under his/her responsibility. On this issue, Philippe Maystadt offered the following comments in January 1997: "As far as regards the heart of the matter: it is correct that the Treasury has been involved in one unfortunate operation, which appeared to be too risky. The administration had not informed me, nor was it required to do so. I am rather prudent by nature. If I had known about it, I might not have allowed them to go along with it – which is easy to say in retrospect of course. Nevertheless, I want to defend my administration completely on this issue. They have done an excellent job during the past years. The public debt is costing us billions of francs less than before. Our debt portfolio is less expensive and less risky today than it was in 1988".[12]

We would like to suppose that a Minister, even if he does not wish to be kept informed on the daily transactions by his administration, would at least define the limits of acceptable risk/price ratios of the financial transactions that are being executed under his responsibility. If he fails to do even that, the Minister is neglecting to fulfill his basic duty. The decision to sell knock-out options in 1992 for a nominal value of 75 billion can in no way be described as an ordinary transaction, which needs no specific approval by the Minister. The Minister is responsible for structural changes in current policies which have a lasting and significant impact on the public debt (as was the case with the swap rescheduling and the option policies of 1992), and he is also politically responsible for the actions of the staff

---

[12] Interview with Maystadt in *De Standaard*, 31 January 1997, p. 13.

members which he directly appoints (as was the case for the members of the so-called Market Committee to whom Jean Basecq reported, and especially for Olivier Lefebvre, member of the committee and Maystadt's Chief of Staff). Thus, even if the Market Committee would prove to be the main culprit, the Minister should be held directly accountable.

One would expect the members of Parliament to follow a similar line of reasoning and critique. In Belgium, there is much public debate going on about a 'new political culture'. Parliamentary investigation committees have been organised to examine different political and judicial scandals, and to formulate appropriate reform proposals.

The same Parliament was never correctly informed about the 'arbitrage swaps' and their effects up to October 1996. The official 'Annual Reports of the Treasury on Sovereign Debt' between 1990 and 1995 offered insufficient data to determine correct estimates of the current debt policy, and a fortiori of the incurred losses. The Minister regularly invoked the argument of confidentiality, contending that by revealing the positions of the Treasury on ongoing financial transactions, he would increase the risk of speculation against the Belgian franc. That argument may be true to some extent (even if some commentators reply that this affirmation only confirms how badly the Treasury covered his positions in the first place), but it does not explain why the Minister did not inform Parliament on the losses that the Treasury had already taken, some of them three or four years earlier.

The provision fund, which has been set up to pay for the losses incurred, was booked outside the balance of state accounts, and did not appear, therefore, in the annual state budget. This may be correct according to accounting standards, also in the private sector, but in that case the Minister should inform parliament about the existence of such 'off balance' funds, and of their results, at least on a yearly basis. Furthermore, he is not allowed to keep the incoming money of such funds on foreign accounts, as seems to have been the case (located at the banks acting as intermediaries in London).

Consequently, one may safely conclude that the Minister failed to inform Parliament in due time. This is also confirmed by an exchange of correspondence between the president of the Controller of Accounts and Minister Maystadt in 1996.

In 1997, the Finance Committee of the House negotiated with representatives of the Ministry and of the Controller of Accounts in order to install some type of permanent parliamentary control of debt management policies. A correct balance should be found between the need for confidentiality (in those cases where it is proven necessary, not as a general line of policy!) and the right of full budgetary control of Parliament. The Minister has formulated two proposals to that effect. First, he is willing to have a yearly debate in the Finance Committee on the strategic options of debt management. Secondly, he is ready to offer full disclosure on open positions and current transactions to a select committee including the president of the House, the president of the Controller of Accounts and a representative of the Treasury. The members would be required to respect confidentiality on the data received. These proposals are moving in the right direction, but still remain below democratic standards. It would be necessary, e.g. to add at least three or four members of the House to the select committee. Disclosure to the President of the House does not offer a sufficient guarantee of parliamentary control.[13]

4. Conclusions

At this moment, the case has not yet been closed. A number of precise data on the financial transactions involved are still kept secret, and the final results will only be known after 2002, when the term of the last transaction has expired. But as citizens and observers, we think we have the right, and the duty to produce tentative analyses and conclusions on the present situation. We have two main conclusions:

(i) It seems astonishing that a Minister, under the given circumstances, would not offer his resignation, nor would he be forced by

[13] In its session of 14 July 1997, the House of Representatives came to a new proposal for controlling the management of sovereign debt, involving three sorts of House committees: the Finance committee for the budget, a sub-committee for the benchmarks of the portfolio, and a select committee of four members (two of the majority, two of the opposition), which would be allowed to look into confidential transactions, after the Controller of Accounts has informed the sub-committee of possible serious irregularities ('Report of Finance and Budget Committee in the House of Representatives', 1131/1-96-97).

the House to resign.[14] Nevertheless, core principles of democratic government are at stake in this case: the principle of accountability in government, and the right of the House to be correctly informed on current expenses and policies. No amount of utilitarian arguments ("the losses are less than initially expected", "the total result of my debt policy is a positive one", "we have learned from our mistakes", etc.) can offer a valid excuse for the failure to abide by these basic principles. The fact that both the Minister and the majority of representatives seem to accept these utilitarian arguments as convincing reveals once more the problematic nature of the 'old political culture' in Belgium: a boundless readiness to compromise.

(ii) This national case of debt management has a number of consequences on the international level, which have not yet been taken into account in the present debate. Most people presuppose that markets should be regulated by governments, which are presumed to formulate common rules in pursuit of the general interest. On the international level, such presumption already meets with serious difficulties, because no supranational institutions exist that could fulfill this role effectively. A consensus between the most powerful national states meeting in several instances (the G7, G10, OECD, IMF, etc.) has had to function as a second best solution. When we take into account that the same national governments are actively involved in the transactions of financial markets, even as speculators against each other's currencies, their role as regulators becomes all the more questionable.[15] Should we turn instead to the Governors of the Central Banks to play this role of regulators of the market? That is the subject for another study. In any case, we can no longer expect our national governments to play the role of impartial regulators of financial markets. This myth ought to be discarded.

[14] Minister Maystadt affirmed in May 1997 that he had briefly considered resigning in 1996. But after the majority of the House had voted in his favour in the vote of confidence, and following a plea of the Prime Minister to stay on, he had not taken this line of action. (*De Standaard*, 26 April 1997, p. 3. He withdrew from his office in June 1998, in order to become the president of the PSC (Christian-Democratic party).

[15] We have not been investigating here a fourth moral critique on the Belgian debt policy, stating that this policy, and especially the buying of options in 1992, was undermining the solidarity between Member States within the European Union. This argument could not be accepted without further specification; however, it seems evident that the actions of European governments in 1992 did demonstrate the predominance of national interests over European solidarity. One could hardly expect otherwise in the context of an incomplete Monetary Union.

CURRENCY CRISES, TOBIN TAX AND INTERNATIONAL JUSTICE

Luc Van Liedekerke

1. Currency Crises in the 1990s and their Welfare Effects

Currency crises are spectacular events that hit the news headlines. Far less publicised, however, are the welfare effects of such crises. It seems to me that any normative analysis of currency crises should start from the real impact they have on the people involved. This, however, is difficult to determine. I therefore concentrate hereafter on some indicative macro-economic variables that give a rough idea about the possible welfare effects.

The 1990s offered the spectacle of three distinct regional waves of currency crises: Europe in 1992-93, Latin-America in 1994-95, and the Asian crisis that is still unfolding at this moment. In the case of the much studied ERM crisis, it is remarkable to see that the countries which 'failed' and left the system scored much better afterwards than those which remained in the system. Almost all macro-economic variables improved. Unemployment figures dropped dramatically in the U.K. and Italy experienced a major upturn of the economy. From a pure welfare point of view, it would seem that this crisis was rather positive for the victimised countries. Still, this is by no means a justification for the way in which the crisis materialised. It might well be that other, less dramatic means to change the value of the pound and lira would have been preferable.

Contrary to the ERM crisis, the Latin American crisis was long anticipated by economists who warned about problems with fundamentals from the beginning of 1993 (e.g. Dornbush, 1993). Financial markets, however, neglected these warnings – interest premiums on the peso remained low through the whole of 1993 and until the end of 1994, when political turmoil, combined with a badly managed devaluation led to a near complete loss of confidence in Mexican policies and prospects. The peso quickly fell to half its pre-crisis value, interest rates sky-rocketed to 80%, and the subsequent welfare effects were dramatic. Real GDP fell by seven percent; the real hardship was felt in Mexican homes. Argentina, which initially had hoped to escape the crisis, experienced the same rapid outflow of capital which resulted in a severe banking crisis and an almost complete dry-up of credit. This in its turn caused serious negative welfare effects in 1995. International official loans to Mexico as well as Argentina eased the crisis and eventually the economies of both countries picked up again in 1996.

The Asian crisis, which is still developing at the time of writing, has had the same extreme negative welfare effects. I give an early assessment of the social impact of the crisis on three countries: Indonesia, the Republic of Korea, and Thailand.

unemployment: open unemployment has increased significantly relative to the pre-crisis year 1996: in Indonesia the projected official unemployment rate will increase from about 5% in 1996 to between 8 and 10% at the end of 1998; in the Republic of Korea, it grew from 2% in 1996 to 4.7% in February 1998 and a projected 6.2% at the end of 1998; in Thailand, an increase from 1.5% in 1996 to 5.6% at the end of 1998 is projected. Additionally, under-employment, which is far more difficult to measure, is said to have highly increased. Especially in the Republic of Korea, the crisis has put an end to the psychological myth of secured lifetime employment. More than occasional cases of suicide, due to loss of employment, have been reported. Most of those losing their jobs have little choice than to become active in the informal sector.

real wage levels: moreover, the strong increase in real wages of the past few years was abruptly halted in 1997 and turned negative in 1998. As an example, in the Republic of Korea, real wage growth which was on average 6.5% during 1995-96, was reduced to 2.7% during the third quarter of 1997, and -2.3% during the last quarter of 1997. This decline particularly reflects the bonus element in wages.

change in poverty levels: direct statistical material on the number of people falling below poverty level as a result of the crisis is non-existent. Nevertheless, some indirect figures give some indication: in the Republic of Korea, at least an additional 100.000 people are luckily to become recipients of the state's 'livelihood protection scheme'. In Indonesia, it is believed that the crisis would add "a substantial number" of people to the 22 million already living below the poverty line.

price increases due to inflation and import curbs: especially since the last quarter of 1997, increases of basic food prices have started to accelerate, exceeding the rate of increase of overall consumer prices; the price of some basic drugs (which have to be imported) has tripled since the beginning of 1998. In Indonesia, the rice equivalent of the daily minimum wage (Rp.5800) fell from 6.28kg in January 1997 to 4.76kg at the end of December 1997. The import curbs has also affected the availability of basic food, such as rice in Indonesia: as a consequence, president Habibie has asked the people to fast twice a week to save on rice.

fragility of social protection: due to the absence of a meaningful official social safety-net, loss of employment also leads to a large decline in social protections, since social security is by and large enjoyed by virtue of formal sector employment. The pressure on existing official schemes will be intensified, in a time where pressure on the overall government budget will not make it easy to ensure that adequate resources are available to meet the intensified demand. In Indonesia, for instance, demand for subsidised public health-care service is estimated to double in 1998 to 68% of the population.

increased violence and unrest: increased cases of violence within the family have been reported. Also ethnic tension and violence is increasing heavily; pressure is particularly put on the migrant labour force. The purchasing power decrease of income has also increased petty criminality. In Indonesia some 40 towns have seen violence against the minority Chinese and Catholic populations (38 churches trashed in February 98 alone).

Currency crises are almost never contained to the countries under siege. The Asian currency crisis had direct contagion effects on countries such as the Philippines and Singapore, and ultimately, because of the real economic linkages, to the whole world. The direct costs are huge: the Asian currency crisis has lowered current world growth projection for 1998 alone by about 1%. Since world GDP is about US $30,000 billion, total costs can be estimated at US $300 billion at least. Moreover, as the World Bank indicates, the impact of the Asian crisis on economic growth in developing countries will be twice as large as it is for the world as a whole. For a country like Mozambique, which spends twice as much on servicing its debt than on basic services, such as primary health care and education, this means the (temporary) end of development.

Welfare effects of currency crises can be dramatic, certainly for those who have no cushion against periods of hardship. It is clear that a world in which a major currency crisis occurs at an average rate of one every 19 months, is not a very comfortable world to live in. We should, therefore, consider measures to prevent, or at least contain, currency crises more efficiently.

This article first sets out to discuss the nature of currency crises in an informal way. Next I will discuss one proposal aimed at reducing the probability and severity of currency crises: the Tobin tax. I then present Tobin's idea, discussing its merits and demerits, and make a new proposal that might better live up to Tobin's aims.

2. The Nature of Currency Crises

On July 2, 1997 Thai Government abandoned its effort to maintain a fixed exchange rate for the bath. For months the government had asserted that it would do no such thing, and for months it had defended the currency with what initially seemed a enormous war chest of foreign exchange. Massive speculation, however, emptied the war chest and forced the government to devalue. And why did speculators bet against the bath? Because they expected it to be devalued. This kind of circular logic – in which investors flee a currency because they expect it to be devalued and much of the pressure on the currency comes because of this investors lack of confidence – has become the defining nature of currency crises.

The first currency crisis models (Krugman, 1979, and Garber & Flood, 1984) explain a crisis as the result of a fundamental inconsistency among domestic policies. Typically, on the one hand we have a government financing its budget deficit by printing money, and on the other hand a central bank that tries to hold on to a fixed exchange rate using a stock of foreign reserves that it is ready to sell at the target rate. Speculators recognise this inconsistency and – foresighted as they are – start selling the currency and in so doing advance the date of the collapse. The abrupt character of such an attack – billions lost in a day – is the consequence of the foresightedness of market participants. The speculative attack is the main reason for devaluation, yet the whole process is ultimately caused by the inconsistent policies of the attacked country. Financial markets simply bring home the news, albeit sooner than the country might have wished to hear it. Under this type of model, politicians take all the blame. It is their task to balance different goals, a task with a notoriously ethical component, and if they fail, they must bear the blame.

Nevertheless, many countries complain about being unfairly or arbitrarily attacked, and recently economists are beginning to take these complaints seriously. The new branch of currency crisis models that treats agents less mechanically – Obstfeld (1994) is a good example – opens up the possibility of self-fulfilling exchange rate crises. This does not mean, however, that any currency can be subject to an attack or that all speculative attacks are unjustified by fundamentals. It is clear that a country whose fundamentals (e.g. the foreign exchange reserves, the fiscal position, the political commitment to the exchange rate, etc.) are persistently and predictably deteriorating will necessarily have a crisis at some point, and a country which holds on firmly to its position will probably not have to defend its currency. Still, there is an intermediate range in which a crisis can happen, but need not happen. Exactly how broad this range may be, is an empirical question and remains at this point unclear. But even if this range is small, the new orthodoxy on currency crises implies that financial markets are no longer blameless: they play an essential part in provoking currency crises.

The new models play down the all-importance of fundamentals and thereby focuses attention on the institutional structure of capital markets, and more precisely on the foreign exchange market and its participants. Some features of this market are regularly indicated as crucial factors contributing to a crisis. I submit them briefly.

Herding: In his remarkable survey, Shiller (1989) found that when the stock market crashed in 1987 the only reason consistently given by those selling stocks for their actions was that prices were going down. In the context of a currency crisis this means that a wave of selling, whatever its cause, could be magnified through imitation into a real stampede out of a currency. Two reasons have been put forward for this conduct. One involves bandwagon effects driven by the knowledge that some investors have private information. Bandwagon effects in markets with private information create 'hot money' that can cause markets to overreact to positive or negative news. The second reason focuses on the principal-agent situation in which most money managers find themselves. Money managers are often compensated in comparison with other money managers.

When the losses one accumulates are more or less like those of all the others, there is not much cause for concern; but if one happens to be the only one losing money in Asia, one had better start looking for another job. There is therefore a strong incentive not to behave too differently from all the rest. Such a theory could also explain the passivity of financial markets in the face of crisis (e.g. the Latin-America crisis). As long as everybody else stays in the market, there is not much reason for one to leave; but once they start pulling out, one has to follow as quickly as possible.

Market Manipulation: Since the ERM crisis, Soros has become the arch-example of a market manipulator (though he is probably not the best example). If herding or self-fulfilling crises occur, there is room for market manipulation. The manipulator might be looked upon as an insider, and once it becomes clear that he/she bets on devaluation, the rest follow. The manipulator will bet because, if his/her position is sufficiently strong, he/she stands to make a big gain, as in the case of Soros.

Contagion: One remarkable aspect about currency crises in the 1990s is their regional spread. A simple explanation for regional waves is that there exist strong real linkages between the countries involved. Devaluing the pound in 1992 affected the trade and unemployment prospects of France adversely and thus increased the pressure to devalue. This, however, is not the full story. Trade links between Mexico and Argentina were virtually nil, and still Argentina was attacked. Likewise, South Korea differs substantially both in its policy and basket of traded goods from Thailand and Malaysia, yet it was also caught in the middle. Contagion works both ways; once the Mexican economy picked up again, the wave of optimism also spread to Argentina.

Self-fulfilling crises: Suppose the fundamentals of a country are in the intermediate range in which a currency crisis is possible but not certain. At that moment, a crisis will materialise if many investors pull out, and will not materialise if they stay. The mood of the market now becomes extremely important, and optimism or pessimism tends to become self-confirming.

In such an intermediate situation, market participants are faced with a one-sided bet. Suppose one pulls out of the market and the currency devalues, then one has either made a big gain or avoided a big loss. If, however, the currency does not move, one only has the transaction costs to lament over. This unevenness in returns must make one react to even the slightest hint of crisis. At the same time, this mechanism reveals the importance of transaction costs and the free flow of capital. In a very liquid, deregulated market with small transaction costs (e.g. the foreign exchange market), self-fulfilling currency crises should therefore become more common.[1]

It is at this point that one can introduce the idea of a tax on foreign exchange transactions, as originally proposed by James Tobin in 1972. Essentially what Tobin wanted to do is raise the cost of moving capital. But this is done in an asymmetric way: people trading on a very short-term horizon (speculators in his view) will pay more than those who reallocate money on a long-term basis (investors). The instrument used is a tax on the nominal value of any contract which implies conversion of one currency into another.

3. The Tobin Tax as a Instrument of Financial Policy

In a famous passage in his *General Theory*, Keynes compares the price formation process in the (New York) stock exchange to 'those beauty contests' organised by magazines in which the participants were asked not to determine their own favourite girl, but rather the average choice of the other participants (Keynes, 1993, p. 156). Translated in more modern terms, the basic problem with this contest is that the final choice is not determined by any consensus on fundamentals (the nicest girl), but by readers in the game of guessing what other readers are going to think. Replace 'readers' by 'traders' and one has a perfect description of the price formation process in capital markets. His suspicion of speculators brings Keynes to the point where he advocates a "substantial transfer tax with a view of mitigating the predominance of speculation over enterprise" (Tobin, 1984, p. 8). Tobin shares this suspicion. That there are excessive capital flows is in itself not too much of a problem, but the real world effects generated by these sudden swings in capital and prices are far more

---

[1] The problem of the one-sided bet is at this point not standard in second generation currency crises models. However, Krugman (1997, p. 6) points out that it might be an interesting avenue for theoretical research. From this point of view the safety net of government or IMF bail-outs gains a cynical tone. It does not attack the speculative nature of financial operations, instead it looks more like "officially subsidized speculation, generating private profits and socialised losses that are covered by governments" (Raffer, 1998, p. 531).

problematic. These macro-economic disturbances and their negative welfare effects form the background for Tobin's proposal.

He starts from a simple observation: "goods and labour move, in response to international price signals, much more sluggishly than fluid funds" (Tobin, 1978, p. 154).[2] In large capital markets, funds flow very quickly and prices adjust immediately to new (public) information. Adjustments in labour and goods markets are sluggish or limited by institutional barriers, transactions are costly, transportation is slow and expensive, substitutions are imperfect and expectations are fuzzy. The prime concern of an economist must undoubtedly be to improve the functioning of these markets. Some of these differences, however, have a structural character and cannot be solved easily. The physical nature of goods for instance, limits goods arbitrage possibilities. A minimum wage is an institutional barrier that curbs the adaptation potential of the labour market, but other than economic objectives, notably social concerns, justify the imposition of this barrier. Therefore, excessive capital flows will *always* induce disturbances in the real economy.

Currency crises are undoubtedly the most spectacular examples of massive capital flows with immediate effect on relative prices of goods and labour, as well as serious welfare effects. Industry, and even government, has to live with this almost overnight reshuffling of competitive positions dictated by financial markets looking for speculative gains. Such real effects are too important to be neglected. Consequently, Tobin seeks to throw some sand in the super efficient wheels of financial markets.

4. The Target: Short-term Trading in the Foreign Exchange Market

The Tobin tax focuses on one financial market: the foreign exchange market. It is by far the largest financial market with a daily trading volume now estimated at $2 trillion, up twenty-fold since 1972, when Tobin launched his proposal.[3] About 95% of this trading has a purely

---

[2] Dornbush celebrated overshooting model uses this discrepancy to point out that in the short-term exchange rates can seriously break away from equilibrium rates (Dornbush, 1976).

[3] By comparison, annual global turnover in equity markets in 1995 was $21 trillion, or 17 days of trading on the foreign exchange. Annual global trade in goods and services was a mere $4.3 trillion, or not even 4 days of trading. (Langmore, 1996, p.3)

financial character; only 5% involves real transactions directed towards end-users (Hamende, 1996, p. 237). Data from BIS further indicate that about 80% of all transactions involve round trips of seven days or less, and more than 40% of two days or less.

When Bretton Woods collapsed, the switch from fixed to floating exchange rates was not only accompanied by an increase in volume, but also by an increase in volatility of the nominal and real exchange rates. Exchange rates have also been more volatile than the prices of goods and services, and more volatile than the monetary fundamentals (interest rate, money growth,....).[4] It therefore becomes very difficult to explain (short-term) exchange rate movements exclusively in terms of fundamentals. Let us label exchange rate movements not supported by fundamentals as excessive volatility.

This brings us to the following question: how harmful is volatility in actuality? There is a strong suspicion among economists that volatility is harmful for the economy, especially trade, but unfortunately there are few convincing studies to underpin this suspicion. Development of financial markets has included many instruments that protect against exchange rate volatility at a reasonable price, so the cost of volatility to trade should be minimal. Nevertheless, long-term misalignments, like that of the dollar, have undeniably generated serious economic costs for companies and governments alike. Although hard evidence is difficult to gather, there is a presumption that constant cycles of overvaluation and undervaluation may have stimulated protectionist pressures, thereby harming international trade.[5] Negative trade effects have certainly been one of the main arguments for European countries to proceed with monetary union, in order to banish all volatility in currency prices once and for all. Volatility might also have a negative effect on investment. Volatility creates uncertainty, which in its turn tilts the balance between a irreversible real investment on the one hand and a very reversible financial investment in favour of the former on the other.[6] The net-result is under-investment when compared to a world

[4] The volatility of exchange rates relative to fundamentals has been extensively documented (Frankel, 1996, p. 13).

[5] Ultimately, this may have contributed to the major slow-down of economic growth that has been observed in the industrialised world since 1973. (See also De Grauwe, 1996, ch. 12).

[6] On this aspect of volatility and the possible role of the Tobin tax see Tornell, 1990.

without excessive volatility. Finally, there might also be a link between volatility and the stability of the financial system. Sudden swings in prices are undoubtedly dangerous episodes for the financial system. A good example is the case of Argentina, where almost the entire banking sector came under pressure after the unanticipated attack on the Argentine peso.

Accordingly, let us presume that volatility actually implies significant economic costs. We still are not home yet. Now I have to prove: (i) that this excessive and harmful volatility is caused by speculative trading and (ii) that a Tobin tax can in fact reduce speculative trading.

There is ample evidence that traders trying to determine the price on a short-term horizon (less than three months), rely heavily on the extrapolation of present prices. This creates the possibility of band-wagon effects. One small slip of the price can cause expectations of future depreciation, which puts a self-fulfilling mechanism at work.[7] This sort of speculation would be seriously destabilising.[8] On a longer-term horizon, however, traders seem to deviate from simple extrapolation and perform in the way Friedman suggested – buying low and selling high – thereby stabilising prices. If all this is true, the real question becomes: which horizon dominates currency trading? The answer is clear cut: it is an often cited stylised fact of currency markets that the bulk of trading activity takes place on a horizon less then a couple of hours. There is thus a presumption that speculative trading is responsible for much of the volatility in currency markets.

How would a Tobin tax counteract this? Simply by penalising the short-term transactions more than the long-term ones. Dornbush and Frankel (1988), Frankel (1996) and a number of other authors have demonstrated how a simple transaction tax has a progressive nature in terms of the duration of the investment. With a modest tax rate of 0,001 % of the total amount invested, a dealer on the foreign exchange market with a one day horizon would need an annual

---

[7] Technical analysis is often blamed for this. Most rules of technical analysis, like the momentum model which advises traders to buy when the current price exceeds the price of five days ago, imply destabilising results. Moreover, a questionnaire survey by Taylor and Allen (1992) indicates that 90% of all traders place some weight on technical analysis and that this weight increases with the shortness of the horizon.

[8] Frankel & Froot (1990) and Ito (1994) give ample evidence for the existence of this type of speculation.

return of 46.5% to make his/her investment attractive. An investment with a one year horizon would only incur the 0,001% cost, which is marginal.[9] Given the fact that most trading takes place on a very short horizon, it is clear that even such a minimal tax, if it were implemented effectively, would wipe out a very large part of current trading activity and stand a good chance of reducing volatility. At least, that is what proponents of the Tobin tax expect.

Adversaries of the Tobin tax point out that there are several flows in the argument. I can summarise the argument so far in five points:

(i)   The foreign exchange market exhibits signs of excessive volatility.

(ii) Excessive volatility implies serious economic costs.

(iii) Excessive volatility is caused by speculative trading.

(iv) Speculative trading is to a great extent equal to short-term trading.

(v)   The Tobin tax reduces short-term trading and thus volatility.

There is consensus on (i) and may be (ii), but all the rest are seriously disputed. The most contested step in the argument is undoubtedly the last one. A tax equals an increase in transaction costs and thus the argument would be that higher transaction costs imply lower volatility, but there is no empirical evidence to support this view; on the contrary, the evidence seems to point the other way.[10] I shall not take up this discussion here, but simply point out that something as radical as a global tax has never been tried, so there cannot be at this point any conclusive empirical evidence on the link between such a tax and volatility.

The second and most important argument raised by adversaries concentrates precisely on the world-wide nature of the tax and can be summed up in one word: impossible. It is impossible to implement such a tax on a world-wide scale.

[9] The calculation behind this numerical example can be found in Frankel, 1996, p. 22.

[10] Umlauf (1993) concentrates on the Swedish experience and points out that the introduction of a securities transaction tax in Sweden actually increased, rather than decreased, volatility. The most recent study on the link between transaction costs and volatility is Jones and Seguin (1997) and is again not very supportive for a Tobin tax.

The implementation problem is characterised by the public goods nature of the tax. This implies two things: unilateral action is totally ineffective and concerted action will be confronted with the free-rider problem.

(i) Unilateral action is ineffective: Consider a situation where the Belgian government decides to tax all conversions in and out of the Belgian franc. At that moment currency dealers would immediately switch to Euro-markets where Belgian monetary authorities hold no power. If for some reason the Euro-market in Belgian currencies is too small to contain all orders, Belgian banks could drain untaxed Belgian francs to their foreign branches and then do the exchange transaction. A unilateral tax is clearly ineffective. Global coordination is a necessity.

(ii) The free-rider problem: A free-rider not only lessens the effectiveness of the tax, but also has a demonstration effect towards the others which implies that even a limited amount of free-riding could potentially be very harmful. Free-riding can go two ways: either the trader changes physical location to escape the tax or looks for a financial instrument that is not taxed.

Physical delocation: At this moment foreign exchange transactions are very much concentrated. London, New York and Tokyo entail the bulk of all transactions. But it would not be sufficient to introduce the tax only in those places. Traders could easily switch to non-regulated financial centres. Again global coordination is a necessity. Though this is a difficult task indeed – why for instance would the Cayman Islands be interested in such a tax – it is not impossible. It took several years to introduce the Cook rule, but it has now firmly established itself in all the major financial centres, likewise, the WTO has succeeded in implementing trade rules that are much more complicated than a financial transaction tax. At this point, the problem takes on a political dimension: how to convince all the countries involved that imposing such a tax is a good thing to do. One practical way out could be to add the tax as an extra condition for becoming a member of the IMF. If all IMF members were included, the tax would stand a good chance.

Financial delocation: Originally, Tobin wanted to tax only the spot market, but this would be totally ineffective as trading would simply switch to the forward market. Suppose we tax spot and forward trading, can we stop here? Certainly not, traders could for instance swap Belgian Government bonds against American treasury bills, or Bel 20 equities against Dow Jones equities. It seems that the tax would have to be applied in an ever-widening circle, thereby increasing the burden associated with the tax. But surely there is a limit. Exchanging equity indices is simply not equivalent to exchanging currencies. At a certain point the extra costs incurred by stepping over to a different instrument match the cost of the Tobin tax, and at this point the circle stops. It is off course very likely that financial wiz-kids will invent derivatives that escape the tax, but at that point the taxing authority should be flexible enough to intervene immediately and close these loopholes (Garber & Taylor, 1995, p. 179).

Financial economists are at this point certainly not ready to endorse the Tobin tax, on the contrary. But the least one could ask for is a serious study of the proposal, and that has not been the case. That Tobin's proposal has been so easily dismissed has, I think, to do with another strand of literature on the tax which concentrates on the fiscal nature of the tax and looks upon it as an income generating device, rather than a measure for monetary policy.

5. The Tobin Tax as an Income Generating Device

More problems are becoming global: the environment, poverty, security. Yet the international community has limited resources to address these. Governments recycle on average 30% of their income through the government budget, but international public spending is limited to 0.3% of the budget of just a few countries. Winning political support to provide more means is often very difficult. As such, a source of revenue that is not too closely linked to domestic activity and domestic politics is needed. Tapping international economic activities to generate funds for international cooperation in support of world-wide public goods seems a logical thing to do and analogous to what happens at the national level. This is how international organisations like the U.N. look upon the problem. It redefines the goal of the tax from a cure for financial markets to a source of income for international organisations. The strongest argument for the tax at this point is that there is no other instrument for raising that much money in a less distorting way. If, for instance, we were to tax international trade at the same level by increasing import tariffs, this would undoubtedly induce much stronger distortions and economic losses.

The revenue of the tax is difficult to estimate. Figures range from a massive $3.000 billion a year by the most optimistic projections, to $140 billion which is still a lot of money.[11] Tobin himself projected a revenue of $1.500 billion. This, however, is when only currency markets are taxed. But if income is the target, why limit it to currency markets alone? Respected economists like Dornbush have on occasion argued for such an extension in a language that leaves no room for doubt:

> There is no reason only to tax foreign exchange transactions. Since asset market instability suggests short-horizon speculation in all asset markets, the response should be a world-wide financial transactions tax. A moderate world-wide tax on all financial transactions would force asset markets to take a long-run view of the assets they price. As a result there would be more stabilising speculation. (Kelly, 1993, p. 18)

On other occasions, Dornbush has been somewhat more emotional about why a tax on international capital is warranted.

> Ultimately a more severe control of international capital flows may be unavoidable. Most international capital flows today involve tax sheltering or tax evasion rather than socially productive resource transfers. Shifting international capital in search of tax havens has become a nasty evasion of ordinary tax discipline…. This footloose capital is parked tax free in shelters, helping promote an overvalued dollar and serious fiscal and social problems in the country of origin. (Dornbush, 1986, p. 224)

The Tobin tax seems in this sense a first step in the direction of a more universal tax on all capital transactions. Arguments for or against the tax often mimic arguments for or against a general securities transaction tax (STT), the argument over which has been – at least in the States – much more fervent and with a deeper political impact than the argument over Tobin taxes.

Most industrial countries have or have had such a tax, Campbell and Froot (1994) provide an extensive list. The textbook example is the 'stamp duty' tax in the UK. Not only does it collect a very high

---

[11] By comparison: Larsen and Shah (1995, p. 122) estimate that a carbon tax of $10 per ton imposed by all nations would yield $55 billion in its first year of operation.

yield (about £830 million in 1993), but it is functioning in what is called one of the most sophisticated markets (the City of London) without triggering massive tax evasion. Belgium also has a stamp duty of 0.17% on the nominal value of the contract on the buying or selling of securities, but with a maximum of 10.000 BF ($270). This kind of upper limits are common in most countries and curtail the income potential of existing transaction taxes.[12] Higher taxes would simply induce evasion, as the case of Sweden made abundantly clear.[13] Only a universal tax, like the Tobin tax, could generate substantial income.

The ultimate arguments for such a tax rely on distributive justice: the tax is advocated because one believes that capital does not share its part of the burden or because it is seen as a good instrument to reduce (income) inequality on the national or global scale. Here are some arguments one might use to defend a Tobin tax or a general securities transaction tax. I will not dig too deeply into any of these arguments, since that would lead us into another debate.

(i) The installation of progressive tax systems have reduced income inequality in Western societies. Unfortunately, the very unequal distribution of wealth remained. A conservative estimation for Belgium holds that the top 20% of population holds around 50% of wealth, while the poorest half of the population owns only 20% (Vuchelen, 1995, p. 162). If we concentrate on financial property only, the inequality increases. Furthermore, financial property represents about 60% of all wealth. Taxation of real property is difficult, but not impossible and part of most tax schemes. Taxation of financial property, however, proves to be very ineffective. The ultimate reason for this implementation failure is the high mobility of capital. This mobility makes national capital registers difficult to compose and unreliable. An international transaction tax, levied in all countries, circumvents this problem. Part of the tax receipts could flow back to national authorities who could use the money for different purposes. Improving access to education, for instance, is known to be a good

---

[12] Nevertheless a country like Switzerland collects about 0.5% of GDP through securities transaction taxes.

[13] Sweden introduced a securities transaction tax, but was forced to withdraw this measure because of massive evasion. In the futures bond market, for example, 98% of trading moved off-shore in just a few months time, rendering the tax totally ineffective.

long-term instrument for reducing inequality and stimulating economic growth.[14]

Exactly how effective a Tobin tax would be as a surrogate capital income tax has never been studied and remains unclear at this point (one exception is Reinhart, 1991). It is a blind tax, which means that its distributive effects are also unclear. The only thing certain is that the poorest part of the population would not carry any burden, simply because they have no access to capital markets and often not even to the local banking system.

(ii) European countries have burdened the labour factor with high progressive taxes. The net result of this evolution has been the replacement of expensive labour for cheaper capital and, as an ultimate result, high unemployment. This new form of social exclusion must be looked upon as the most important problem for Western democracies. In order to restore the balance between capital and labour, we must tax capital more and labour less. A Tobin tax is a first step in that direction.

(iii) Since 1980, daily turnover in the US foreign exchange market has on average doubled every 3 years (Frankel, 1996, figure 1). Other capital markets have followed this trend. This is mainly due to a higher speed in transactions, but also to an enormous influx of new money. New money stayed in the financial sphere – preferably in the form of short-term financial titles – because real investment could not offer the same combination of high return and liquidity which is characteristic of financial markets. This imbalance is partly due to the fact that deregulation freed international capital from all tax burdens, while return brought about by labour and real investment remains heavily taxed. A Tobin tax addresses this imbalance and gives the real economy the opportunity to attract more new capital, which increases job creation.

(iv) Whether we like it or not, the world is becoming more and more globalised. For the world as a whole, the benefits of globalisation should clearly exceed the costs. It is estimated that, during 1995-2001, the results of the Uruguay round of the GATT (General Agreement on Tariffs and Trade) could increase global income by an estimated $212-500 billion, due to gains from greater efficiency and higher

---

[14] See, for instance, Perotti, 1996.

returns on capital, as well as from the expansion of trade. However, without an explicit policy of redistribution of the overall gains, they will not result in a situation where all are winners; rather, it will represent a "complex balance sheet of winners and losers, where the losses tend to be concentrated in a group of countries that can least afford them" (Human Development Report 1997, p. 82). It is estimated that, during the same 1995-2001 period, the least developed countries stand to lose up to US $600 million a year, and Sub-Saharan Africa up to US $1.2 billion. Without explicit action, resulting in a redistribution of overall gains, an 'everybody wins' situation will not be accomplished. An efficient and effective instrument of redistribution can be a truly global source of finance, such as a global tax instrument. Because it generates revenue, a tax instrument, levied on some general tax base or levied more particularly on the cause that hampers attaining the global common good, is most appropriate, provided it can be installed in an efficient and effective way.

(v) Within the context of the Second UN Development Program, the industrialised countries have promised to spend 0.7% of GNP to development aid by 1975. In 1996, only three countries had reached this goal. The gap between the richest and poorest nations has only increased.[15] In fact, between 1992 and 1996 net official aid to developing countries from industrial countries and multilateral institutions fell by 16% in real terms.[16] The fiscal crisis, experienced by many donor countries, is undoubtedly an important explanation for this. But even in times of crisis governments decide upon what the priorities are and the conclusion so far must be that international development cooperation is no longer on their agenda. The deeper explanation for this unfortunate evolution must be found on the ideological level. Up to now the only rationale for international development support has been the aid factor and precisely this aid-rationale has lost much of its appeal. Let me single out two reasons for this.

[15] The rich industrialised economies represent 10% of the world population. This 10% has about 54% of GNP and 69% of trade. But the inequality is much stronger when we consider capital markets. This 10% owns 85% of world stock market capitalisation and 89% of all borrowing on international capital markets. (Source: *The Economist*, 14 September 1996).

[16] Source: *The Economist*, 14 February 1998.

— Aid projects have remained lonely islands, too small to affect the macro-economy of a country in any deep manner. The net result has been that many problems return or persist, which in turn has caused a loss of confidence. The aid-fatigue is part of the political climate and of public opinion.
— Some of the 'poor' countries that needed our help, developed new markets that became strong competitors for the donor countries. Loss of jobs in donor countries was often attributed to this new competition and created an ambivalent attitude towards aid.

We need a new rationale for international cooperation to increase donations. A possible rationale could be given in terms of the international public good. Many critical problems today are of a global nature: air and water pollution, deforestation, preserving bio-diversity, international peace, terrorism and organised crime, migration, the spread of aids, free trade, and we could add here the problem of a stable financial system. The nature of the public good in all these problems implies that effective management requires a supranational perspective. If one could explain to the general public and politicians that these problems are crucial and require an international approach, this could give us a new rationale for international cooperation. Stated differently: there is probably no fatigue at this point with respect to problems like aids or international financial stability. An international tax on capital transactions, intended to raise the revenue necessary to tackle some of these problems, could gain public support quite easily (Langmore, 1996, p. 264).

It is clear that this type of argument has appealed to many leftist organisations and made the Tobin tax a darling of leftist think-tanks (e.g. Fabian Society, Left Financial Observer). In a certain sense this leftist support has been unfortunate. It obscured the original idea in which the tax was meant to be an instrument of financial policy and it made many an economist and central banker suspicious about the entire proposal. A vicious circle developed in which the proposal was not studied because it was looked upon as a purely ideological device and the lack of serious research confirmed the ideological interpretation. This is only slowly changing.[17] The UN study (Kaul, 1996) is a good example.

[17] A number of studies on the Tobin tax by financial economists have recently been published. Examples include: Eichengreen, Tobin & Wyplosz (1995, 1996), Garber & Taylor (1995), Kenen (1995), Spahn (1996), Frankel (1996), Jeanne (1996), Caminal (1997), and Davidson (1997).

6. Combining both Targets: The Double Dividend Hypothesis and its Dilemmas

Most of the time the argument in favour of the Tobin tax combines both goals mentioned above. The basic argument is in terms of the impact of the tax on financial markets, but is ultimately driven by the income potential of the tax. I would call this the double dividend hypothesis. Punish speculative trading and generate at the same time income for international organisations (Langmore, 1996, is an example). This type of 'brilliant' idea has been used on other occasions, for instance to support a carbon tax. The idea is simple: tax CO emissions to create a cleaner environment and use the proceeds to reduce taxes on labour which increases employment. Many economists have criticised this ideology and insisted that one instrument cannot serve two goals in an optimal way. The same is true for the Tobin tax. If one insists on both targets, one ends up in a three-fold dilemma discussed below.

1. *How high should the tax rate be?* A low tax rate is unlikely to deter speculators who bet on a short-term devaluation. According to Davidson (1997), and I believe he has a point, not grains of sand but boulders should be thrown in the wheels of finance to stop speculative trading. This very high tax rate would induce massive evasion, which would render the tax inefficient and jeopardise the income objective.

2. *Who should be taxed?* The tax base should in principle be as broad as possible in order to limit tax avoidance and market distortions. There are nevertheless deviations of this rule. Exemptions should reasonably apply to central banks intervening to support a currency. Transactions between governments and international organisations or aid to third world countries could also be exempted. One might even argue that market-makers, who are crucial players in the functioning of the market, should be excluded. Certainly with a high tax rate more and more participants would argue in favour of exclusion. This however would create loopholes for tax evasion and render the instrument inefficient. The basic problem here is that it is difficult to discriminate between normal trading and destabilising noise trading. Therefore, one should tax everybody, but this would increase the burden associated with a high tax rate.

3. *What should be taxed?* As indicated above, it is not sufficient to tax only the spot market, this would simply move trading towards the forward market, and if we tax both, trading currencies could switch towards the bond or equity market. A high tax applied in ever-widening circles, would imply serious distortions of financial markets. If for instance we tax derivatives like swaps in the same way as spot conversions, we risk losing the entire market because these instruments become too expensive. But a currency market without swaps is almost unimaginable and would greatly increase the cost of capital and endanger the stability of financial markets. If one introduces a selective tax rate, linked to different classes of financial instruments, one ends up with an administrative nightmare.

In the end, one is always caught between two ends: one pointing in the direction of a higher rate, the other the opposite way. The way out is I believe introduced by Spahn (1995).

7. A Two-tier Rate Tax System

If one has two targets, why not introduce two instruments: a low tax to generate income and a very high one to scare off currency speculators. This is the essence of Spahn's proposal. I will sketch the broad lines of this practical and realistic proposal.[18]

We begin with the introduction of a low tax of one basis point (.001%) on the nominal value of all currency transactions.[19] Though this might seem a very low tax, one should keep in mind that the (gross) profit margin on most liquid transactions is estimated at four basis points. This tax would raise the cost of capital only marginally and create no distortions (capital streams would not react upon the introduction of the tax). Because the tax is so low, the incentive to evade the tax would be minimal and thus implementation relatively easy. At the same time, the income generating capacity of the tax would still be considerable: around $25 billion per year (by comparison, the UN estimated the cost of international peace-keeping in 1994 to be $16 billion).

---

[18] Paul Bernhard Spahn is a professor of public finance at the University of Frankfurt am Main, and was a consultant to the fiscal affairs department of the IMF at the time of presenting his Tobin-tax variant.

[19] It remains necessary, however, to put the tax on derivatives at an even lower rate in order to prevent major disturbances in this market. See Spahn, 1995, p. 31.

Apart from the income objective, such a tax could function as a monitoring device. It would allow the administrator of the tax to follow up any movements in currency markets closely. A second step in the monitoring role could be that the administrator licenses all financial institutions and traders engaging in international currency contracts. Again this would allow the administrator or international organisations like the IMF to follow up currency markets.

The factual administration of the tax would be the task of licensed currency operators, who should collect the tax before the contract is executed and transfer the proceeds to the central administrator. Anyone trying to escape this scheme would lose his/her licence. Countries or financial institutions not willing to enter the tax scheme might face much higher charges on any contracts involving transfers from and to this country/institution. This punitive tax would thus operate like a blocking tariff on goods. But again, given the very small tax rate, it is unlikely that major financial institutions will engage in setting up other branches in order to escape the tax, as this is an expensive investment.

Secondly, we introduce a far higher exchange surcharge, administered in conjunction with the underlying low charge. The objective of this tax is to tax negative externalities associated with excessive volatility. In normal times, this tax would be zero; only during phases of speculative trading would the tax be levied. Ideally, revenue from this surcharge would be nil, only in that case could we say that the tax had reached its objective. In fact, the tax is so high that it would work like a circuit breaker, as has been introduced in stock markets after the 1987 crash.

The remaining problem is: how do we identify a 'phase of speculative trading'? Spahn proposes a system that mimics the old EMS system. Each currency is attributed a target rate, this could be done in a rather mechanical way, leaving the market forces to do their work. Take for instance a crawling peg (like a moving average of the last twenty business days). This would set the central rate. Secondly, a band within which the currency is allowed to float is defined. Whenever the exchange rate transgresses the band, the difference between the band rate and the effective exchange rate is considered a negative externality and an excess profit that is taxed away. The main difference with the European Monetary System is the technique used to defend a currency. In the case of the EMS defence is centred around the use of valuable foreign exchange reserves and the interest rate. Certainly using the interest rate as a defence is not without its costs. Raising domestic interest rates over a considerable time period most of the time punishes the local real economy more than the currency speculator. High interest rates drive companies with short-term debt into bankruptcy and induce a credit crunch. In fact, financial markets often look upon raising domestic interest rates as an act of desperation and an indicator that defence of the currency will not hold much longer. An exchange surcharge would cost neither the central bank nor the economy anything at all.

Contrary to the original Tobin proposal, the tax used to curtail speculators can be set very high without hurting capital markets in their normal daily operations. In fact, Spahn's proposal is a crude instrument to discriminate between speculative and non-speculative trading, with the speculative trading defined as any trading that leaves the currency band. Tobin's original proposal could not make such a distinction at all.

Will this scheme stop all speculative trading? Certainly not, nor is this the intention. Markets should be allowed to do their work and choose against policy-makers who go against fundamentals. The most likely effect is that changes in currency value will be smoothed out. If we define a central rate around a moving average, this implies that at times of crisis the rate will go up and thus also the band around it. Over time, the value of a currency will reach the same height as without the tax scheme, only the adaptation process will work much more smoothly and slowly. This gives policy-makers and the real economy (goods and labour markets) some time to adapt to the new situation.

The scheme would ideally work on a global scale, like the tax originally proposed by Tobin; it is not, however, impossible to start up the mechanism unilaterally with a limited number of participants holding a sufficiently large share of the foreign exchange market. Usually the critique against a unilateral introduction of a transaction tax is that it is highly distorting and results in massive evasion which renders the tax scheme ineffective (remember Sweden). A two-tier Tobin tax, however, would stand a better chance. Setting up a parallel market for the conversion of domestic currency is costly and will only be profitable if transaction costs are higher on a consistent and permanent basis. This would probably be the case under a single rate Tobin tax, but not with a very low basis rate and the high rate only coming into effect occasionally and for a short time period.

An additional advantage of the tax scheme is that it might influence investors' expectations. Short-term speculative investment in countries with weak fundamentals becomes less attractive because it will be difficult to pull out one's money at times of crisis without bouncing into the exchange surcharge reaping away the windfall gains. Reduced inflows of capital also lessen the vulnerability of a country at times of crisis because the potential outflow is much smaller. Rational investors will choose their countries for investment more carefully, taking into account long-term fundamentals, rather than potential speculative gains. This was precisely the original intention of Tobin.

8. Distributing the Proceeds

Spahn's attractive study leaves two strongly related questions unanswered: who can claim the proceeds and what should they be used for? These are tricky political questions, which might prove to be the main obstacle for implementing the tax scheme. I shall treat some aspects of this problem.

Again it seems to me that the answer to both questions very much depends upon what one considers to be the basic target of the tax. Suppose one looks upon the tax as a monetary instrument that helps one internalise the costs connected to excessive capital mobility. At that point, it would seem logical to let an international monetary authority manage the tax and (part of) its proceeds. This could be either the IMF or the BIS, both of which have been suggested by Tobin. The Mexico crisis as well as the Asian crisis seem to confirm the role of the IMF as a sort of global insurer against currency crises. Extensive aid packages protect countries from total collapse and support the stability of the financial system. But this insurance function calls for ever bigger loans and thus for an extension of the IMF means. The proceeds of the tax could be part of a fund available at times of crisis. At the same time, this gives an incentive to IMF members countries to levy the tax: it is simply part of the insurance premium to be paid for protection. Countries unwilling to enter in the tax scheme could be excluded from IMF help, which would be a serious risk to take.

A completely different approach is provided by Langmore and Kaul (1996). Here the income objective prevails. At this point, it becomes much harder to answer the above questions.

One possible answer is the derivation principle: the one who levies the tax can claim its proceeds and decide what to do with it. Given the fact that the foreign exchange market is so concentrated (London, New York and Tokyo combine about 60% of world market operations) this would result in a very unequal distribution at the global level. Table 1 exhibits this.

Table 1: distribution of proceeds from a 0.05% tax applied to 1995 foreign exchange volumes (source: Michalos, 1997, p. 27)

Industrial countries	proceeds in billion US$
United Kingdom	28.7
United States	15.1
Japan	9.9
Switzerland	5.3
Germany	4.5
France	3.6
Australia	2.4
Denmark	1.8
Canada	1.7
Netherlands	1.4
Sweden	1.2
Other OECD Countries	8.1
Developing Countries	
Singapore	6.4
Hong Kong	5.5
South Africa	0.3
Bahrain	0.1
Other Less Developed Countries	1.1
Total for all countries	97.1

What can be said against this? One might point out that the regional distribution of the tax is the consequence of historical fortune and that in itself does not seem a good argument for claiming the proceeds. Not only is the fact that London became the centerpiece of international finance a historical contingency, but the services it renders have a truly global character and are not at all contained to England alone. In fact, the regional incidence pattern of financial services is so hard to detect that Tobin's original suggestion that the proceeds should be handed over to an international body, seems the most logical thing to do.

A parallel problem exists with respect to customs duties in Europe. Rotterdam and Antwerp receive a major proportion of custom duties on goods that are distributed over the entire European Union. It would be preposterous if the incidence principle were put in place here. A far better solution has been found which transfers the proceeds to the supranational budget of the European Union, where it becomes part of the democratic political process which decides over the distribution of all European means. A similar solution could be envisaged for the Tobin tax. The proceeds could be given to the IMF and its distribution linked to the IMF quota system. It is clear that the balance of power at the IMF is tilted towards the West, especially the United States, but even with the present quota system, redistribution of the proceeds would favour small and less developed countries which often lack a well-developed exchange market.[20]

If London were to reject this argument, how could it be convinced to share the proceeds? The strongest argument is undoubtedly that other countries can threaten to leave the tax scheme and start up their own financial centre where the tax is not levied. The global nature of the tax and the possibility to free-ride is the best argument for sharing. Still, very poor countries like Mozambique can hardly threaten to free-ride because the facilities to put up a major financial centre are simply not available to it. Most countries fall into the Mozambique category, and certainly the very poor countries do. They can only argue in terms of distributive justice to claim their share of the pie. Unfortunately, as indicated above, distributive justice arguments seem to have worn out. Let me briefly indicate one way to rekindle this argument.

9. A Rawlsian Framework for International Justice

Justice, Rawls says, is the first virtue of social institutions. Its primary subject is the basic structure of society, or more exactly, the way in which major institutions distribute fundamental rights and duties, determining the division of advantages from social cooperation. Two principles ultimately characterise the just state, but these principles are not at the same time used to characterise the justice of the law of nations and of relations between states (Rawls, 1972, p. 7).

---

[20] A notable exception is of course Singapore. A separate solution is needed here.

On the contrary, the justice of the law of nations is to him a secondary problem, only to be tackled when the internal just structure in nation states has been put in place. The basic reason for this is that the contractarian framework can only work within the boundaries of an 'ongoing scheme of social cooperation', and as Rawls assumes, the boundaries of such cooperative schemes are given by the notion of a self-contained national community. This roughly coincides with national boundaries. It is these boundaries which determine discrete schemes of social cooperation (Rawls, 1972, p. 457). In paragraph 58 of his *A Theory of Justice* Rawls organised a meeting between representatives of different national states who found themselves in an extended original position where one's nationality is unknown. Because they are representatives of separate social schemes, their attention is turned inward, not outward. The basic element on which all can agree is one of equality between nations and their main interest is ultimately to provide conditions in which just domestic social orders can flourish. But this might result in a justification of inequality at the global scale in terms of the creation of a just society at the national level. In other words, making the problem of justice between nations a secondary problem opens up the possibility of gross injustice. This problem has been pointed out by several authors, and the logical way out seems to be an extension of the original position to the world as a whole.[21] But this is only possible when one either believes that an 'ongoing scheme of social cooperation' is not a prerequisite for a contractarian argument or when one denies the link between national boundaries and schemes of social cooperation.

The second way out is the most attractive. All we have to do is prove that national states are no longer the self-sufficient entities presupposed by Rawls. And here we can turn back to financial markets and currency crises: the evolution of the 1990s has clearly been one of increased interdependence and the contagion effect demonstrates that at least on the financial side nations states are no longer independent. In fact, political evolution has been one of a continuous loss of national autonomy, and the only way in which national states can regain some autonomy is by extending their international cooperation. The case of the European Union is a key example. Only by enlarging the scale of management can politicians still influence national economies.

---

[21] See Brian Barry (1973), Thomas Scanlon (1973) and Charles Beitz (1985).

The evolution in financial markets is just one aspect of a globalisation movement that points out the increasing interdependence of national states. Another aspect of globalisation is used by Langmore and Kaul (1996) as a starting point for their defence of a Tobin tax: the growing number of international problems. Key examples include: air and water pollution, deforestation, preserving bio-diversity, international peace, terrorism and organised crime, migration, the spread of aids, and free trade. According to Langmore and Kaul, endorsing the Tobin tax is simply a question of correct cost-benefit analysis. The tax allows one to tackle some of these problems on a permanent base, and as every nation stands to gain from this, putting up the money should be no problem: it is well spent. The advantage of limiting oneself to the cost-benefit perspective is that it allows one to convince self-interested politicians to support the tax.[22] The disadvantage is that one offers the international justice perspective to narrow national self-interest. And this shows itself when Langmore and Kaul develop an implementation scheme for the tax. Governments are lured into accepting the tax by pointing out their painful fiscal position. All the countries mentioned in table 1 – with the exception of Singapore – all face more or less serious budget deficits. Langmore and Kaul hand over a generous 80% of the proceeds of the tax to the industrialised countries in order to ease the fiscal burden and demand a meager 20% for international funding (Langmore, 1996, p. 267). Because donor countries would also benefit from the international funds, the final distribution would even be more skewed to the West and would in fact mimic the initial distribution of proceeds of the Tobin tax. In other words: there would be practically no transfer at all! All this follows almost directly from giving in to a condition which game theorists would call *individual rationality*: the fact that the benefits of entering into the tax scheme should be higher than the cost, and this for each individual country involved. Accepting such a condition means abandoning the justice perspective.

In a certain sense it is strange that Langmore and Kaul accept individual rationality so easily. Their global public good perspective is precisely an ideal starting point to criticise this condition. Many global problems of the type mentioned above are left unanswered

---

[22] If, however, the cost-benefit calculation is so obvious, it is unclear why nations do not already provide the means for combatting these problems.

because individual countries are caught up in a strictly individual cost-benefit analysis. It is this point of view which drives them into a collective prisoner's dilemma. National states agree that global problems should be tackled and that this is ultimately in their own self-interest. But from the point of view of individual rationality, it is much cheaper for a nation to free-ride on the efforts of other nations than to undertake any effort for itself. Besides, if a nation were to assume efforts unilaterally, not only would its action be ineffective (the problem is global), but others would free-ride on its efforts. The end result is under development of the global public good. It seems to me that this is a not too unrealistic description of the world, and to a great extent due to the narrow point of view of individual rationality. Remember that industrialised states recycle about 30% of their GDP through the government budget, but spent only 0.3% internationally. We need to break this deadlock.

Globalisation and interdependence create a new basis for international morality. How would a just world look like? In his *Liberal Theory of Justice*, Barry simply transposes the Rawlsian conditions to the international level; but this might be too easy. Though the world is certainly not a collection of self-sufficient, independent nation states (the *Theory of Justice* perspective) neither is it one global community. We are somewhere in the middle, heading for globalisation, certainly in the economic sphere of our society, and increasingly also in the cultural sphere (the overall presence of jeans, CDs, Coca-Cola, Soap opera's, McDonalds, materialism as a global religion, etc.). Growing interdependence should be linked to a growing role for global institutions in order to escape the collective prisoner's dilemma. Stable funding of these institutions is a prerequisite for their efficient functioning. The Tobin tax is one tiny step in that direction.

10. Conclusion

Liberalisation of capital markets have increased the access to global financial markets for emerging economies. This has brought them great benefit, but it has also made them vulnerable to sudden shifts in investor sentiment and attacks on their currencies. The welfare effects of such a shift can be quite dramatic and provide the basic reason for reconsidering the functioning of the foreign exchange market. Already in 1972, Tobin proposed to increase the transaction costs of currency exchange in order to increase the costs of speculative transactions, which at this point resemble too much a one-sided bet. His proposal, however, was never taken very seriously. This is partly due to the double dividend ideology that is often used to defend the Tobin tax.[23] But as Spahn has made abundantly clear, one tax rate cannot at the same time be an optimal deterrent for speculative transactions and an optimal income generating device. Therefore, the only way out is to introduce two tax rates: a very small one that could be extended to all capital transactions and a high tax rate that only becomes effective at times of currency tension.

Spahn's proposal is both practical and realistic. Implementing it would certainly be a formidable task, but not impossible. The major obstacles at this point are the political questions: who can claim the proceeds of the tax? and what should they be used for? Answering both questions means developing a framework for international cooperation. Such a framework is indicated by Langmore and Kaul in terms of caring for the global public good. Unfortunately, they allow principles of justice to collapse into utilitarianism and miss the opportunity to link the problem of caring for the global common good to that of putting up the necessary framework for a just international community.

The major task ahead is to convince individual countries that they are interdependent and that the only way to regain some national autonomy is to coordinate their actions at the international level. One of the most obvious proofs for this is precisely the functioning of international capital markets, where unilateral action is completely ineffective and international organisations like the IMF have become indispensable to ease tensions. Implementing the Tobin tax would give the international community another instrument in its effort to preserve the common good.

[23] The main obstacle is off course political. Political resentment with respect to Tobin's proposal is felt most strongly in the US, where the proposition of the 'Prohibition on United Nations Taxation Act of 1996', designed to prohibit UN officials from developing or promoting Tobin-tax or other global tax proposals, was introduced to the US Congress. This proposition successfully stopped at least UN agencies and officials, who were at that time central to discussions on global taxes (see e.g. Kaul e.a., 1996), from continuing to mentioning Tobin-tax proposals. It was a ridiculous and short-sighted form of censorship.

References

BARRY, Brian (1973), *The Liberal Theory of Justice*. Oxford, Oxford University Press.

BEITZ, Charles (1985), 'Justice and International Relations' in Charles Beitz et al. (eds.), *International Ethics*. Princeton, Princeton University Press, pp. 282-311.

CAMPBELL, John and Kenneth FROOT (1994), 'Securities Transaction Taxes: Lessons from International Experience' in J. FRANKEL (ed.), *The Internationalization of Equity Markets*. Chicago, University of Chicago Press, pp. 65-90.

DE GRAUWE, Paul (1996), *International Money: Postwar Trends and Theories*. Oxford, Oxford University Press, 268p.

DORNBUSH, Rudiger (1976), 'Expectations and Exchange Rate Dynamics' in *Journal of Political Economy*, 84(1976), pp. 1161-1176.

DORNBUSH, Rudiger (1986), 'Flexible Exchange Rates and Excess Capital Mobility' in *Brookings Papers on Economic Activity*, 1, pp. 209-235.

DORNBUSH, Rudiger (1990), 'Flexible Exchange Rates and Excess Capital Mobility' in LLEWELLYN and MILLER (eds.), *Current Issues in International Monetary Economics*. MacMillan, pp. 209-226.

DORNBUSH, Rudiger (1993), 'Mexico, Stabilization, Reform and No Growth' in *Brooking Papers on Economic Activity*.

DORNBUSH, Rudiger and Jeffrey FRANKEL, (1988), 'The Flexible Exchange Rate System: Experience and Alternatives' in Silvio BORNER (ed.), *International Finance and Trade*. MacMillan.

EICHENGREEN, Barry, James TOBIN and Charles WYPLOSZ (1995), 'Two Cases for Sand in the Wheels of International Finance' in *The Economic Journal*, 105(1995)1, pp. 162-172.

EICHENGREEN, Barry and Charles WYPLOSZ (1996), 'Taxing International Financial Transactions to Enhance the Operation of the International Monetary System' in Inge KAUL, Mahbub UL HAQ and Isabelle GRUNBERG (eds.), *The Tobin Tax: Coping with Financial Volatility*. Oxford, Oxford University Press, pp. 15-39.

FRANKEL, Jeffrey A. (1996), 'How Well Do Foreign Exchange Markets Function: Might a Tobin Tax Help?' in *NBER Working Paper Series*, n° 5422.

FRANKEL, Jeffrey A. and Kenneth FROOT (1990), 'Chartist, Fundamentalists, and the Demand for Dollars' in Anthony COURAKIS and Mark TAYLOR (eds.), *Private Behaviour and Government Policy in Interdependent Economies*. London, Clarendon Press.

GARBER, Peter and R. FLOOD (1984), 'Collapsing Exchange Rate Regimes: Some Linear Examples' in *Journal of International Economics*, 17(1984), pp. 1-13.

GARBER, Peter and Mark P. TAYLOR (1995), 'Sand in the Wheels of Foreign Exchange Markets: A Sceptical Note' in *The Economic Journal*, 105(1995)1, pp. 173-180.

HAMENDE, Geneviève (1996), 'Un Frein a la Speculation sur les Marchés des Changes, in: douzième congrès des économistes belges de langue française' in *Les Grandes Interrogations de l'an 2000: Croissance, Emploi, Sécurité Sociale*, commission 3: le système financière, pp. 231-258.

JONES, Charles and Paul SEGUIN (19), 'Transaction Costs and Price Volatility' in *American Economic Review*, 87(19)4, pp. 28-737.

ILO (1998), *The Social Impact of the Asian Financial Crisis*. Technical Report for the High-Level Tripartite Meeting on Social Responses to the Financial Crisis in East and South-East Asia (Bangkok, 22-24 April 1998).

ITO, Takatoshi (1994), 'Short-run and Long-run Expectations of the Yen/Dollar Exchange Rate' in *Journal of the Japanese and International Economies*, 8(1994)2, pp. 119-143.

KAUL, Inge, Mahbub UL HAQ and Isabelle GRUNBERG (eds.) (1996), *The Tobin Tax: Coping with Financial Volatility*. Oxford, Oxford University Press, 318p.

KELLY, Ruth (1993), 'Taxing the Speculator: the Route to Forex Stability' Fabian Society, discussion paper n° 15.

KENEN, Peter B. (1995), 'Capital Controls, the EMS and the EMU' in *The Economic Journal*, 105(1995)1, pp. 181-192.

KEYNES, John Maynard (1993), *The General Theory of Employment, Interest and Money*. 9th ed., New York, MacMillan, 428p.

KRUGMAN, Paul (1979), 'A Model of Balance of Payments Crises' in *Journal of Money, Credit and Banking*, 11(1979), pp. 311-325.

KRUGMAN, Paul (1997), 'Currency Crises', unpublished paper presented at NBER conference October 1997,
http:// web.mit.edu/krugman/www/crises.html.

KRUGMAN, Paul (1998), 'What Happened to Asia?', unpublished paper presented at a conference in Japan,
http://web.mit.edu/krugman/ www/asia.html.

KULESSA, Margareta E. (1996), 'The Tobin Tax: A Tool for Allocative or Distributional Policies?' in *Intereconomics*, (1996)May/June, pp. 122-131.

LANGMORE, John and Inge KAUL (1996), 'Potential Uses of the Revenue from a Tobin Tax' in Inge KAUL, Mahbub UL HAQ and Isabelle GRUNBERG (eds.) *The Tobin Tax: Coping with Financial Volatility*. Oxford, Oxford University Press, pp. 255-272.

LARSEN Bjork and Anwar SHAH (1995), 'Global Climate Change, Energy Subsidies and National Carbon Taxes' in Lans BOVENBERG and Sijbren CNOSSEN (eds.), *Public Economics and the Environment in an Imperfect World*. Dordrecht, Kluwer Academic Publishers, pp. 113-132.

MᴄLᴜʀᴇ, Charles E. (1997), 'Tax Policies for the XXIst Century' in International Fiscal Association, *Visions of the Tax Systems of the XXIst Century*. Dordrecht, Kluwer Academic Publishers, pp. 9-52.

Mɪᴄʜᴀʟᴏs, Alex C. (1997), *Good Taxes: The Case for Taxing Foreign Currency Exchange and Other Financial Transactions*. Toronto, Dundurn Press.

Oʙsᴛғᴇʟᴅ, M. (1994), 'The Logic of Currency Crises' in *Cahiers Economiques et Monétaires*, 43(1994), pp. 189-213.

Pᴇʀᴏᴛᴛɪ, Robert (1996), 'Growth, Income Distribution, and Democracy: What the Data Say' in *Journal of Economic Growth*, (1996)June.

Rᴀғғᴇʀ, Kunibert (1998), 'The Tobin Tax: Reviving a Discussion' in *World Development*, 26(1998)3, pp. 529-538.

Rᴀᴡʟs, John (1972), *A Theory of Justice*, Cambridge (MA).

Rᴏsᴇ, Andrew (1994), 'Are Exchange Rates Macroeconomic Phenomena?' in *Federal Reserve Bank of San Francisco Economic Review*, 1(1994), pp. 19-30.

Rᴇɪɴʜᴀʀᴛ, Vincent (1991), 'The Tobin Tax, Asset Accumulation, and the Real Exchange Rate' in *Journal of International Money and Finance*, 10(1991), pp. 420-431.

Sᴄᴀɴʟᴏɴ, Thomas (1973), 'Rawls' Theory of Justice' in *University of Pennsylvania Law Review*, 121(1973)5, pp. 1066-1067.

Sʜɪʟʟᴇʀ, Robert (1989), *Market Volatility*. Cambridge (MA), MIT Press, 464p.

Sᴘᴀʜɴ, Paul Bernhard (1995), International Financial Flows and Transactions Taxes: Survey and Options, IMF Working Paper 60 (1995)June, Washington, D.C.

Sᴘᴀʜɴ, Paul Bernhard (1996), 'La Taxe Tobin et la Stabilité des Taux de Change' in *Finances et Développement*, (1996)June, pp. 24-29.

Tᴀʏʟᴏʀ, Mark and Allen Hᴇʟᴇɴ (1992), 'The Use of Technical Analysis in the Foreign Exchange Market' in *Journal of International Money and Finance*, 11(1992)3, pp. 304-314.

Tᴏʙɪɴ, James (1978), 'A Proposal for International Monetary Reform' in *The Eastern Economic Journal*, 4(1978)3-4, pp. 153-159.

Tᴏʙɪɴ, James (1984), 'On the Efficiency of the Financial System' in *Lloyds Bank Review*, (1984)July, pp. 1-15.

Tᴏʀɴᴇʟʟ, Aaron (1990), 'Real vs Financial Investment: Can Tobin Taxes Eliminate the Irreversibility Distortion?' in *Journal of Development Economics*, 32(1990), pp. 419-444.

Uᴍʟᴀᴜғ, Steven (1993), 'Transaction Taxes and the Behaviour of the Swedish Stock Market' in *Journal of Financial Economics*, 33(1993)2, pp. 227-240.

Vᴜᴄʜᴇʟᴇɴ, Jef and Koen Rᴀᴅᴇᴍᴀᴋᴇʀs (1995), 'De Inkomensverdeling en Mogelijke Fyscale Oplossingen voor de Overheidsschuld' in *Documentatieblad Ministerie van Financiën*, (1995)May-June, pp. 149-176.

Wᴏᴏ, Wing T. (1985), 'The Monetary Approach to Exchange Rate Determination under Rational Expectations' in *Journal of International Economics*, 15(1985), p. 1-16.

HOW TO REMOVE SAND OUT OF THE WHEELS OF LOCAL FINANCIAL MARKETS

Financial Institution Building in Rural Nicaragua

Johan Bastiaensen

1. Introduction

Today's world-wide financial markets represent the closest real-world approximation of the perfect market. Even though the concrete institutional forms continue to influence outcomes and relative benefits, there is no doubt that today's efficiency in communication, minimum regulation and an extremely competitive environment contribute to almost instantaneous transactions based on close to perfect information. Several contributions in this volume focus on the consequences of these – in a sense – too perfectly functioning markets which entail dangers of system instability as well as destroying the margins for national economic policy. Tobin took this even as a starting point for a highly unorthodox – at least for a mainstream economist – argument to put 'sand into the wheels' in order to create more friction and drag in the world financial system.

In this contribution, we deal with a completely different world of shaky financial configurations in rural Nicaragua. Nicaragua is a country that might be considered exemplary of many low income countries where the institutional conditions, necessary for the functioning of financial and other markets, are highly deficient. Using Tobin's metaphor, one might say that because of 'too much sand, the wheels turn slow and wear down rapidly'. Even though internally Nicaragua is far off from embodying a realm of perfectly functioning financial markets, it can not escape the discipline imposed by the smoothly functioning world financial system. With the disappearance of the socialist bloc, there is no alternative but the economic collapse that would follow a de-linking option. As one of the most indebted countries in the world with a persistent and huge balance of payment deficit, Nicaragua crucially depends on net capital flows from the world financial system. Most of these represent aid or fresh loans from donor countries and multilateral institutions. The securing of the bulk of these capital flows crucially depends on Nicaragua's compliance with the macro-economic conditionality imposed by the IMF under the subsequent Extended Structural Adjustment Facility agreements. In the first place, these agreements have imposed substantial expenditure reductions by increasing taxation of all kinds and by severely cutting back on the public sector. On the other hand, privatisation and liberalisation measures were expected to generate the required expenditure switching that would bring Nicaragua back to a healthy development path. More structural policy measures, of which the institutional development of the financial sector is but an example, have only slowly entered the agenda. It nevertheless became rapidly clear that market liberalisation alone failed to meet optimistic expectations due to the deficiencies of the (especially rural) institutional environment. As a consequence of this neo-liberal myopia, the country experienced slow economic reactivation, increasing income disparities and an unacceptable rise in (rural) poverty.

The shortcomings of the standard structural adjustment paradigm imposed by the IMF are largely explained by the failure to acknowledge the consequences of 'too much sand in the wheels' of real markets impeding them from working properly. In our view, Nicaragua's economic crisis is primordially engendered by its institutional incapacity to organise socio-economic processes in ways that avoid a squandering of opportunities and resources due to disorganisation, chaos and conflict. This cannot be resolved by sound macro-economic policies alone, but requires audacious and innovative structural policies that enhance institutional conditions such that the functioning of existing imperfect markets improves and presently missing markets can emerge. In this perspective, this contribution focusses on the creation of an institutional framework capable of governing financial transactions with small rural producers. This analysis will be undertaken and illustrated by practical experiences with the creation of an innovative financial system by Nitlapán, a research and development institute of the Universidad Centroamericana of Managua. We will also elaborate on the relation between the institutional framework for financial transactions and that of real world transactions of goods, services and information. We will argue that the governance structures for financial transactions have the potential to contribute to broader institutional innovation and development. Instead of an unfettered competitive world financial system disrupting the evolution of real world fundamentals, we detect a potential confidence, cooperation and competition enhancing effect of financial institutions building on real world development.

2. A Framework of Interpretation

The overall framework of our analysis is inspired by a general model proposed by 'the new institutional' economist O. Williamson (1994, p. 80) and a quite similar, more elaborated model of the 'institutional sociologist' W.R. Scott (Scott & Meyer, 1994, p. 57). Both models suggest distinguishing three interacting layers in the analysis (see Figure 1):

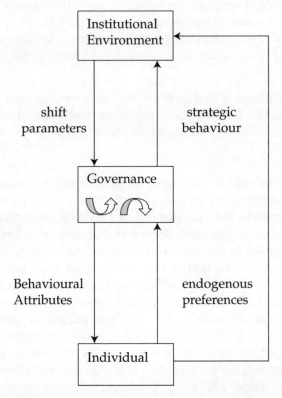

Figure 1: Framework of analysis, a layer scheme

(i) The first layer is that of the *institutional environment*, which is understood as the general and usually relatively stable societal background conditions that 'define the rules of the game'. In the words of Davis and North, it is "the set of fundamental political, social and legal ground rules that establishes the basis for production, exchange and distribution" (Quoted in Williamson, 1994, p. 79). At this level, Scott identifies "meaning systems and related behaviour patterns, which contain symbolic elements, including representational, constitutive and normative components, that are enforced by regulatory processes" (Scott & Meyer, 1994, p. 56). N. Uphoff reserves the term 'institution', as distinct from 'organisation', for this level of "complexes of norms and behaviours that persist over time by serving collectively valued purposes" (Uphoff, 1993, p. 614).

(ii) the second layer is that of *governance structure*, sometimes called the *institutional arrangement*. This layer refers to the consciously designed rules of specific organisations, i.e. "structures of recognised and accepted roles" (Uphoff, 1993, p. 416). For Davis and North, it refers to the "arrangement between economic units that governs the way in which these units can cooperate and/or compete" (Williamson, 1994, p. 79).

(iii) the third layer is that of the *individual actors*, 'created', structured and constrained by both the embracing institutional environment and the concrete organisations in which they do or do not participate.

Following this model, the financial system under creation by Nitlapán can be viewed as an incipient alternative governance structure that must sustain the functioning of financial enterprise with the poorer sections of the rural society in Nicaragua. A first challenge can be identified in the need to articulate this institutional arrangement in such a way that it allows financial transactions to take place without incurring prohibitively high transaction costs. With its behavioural hypothesis of bounded rationality and opportunism, transaction cost economics provides the analytical tools to study this challenge. The three-layer model, however, suggests that the functioning of the financial governance structure also needs to be analysed against the background of the broader institutional environment since this will have a profound influence on the actions of individuals and on the governance structure itself. Williamson views the institutional environment as a relatively stable, but potentially changing background condition that can alter the "comparative costs of governance" thereby implying "a reconfiguration of economic organization" (Williamson, 1994, p. 80) According to this transaction cost approach to institutional evolution, shift parameters in the institutional environment can alter the cost-effectiveness of alternative institutional arrangements and thereby their competitiveness in relation to other arrangements. He nevertheless also recognises that the institutional environment determines the behavioural attributes as well as the endogenous preferences of individuals. With unusual modesty for an economist, he thus admits the limitations of the transaction cost approach with its model of the a-historical individual given that "endogenous preferences are the product of social conditioning" and that "other modes of analysis are often more pertinent" for their study. (Williamson, 1994, p. 81). Scott takes this argument further and argues that one must "recognize that governance structures within organizations are made up of institutional elements: meaning systems, symbolic elements, and regulatory processes. (...) organizational structures incorporate, perhaps even better, instantiate institutional elements" (Scott & Meyer, 1994, p. 70).

In the following analysis, we will therefore search for aspects of the Nicaraguan rural institutional environment that might have a relevant impact on the nature of the governance structure for the financial network. Due to the interaction between governance structures and institutional environment implicit in Scott's view on the former as nothing but 'instantiations' of the latter, the question on how changes in governance structures might transform the institutional environment is immediately raised as well.[1] This, of course, is nothing other than our second question on whether and how the creation of an innovative financial system might have a broader transformative effect on the inherited vertical governance structures.

---

[1] In this context of a broader impact on the institutional environment, Scott introduces the concept of 'organizational field'. Following DiMaggio and Powell, he describes it as a "recognized area of institutional life" and asserts that "the organizational field has emerged as a critical unit bridging the organizational and societal levels in the study of social and community change. Fields identify communities of organizations that participate in the same meaning systems, are defined by similar symbolic processes, and are subject to common regulatory processes" (Scott & Meyer, 1994, p. 71). Thinking of the present-day hype of 'micro-credit systems' (what's in the name?), it becomes immediately clear what is at stake in the shaping of alternative financial systems as a "recognized area of institutional life".

Despite the apparent simplicity of the three layer model, the theoretical and practical methods for its application in empirical analysis
are far from self-evident. A number of complicated issues concerning
path dependency in institutional development as well as the possibilities and avenues for institutional change are raised. Platteau (1996)
indicates that these are the same (unresolved) theoretical issues that
have been at the heart of the development debate since the early
days of modernisation theory. In the same respect, O. Williamson
states that "implementing the intentionality view [i.e. the deliberate
creation of more appropriate institutional arrangements, J.B.] will
require that the microanalytic attributes that define culture, communication codes and routines be uncovered, *which is an ambitious
exercise*" (Williamson, 1994, p. 83, our emphasis). Evidently, the solution to this kind of theoretical problem is far beyond the modest
endeavour of this contribution. We will therefore confine ourselves
to a tentative examination of some of the questions and insights that
might arise from the analytical perspective introduced by the model.

In the following section, we start with an exploration of some of
the characteristics of the institutional environment of rural Nicaragua
that determine the context of both the incipient financial system and
the broader development opportunities.[2] Subsequently, we present
the stylised facts of the financial system of Nitlapán and analyse its
governance structure. In a final section, we make some comments on
the impact of the vertical institutional environment on the functioning
and evolution of the system and explain the solutions that Nitlapán
introduced. Finally, we explore some perspectives as to its impact on
the broader micro-institutional context for development.

3. Some Elements of the Institutional Environment and their Relevance for Rural Development

3.1. *Vertical inheritance*

At the heart of our interpretation of the institutional crisis of rural
society is the idea of a fundamental incompatibility between its inherited and omnipresent vertical-authoritarian governance structures

---

[2] This section summarises and elaborates further on a previous analysis of the
institutional crisis of rural Nicaragua (Bastiaensen, 1997).

and the prerequisites for a dynamic and participative rural development, particularly in the face of the cultural and structural changes that have occurred during the last two decades. Following this idea, one can identify a tremendous lack of appropriate social capital that could facilitate synergy between the local rural producers, especially the poorer sectors among them, and the concrete structures of the adjusting markets and the state. One of the core issues for the future is therefore the need to transform the inherited rural governance structures in order to enhance such a synergy in which appropriate local institutional change can take place. The success of this endeavour will to a large extent determine whether structural adjustment in rural Nicaragua will regress into the exclusionary tendencies of the past or consolidate the more inclusionary development path promised by the land reform process.

There is little doubt that the dominant pattern of socio-economic organisation in the Nicaraguan rural villages before the Sandinista revolution was 'local despotism' of the patron-client type (Marchetti, 1994). This mode of governance entails a number of negative structural characteristics: (1) uncontrolled and non-accountable authority exercised by the local patrons, (2) social fragmentation and familialism, primarily aimed at short-term survival, at the level of the clients, (3) dyadic and ambiguous relations of dependence/resistance between patrons and clients, (4) clientelistic intermediation of externally available information and benefits by the patron. This basic structure of rural society was only partially changed by the Sandinista revolution. It curtailed the influence of the traditional landlords and traders, but its own mode of centralised governance continued to correspond to the inherited vertical structures of clientelistic dependency with the channelling of benefits to local clients through loyal intermediaries (Marchetti, 1994, p. 6).

The prevalence of this 'local despotism' as an omni-present governance structure constitutes a major obstacle for rural development. First of all, as indicated by R. Putnam, vertical governance structures of the patron-client type present but a 'second-best' solution to the problem of social order and cooperation, to be preferred over total Hobbesian chaos, but clearly not the most appropriate for realising development. (Putnam, 1993, pp. 174-175) The patron-client model indeed entails a number of structural deficiencies that restrain both local collective productive capacity and the intensity of economic transactions with the outside as well as within the local community.

A first flaw of the model is the monopolisation of contacts with the external environment by the patron. This severely distorts information flows between the local and the external environment, hampering the development of informationally integrated networks of mutual cooperation for technological learning, supply of inputs and commercialisation. As Putnam (1993, pp. 174-175) indicates, the prevalence of dyadic relations between patrons and clients also undermines the development of horizontal ties between clients. At the level of dependent clients, strong solidarity ties often do exist, but they are typically confined to neatly delimited kinship networks. These co-exist, but do not develop many relationships with other kinship networks. Worse still, among the groups that belong to competing patron-client networks, usually understanding themselves as belonging to different political or religious tendencies, relations are often strained and conflictive.[3] This implies that the crucially important 'weak ties' stretching over the entire range of the local society and thus creating an enabling environment for a more vibrant and civic local economy are largely absent.

Another deficiency of the model relates to the consequences of the arbitrary and absolute power of the local patron. This is contradictory with the prevalence of any stable and just 'rule of law', since it makes the 'upward' imposition of rules impossible and allows for the arbitrary imposition of decisions. For ignorant and powerless clients, the latter contributes to a highly unpredictable and insecure economic environment in which success and survival depends more on luck and the benevolence of the patron than on one's own efforts. This evidently undermines the incentives for personal effort. In this respect, it is also important to stress that this state of affairs is often sustained by the fundamental meaning systems of the people. In their 'non-modern', albeit gradually changing world-view, a conception of 'natural and divine order' that leaves little room for personal effort prevails (Houtart & Lemercinier, 1992, p. 101). In this interpretation of the world, welfare and happiness depend more on a kind of individual symbolic exchange, both with the unquestioned patrons and, of course, with God – intermediated by the saints to whom promises are made. The object of this exchange involves things like

---

[3] For an interesting historical account on the tenacity and violence of confrontation between competing networks of local rural caudillos in the Western Segovias during the Sandino uprising, see Schroeder (1996).

loyalty and intrinsic ethical qualities of personal behaviour, not individual and/or collective productive effort. Such legitimising world-views are necessary to sustain the patron-client relationship since the model intrinsically creates strong incentives on the part of the client to shirk in their relationships with the patron. Viewed from a 'principal-agent' perspective, the relations of the client with the patron are often quite ambiguous since they balance between loyalty and passive resistance, the latter translating into opportunism and abuse whenever possible.[4]

3.2. *Disintegration of the vertical governance structures since the revolution*

In Nicaragua, however, not only do vertical networks in general represent a 'second-best' alternative as a governance structure, a number of recent changes in the society question the appropriateness of the vertical governance structures even further. A first element of importance is the impetus toward a modernisation of the traditional world-view and the redefinition of popular identity by the common people, brought about by the revolutionary change and the long period of war and instability. Although the electoral success of Violeta de Chamorro and the persistent influence of traditional views from the Catholic and other churches (especially among older people and women) cautions against overestimating the impact of the revolution in this respect,[5] it seems clear that an increasing number of people began to see themselves as real actors of their destiny and as citizens with equal rights. Important for the effectiveness of the vertical governance structures is the fact that many people

[4] It is important to stress that some relevant regional differences might exist with respect to this fundamental constellation of meaning systems and world-view. In particular, the peasants of the agricultural frontier regions, who can be viewed as the heirs of an historical tradition of peasant resistance to colonial oppression, seem to have world-views with more space for individual personal effort.

[5] There might even be a clear regress in the sense that the graveness of the present-day social crisis is presented as the 'natural' consequence of the blasphemous challenge of the natural order and the traditional values by the Sandinistas. In this respect, however, it is important not to make the mistake of equating the traditional world-view with anti-sandinism and a modern world-view with sandinism. As Houtart and Lemercinier (1992) have clearly demonstrated for the village El Comejen both 'world-views' are almost equally distributed between sandinistas and non-sandinistas, with a modern world-view even more prominently present among the 'liberal' group.

started to reject the naturalness of their oppression and translated this rejection in a reduction of discipline and obedience, and even in a legitimation for permanent abuse whenever possible. This was even more so after the defeat of the Sandinista party, when knowledge and rumours about the abuses of both old and new 'patrons' became widely spread. As a result, the natural authority of patrons was increasingly delegitimised and the repressive enforcement of compliance with laws and rules by that authority became quite problematic. General disorder and instability further contributed to the worsening of the situation. Today, the prevalence of an extremely familialistic distrusting and skeptical world-view on the part of many Nicaraguans is quite striking.[6] The problem is that this rebellion of the *'güegüense'*[7] against the oppressive vertical structure is mainly destructive and is not effectively translated into a more positive project. Worse, the prevalence of generalised dishonesty and distrust engenders prohibitively high transaction costs, meaning that many opportunities for collective action and productive investment have not been taken advantage of.

A second important 'shift parameter' with influence on the relative efficiency of the vertical governance structures in Nicaragua is the fact that 10 years of revolution and the demobilisation of the official and the rebel armies entailed a substantial redefinition of property rights over land. Thereby, vertical governance has become even more inappropriate since the 'patrons' control substantially less land and production than before. We thus identify an incompatibility between the inherited vertical governance structures and the present-day structure of property rights. A last important element is the shocks and rapid changes imposed by the structural adjustment

---

[6] Nadia Molenaers (1996) made some inquiries with respect to the people's perception of trust of fellow-citizens in poorer neighbourhoods of the capital, Managua. Both in questionnaires and in thematic apperception tests a vast majority of Managuas testified to systematically extreme distrusting attitudes. The answers were much in the line of the attitudes of rural southern Italians whose survival paradigm was first synthesised by Banfield (1954) as to "maximize the material short-run advantage of my nuclear family, assuming that all others do the same".

[7] The güegüense is a literary figure of one of the oldest know written plays from the Latin American continent. The story tells the story of the ambiguous relationship between the Spanish *gobernador* and the colonised indigenous people from the viewpoint of the latter. It cherishes the inventiveness and bravery with which the *güegüense*, as the symbol of the colonised, manages to seduce and circumvent the oppressor without ever confronting him directly. Today, the term *güegüense* is commonly used to denote similar behaviour towards any authority.

program since 1988. The abolition of subsidies and the liberalisation of trade have drastically changed the relative profitability of crops, thereby putting pressure on existing production systems and their articulation to one another.

Since the old institutional arrangements no longer seem to function properly, the main challenge for (rural) development is therefore to identify more appropriate local institutions and viable transition paths towards them. In general terms and in line with Putnam's ideas, Nitlapán's conviction is that a more horizontally structured, as well as civic and rule-governed local polity would have a substantial development enhancing capacity. At the same time, it is less pessimistic than Putnam generally is held to be on the constructability of the social capital required to sustain such a society. In this respect, it is more in line with the conclusions of P. Evans who believes that "(n)orms of cooperation and networks of civic engagement among ordinary citizens can be promoted by public agencies and used for developmental ends" (Evans, p. 1124). In this respect, Evans introduces the idea of 'institutional entrepreneurship' as the deliberate creation and spreading of appropriate institutional forms. He also points out that the spill-over effects from initial social capital building can have very large and transcendental effects.[8] Within this perspective, Nitlapán conceptualises its financial program ambitiously as "a principal means to transform local social organization" (Nitlapán, 1994, p. 30), i.e. as an intent at institutional entrepreneurship. Given this idea of envisaging the construction of a viable alternative financial system as a means of institutional innovation, we now turn to the institutional environment with respect to the rural financial configurations.

3.3. Vertical inheritance and financial configurations

Before the Sandinista revolution, most small-scale rural producers were excluded from formal credit markets and relied mostly on

---

[8] It is worth noting that even Putnam, despite his generally assumed pessimism on the constructability of social capital, seems to recognise such a possibility. Immediately following his analysis of rotating credit associations as an indicator of available social capital and as "a mechanism of strengthening the overall solidarity of the village", he quotes from E. Ostrom's *Governing the Commons*: "Success in *starting small-scale initial institutions* enables a group of individuals to solve larger problems with larger and more complex institutional arrangements. Current theories of collective action do not stress *the process of accretion of institutional capital*". (Putnam, 1993, p. 169, our emphasis).

self-finance for production, supplemented with occasional (often emergency) credit from relatives, friends, local shopkeepers-money-lenders and/or the nearby landlord. Some of the better-off smaller peasants sometimes managed to get access to loans from the national development bank, provided a solid local guarantor (i.e. the local patron) was prepared to give collateral. The poorer section relied strongly on finance provided by landlords in share-cropping arrangements and forward sales by local traders. The formal financial sector, composed of two holding banks of the dominant Nicaraguan business groups and the Somoza-dominated national development bank, only served the richer segments of the rural society. This structure of the financial configuration evidently coincides with the overall vertical institutions of rural society. When smaller scale rural producers had indirect access to formal credit, it was intermediated by local patrons and governed in the patron-client pattern.

A number of characteristics of this constellation changed during the Sandinista revolution. All banks were nationalised and opened up for practically all rural producers. In practise, the Sandinistas used heavily subsidised credit mainly as a planning and procurement instrument financed from the government budget on the basis of forced (inflationary) macro-economic savings. By the middle of the 1980s, credit was practically free, but tied to certain productive activities and therefore – at least officially – not free to use.[9] From the governance point of view, one could say that a 'distant national benevolent patron' largely replaced the local patrons. For a mix of planning and politico-military reasons, this 'patron' channelled credit with priority to state farms, agrarian reform cooperatives, 'strategic' private producers and certain sectors of the historical peasants (e.g. neighbouring the war zone). In this context, enforcement of repayment was only a weak preoccupation. In fact, it became even a political habit to condone uncancelled debts at each anniversary of the revolution. Nevertheless many people, the smaller clients in particular, continued to meet to repayment obligations, while others through all kinds of non-transparent manoeuvring managed never to repay. At the local level, it was often the new or old local 'patrons',

---

[9] A lot of abuse clearly took place such as was reflected in the cyclical upsurge of the black market exchange rate at the time of credit disbursement for the agricultural season in April-May.

monopolising both information and external contacts, that managed to obtain the larger loans and at the same time repaying relatively less of their debts. All this engendered severe deficiencies in the financial configurations. Heavily subsidised credit stimulated allocative irrationality and turned out to be macro-economically unsustainable. At the same time, it undermined previous vertical governance structures and substituted them by weak and non-transparent alternative structures which gave way to an erosion of the usual meaning of credit. Credit became almost a synonym for subsidy since its cost was negative and it was generally repaid only by those with poor political leverage to evade obligations. In short, credit culture was completely undermined.

This general picture changed under the transitional government of Chamorro. Under structural adjustment, the previous policy of heavily subsidised and widely available credit was drastically terminated. With tight monetary programming, official credit became scarce and expensive, with positive real interest rates of over 20% per annum. The national development bank, Banades, drastically cut back on its local branches and loan volume. After the 1992 recapitalisation of the virtually bankrupt public bank, it excluded some 85% of its clients, keeping only the large and some of its medium-sized customers. Emerging private banks in no way filled the rural financing gap, since they restrained their operations mainly to urban commercial activities. Despite this drastic reform of Banades policies, it did not manage to change previous characteristics of its operation. Since access to loans became difficult, the presence of rent seeking activities even intensified and political connections were found to become even more important. Evidently, repayment problems continued to persist and recuperation of pending debts was practically impossible. Substantial arrears rapidly accumulated, and in 1995 a new recapitalisation of the Banades became necessary to avoid its closure. About $200 million (US) in uncancelled debts were passed on to a specialised debt-collection agency that up to now has not been very successful in its mission to recuperate the pending debts. Many of the debtors are influential large producers that contracted short-term productive loans to invest the money in the purchase of land from decapitalised peasants and agrarian reform beneficiaries. Significantly, it was one of the few consensus points between Sandinistas and liberals during the last election campaign that the debt collection efforts should be more flexible. Since more arrears were again accumulating on the post-1995 loans, all this almost logically implied the definitive closure of Banades, to which the new government agreed in 1997.

In this adverse context, the issue of reconstructing the rural financial configurations is posed. Initially, some of the gap for the smaller rural clients was filled in by a large number of private NGO initiatives. Motivated by a rather paternalistic view of the poor, many of them nonetheless repeated a similar pattern of clientelistic grant-credit confusion that was omnipresent in official sandinista finance. For this reason, Nitlapán's research team even found a significant negative correlation of the existence of repayment problems with previous experiences with other NGO-projects (Mendoza, 1993, p. 4). More recently, a number of more professionally run financial NGOs have been gradually consolidating, one of which is the system of Nitlapán. At the same time, the new government says it is thinking of an alternative development bank aimed at the small and medium-sized rural producers. In the following sections, the challenge of the construction of viable financial systems is analysed and evaluated on the basis of the experiences of Nitlapán.

4. The Stylised Facts of the Banking Network

The banking network of Nitlapán consists of 18 semi-independent local banks and a one central refinancing unit: the Local Banks Fund. The vast majority of the local banks area are located in rural areas: nine in the rural areas of the urban periphery of Masaya and Carazo, five in the rural areas of the more developed Pacific region (Rivas and Somotillo) and two larger banks in the more isolated and war affected interior regions of Wiwili and Matiguas. Besides these rural banks, there were two 'artisan' banks in urban Masaya. (See Table 1 in annex).

In 1996, the network provided a total of about $2.6 million in loans to 4688 clients. The larger share of these clients (60%) are poor producers, defined as economic entities with a total estimated wealth of less than $5,000. In practice, these are subsistence producers with little or no land and/or cattle of their own and non-peasant rural families with poorly capitalised artisan or petty-commercial activities often depending on substantial additional wage labour. About

32% of the clients are small, but properly capitalised household producers with an estimated wealth of between $5,000 and $20,000 that allows them to earn a decent local living and to maintain their productive activity in the medium run. These are mainly peasant farmers and small non-agricultural enterprises. A final 8% of clients are medium-sized household producers with more established businesses, such as medium-sized peasant entrepreneurs and rural traders.

About 60% of clients are male and 40% female. The gender balance, however, differs substantially between the different regions, depending on the nature of the local economies and the role of women therein. In monetary-economic terms, women are generally active in and maintain control over income from petty-trade and a number of artisan activities (food processing, textiles, some artisan products like carpets, and certain services). In agricultural activities, the participation of women is much less and control over income from these sources is low, except when they commercialise the produce such as can be the case for fruit, vegetables and processed food (e.g. cheese, corn products). Commerce in the main crops, like food staples, coffee, and cattle, is usually controlled by men. Given this gender constellation, it is not surprising to find the larger share of female clients in urban Masaya and the peri-urban rural areas of Masaya, Carazo and Rivas, where intensive *minifundio* agriculture, with women commercialising fruit and vegetable produce, combines with petty trade and complementary artisan or service activities to provide for survival. In Somotillo, Wiwili and Matiguas, women are largely absent because agriculture and cattle-raising dominate the rural economy and also because the larger share of rural commerce in coffee, cattle, sesame and staple foods is in the hands of men. Because of the nature of their activities (small scale, petty commerce), the women in the network on average tend to have smaller, shorter-term and more rapidly rotating loans than men. Women's share in the total loan volume is therefore lower than the proportion of total clients. Furthermore, they tend to pay on average higher interest rates because of the policy to charge higher rates for small, short-term commercial loans, given the substantially higher profitability of these activities. In the network, women subsidise men's productive activities in agriculture and 'industry'.

By the end of 1996, some three quarters of credit was short-term (less than 18 months) and one quarter 'long'-term, usually between

18 months and three years.[10] Credit is not tied to any specific activity or technological package, and clients are free to ask credit for what they consider suitable and viable projects. Nevertheless, the local banks try to implement a locally concerted 'development' policy that tries to avoid over-concentration on (highly profitable) petty commercial activities and that gives sufficient attention to agricultural and 'industrial' activities as well as 'strategic' rural commerce (e.g. coffee commercialisation). According to the bank's statistics, 44% of the loans in 1996 were directed towards agricultural activities; 46% to petty and other rural commerce; 6% to small-scale industrial and artisan activities, and 4% to others (services, professionals). The relatively large share of agricultural loans and the option to shift towards longer-term investment loans testify to Nitlapán's intention to be an alternative development bank and not just a viable microcredit system. Purely commercial considerations would indeed argue for an almost complete concentration on small, short-term loans for (peri-urban) petty commerce. Nitlapán takes on a balanced view. It recognises the economic reality expressed by the relative profitability of (petty) commercial activities and does not share the neomarxist disdain for activities of 'circulation'. At the same time, it stresses the need for more profound structural change that can resolve the institutional and productive deficiencies that contribute to the higher relative profitability of commercial activities compared to other productive activities. In the short run, the higher profits made from loans for commercial activities permits the system to charge relatively lower rates for agricultural and industrial purposes.

The loans are made both from the accumulated patrimonial capital of the local banks themselves and extra annual loans as well as longer-term credit lines approved by the central refinancing unit. The limited patrimonial capital of the 18 local banks adds up to about $500,000. It is composed of $250,000 in share capital provided by the client-members, $150,000 in accumulated profits and about $100,000 that is left from initial gifts to the local banks during the period 1992-94. The loans provided by the Local Banks Funds totalled about $1.4 million. The funds of the central refinancing unit

---

[10] Nitlapán was creating a special and separately run division for longer-term (up to six years) investment loans of decapitalised agrarian reform beneficiaries and other small peasants, with a special emphasis on farm capitalisation and reforestation in the direction of agro-forestry systems. (see Bastiaensen & D'Exelle, 1997b).

itself originate from two sources. The initial capital fund of about $0.8 million was provided by a number of international NGO's as a gift. This capital is complemented with concessional long-term development loans with an annual interest rate of 2% per annum.

In the past five years a substantial effort of initial enterprise and local organisation building was made. A first component of this effort was intense local animation and organisation of clients to make the concept of the system known and accepted, as well as to create its necessary local organisational structures. This involved the continuous spreading of information with respect to the basic 'rules of the game' and the conscientious cultivation of the image of solidity, transparency, seriousness and trustworthiness of the 'bank', mainly by repeatedly showing compliance with rules and institutional promises. It is in this process that the foundation was laid for constructing a renewed 'credit culture', largely absent in the Nicaraguan countryside. The second component of the enterprise building involved the training of the national and local actors in the basic skills that were required to participate in the administration of the system, i.e. bank promoters, local managers, credit inspectors, cashiers and bookkeepers. Also a modest, but solid physical infrastructure was constructed. By now, most local banks have a secure and functionally equipped office, including a largely symbolical (because mostly empty) strongbox, in an independent (rural) building. Equally important is the creation of a standardised and computerised information and monitoring system that allows week-to-week monitoring of the situation in the local banks and of each individual client by the central unit. This system also permits regular and efficient auditing and control over the local bank records.

The banking system aims at financial sustainability. In this perspective, the supporting NGOs have rapidly cut back on the direct subsidies to the financial system. Their subsidies were used to form the initial equity capital and to finance the animation and training costs for the system. Within the expansion strategy of the system, the sources for additional loan funds are thought to be both concessional loans from external or internal sources (international foundation, BID, the new Nicaraguan development bank) as well as an envisaged collection of voluntary and obligatory savings by the clients. As of today, full financial sustainability has not yet been reached, even when according to the books the system as a whole made a profit of about $50,000. This, however, does not include all depreciation costs, nor does it take the real opportunity costs of money into account. According to the calculations of Nitlapán, the subsidy dependence index of the network of local banks in 1996 was equal to 1.2, which implies that the average interest rate of 26% per year should rise to 57% to reach the break-even point without any form of explicit or implicit subsidy.[11] Planning therefore aims at a further expansion of loan operations, as well as a gradual increase in the average loan per client. The objective is to reach a total loan portfolio of $16 million and some 12,000 clients by the year 2001. According to financial projections, this would enable the system to make a considerable profit. One essential challenge of this expansion plan will be to consolidate, and even improve, the current repayment rate (94.7% in 1996) without a proportional increase of monitoring costs. Beyond these purely financial considerations, it will be critical to continue to guarantee access to the system for the poorer rural clients and to link this access to the entrepreneurial development of these sectors, so that both the financial system and these clients can grow together.

5. The Governance Structure of the Local Bank Network of Nitlapán

As we have said, the financial network of Nitlapán is a two-tier system with two complementary levels: the central refinancing unit (Local Bank Funds-LBF) and the different relatively independent local banks (see Figure 2). The main operational link between the two levels is the bank official who is the local representative of the Local Bank Fund. A secondary but important link is provided by the technical assistance unit of the LBF. This unit gives practical support to the local administrative teams and performs periodic audits of local bookkeeping. Apart from the LBF, both an associated training unit and an independent research and evaluation team (also working for other programs) were functioning at the central level. At the local level, the bank official together with the local administrative team proposes and negotiates a yearly co-management contract with the local board of directors, elected by the general assembly of local

[11] One can, of course, ask whether it is not legitimate to – at least partially – consider concessional development loans as a sustainable source of loanable funds for this kind of rural financial system. Therefore, the subsidy dependence index is probably a too severe criterion of longer-term viability.

client-shareholders. This yearly co-management contract stipulates the conditions of the loans and credit lines that the local bank receives from the LBF. This contract functions as an annually adaptable constitution of the local bank which stipulates banking strategies in terms of interest rates, loan terms, target groups and sectoral aims, criteria for the selection of clients and guarantees that are required for different types of loans, activities to enhance recuperation in case of delinquency, responsibilities of the local banking actors, and so on. This contract also mandates that the bank official and the auditing team closely monitor and control the execution of the contract during the year. It further stipulates the incentives in case of compliance with the 'rules of the game', i.e. access to more and longer term loans in the next year, as well as sanctions in case of violations, i.e. suspension of further access to new loans or curtailment of their increase.

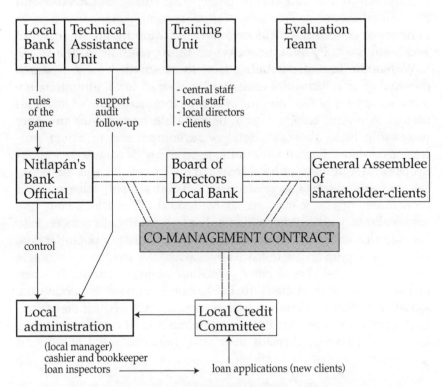

Figure 2: The governance structure of the
banking network (1996)

Each local bank negotiates its own specific co-management contract within the framework of general policies and rules that are imposed by the LBF. In 1996, these general rules defined a minimum ($100) as well as a maximum amount ($5,000) for the loans and imposed a reserve requirement of 5% as a provision for delinquent debtors. It also advocated to keep interest rates at reasonable levels, i.e. up to a maximum of 18% per year for productive activities and 30% per year for commercial activities. It further authorised a maximum of 25% of loans with a term of over 18 months. Furthermore, the framework imposed the obligatory purchase of shares and stipulated the general policies with respect to loan guarantees (see below). The specific negotiation of each contract serves two complementary purposes. The first is to adapt and detail the specific policies within each particular context.[12] The second objective is to annually go through an obligatory process of participation in and consultation of the 'rules of the game' both with local directors and the general assembly. This annual ritual is complemented with more permanent decentralised information spreading in local assemblies and house visits by local inspectors and the bank official.

Within the framework defined by the co-management contract, day-to-day operations are executed by a small local administrative team composed of full- and/or part-time local personnel. The members of this team receive wages or daily allowances that are quite reasonable in local terms, but low in comparison to urban professional wages. Each team minimally consists of a cashier, a bookkeeper and a number of local inspectors. The cashier and the bookkeeper perform the tasks related to the disbursement, collection and registration of the loans and share deposits. The function of the semi-voluntary inspectors, which only receive daily allowances, is to spread information about the bank's services, identify potential new clients, and prepare their loan applications as well as to monitor them afterwards. The number of clients to be monitored by each inspector varies from bank to bank, but is limited by definition. Up to 1996, this local staff was operationally assisted by the voluntary members of the board of directors and a local credit committee. It, however, proved difficult to sustain the substantial amount of

---

[12] In this respect, it must also be pointed out that some local deviations from the general model of organisation of the system that we present here do exist. We will of course not enter into the details of these particularities in each local bank.

voluntary commitment and invested energy over time, which was evident and critical in the initial phase of each bank, so that the work of volunteers must gradually be taken over by professional staff.[13] The need was also felt to liberate the bank official from too close involvement in day-to-day operations and allow him/her to monitor a larger amount of clients/loans as well as to dedicate more attention to complementary development animation tasks. Therefore, a policy was defined to supplement the local administrative teams with a local manager. In 1996, the selected candidates, while receiving formal and on-the-job training, gradually started to function in the local bank under supervision of the bank officials. Candidates were chosen from within the local society: some are committed members of the local boards, others are locally respected youngsters with better schooling.

The crucial task of the selection of clients and approval of loan applications is performed by a locally elected credit committee of volunteers that receive a daily allowance of about twice the rural minimum wage as a compensation for the work-time lost. Members of this committee are selected to guarantee representation from the entire territory of operation, as well as for the different relevant social sectors. In this way, available local knowledge is pooled and used to screen the viability of projects and the solvency and trustworthiness of clients. The credit committee functions within the framework of the general policies. Therefore Nitlapán's officials always participate in the meetings to safeguard compliance with rules and policies. Although this is seldom employed, the bank official has a theoretical veto-power should the credit committee want to advance undue loans to particular clients. Although the credit committee is supposed to take the final decision on loan applications and clients, in practice, the local inspectors under guidance of the local management more and more perform a task of pre-screening since they prepare concrete loan applications for the (new) clients. With time, also the role of the formal credit committees is gradually down-played with local management taking over most of the increasing amount of routine decisions. Former members of the credit committee, as well as other locals, now sometimes tend to serve only as referents for consultation on the trustworthiness of new clients.

---

[13] This evolution corresponds to the conclusions of N. Uphoff on the role and limitations of voluntary efforts in local institution building (Uphoff, 1993, p. 618).

The already mentioned difficulty of permanently mobilising substantial voluntary work is also at play here.

In order to safeguard the contractual compliance of the clients a number of incentive and enforcement mechanisms are put in place. First of all, all clients have to sign a formal 'I Owe You' that constitutes the basic legal document of the transaction and stipulates the modalities and guarantees of the loan. The system, however, does not rely too much on the judicial enforcement of the contracts, except for the exceptional larger loans. A second set of mechanisms provide economic incentives for clients to pay on time. Interest payments are paid on balances and are not 'flat' such as – for simplicity reasons – is the case in many other micro-credit systems in Nicaragua. Delinquent debtors are sanctioned with an additional 2-3% punishment interest rate on the amount in arrears. More important still is the progressivity principle. This principle implies that compliance with the contractual terms at both the client and bank levels is rewarded with a broadened right of access to higher and longer-term loans. Inversely, non-compliance is sanctioned with suspension of access to new loans. At the bank level, this implies that compliance with the rules and policies of the co-management contract is rewarded with higher annual volume loans as well as access to longer-term credit lines from the LBF. In this way, banks are collectively motivated to comply in order to be able to pursue a gradual growth path in terms of both local outreach as well as increasing investment loans. The progressivity principle is also applied at the client level through a rating system based on past bank records (and other loan sources). Only the best rated obtain the right to participate fully in the growth path of the local bank and are thus allowed to demand increasing volumes at longer-terms without, however, ever losing sight of their intrinsic absorption capacity. At the level of the system, the practical application of this mechanism imposes the necessity to grow continuously in loan volume during the initial years of institutional consolidation.

Another type of incentive for compliance is provided by the obligatory purchase of local bank shares. Since 1996, each client has to buy shares in the local bank for an equivalent of 7% of each new loan. These shares cannot be withdrawn during a minimum period of three years. During that period they do however maintain their real value (indexation to the dollar) and give a right to local bank dividends. During the first year, the LBF stipulated that half of the local bank profits would be distributed to local shareholders according to their volume in shares. In many local banks this provided for an annual rate of over 10% per year. Obviously, the shares serve as a loan linked provision against delinquency, since client-shareholders lose their rights over their shares if they fail to repay. The shares also provide an additional means for the capitalisation of the local banks. Still, its main intent is to stimulate the identification of clients with 'their bank'. At first, most clients saw the purchase of the shares as just an additional condition for access that implied a substantial mark-up on the price of the loans. This perception started to change with the first payment of dividends which proved that the 'story' of shareholdership might not just be one of the many beautiful stories told by NGOs and other outsiders. The dividends create an economic incentive for client interest in the affairs of the local banks. At the same time, any remaining local forgiveness for delinquency is further curtailed.

In line with this strategy, the system of Nitlapán intends to promote the collection of voluntary savings as well. Indeed, the spontaneous reactions to the dividend payments indicated a substantial local demand for monetary saving opportunities. As well as being a strong indicator of local trust in the system, savings would further enhance local identification with the 'cause of the bank' and thereby sustain local credit culture. The collection of savings, however, does pose serious legal issues, such as recognition as a financial institution and the supervision by the banking authorities, which in the absence of appropriate rules for 'non-conventional (rural) banks is not evident yet.

Another component of enforcement mechanisms is guarantee policy. A combination of social and material guarantees is utilised. For the poorer clients, joint-liability groups that provide a social guarantee are usually required, particularly when the banks deal with new clients. The combination of the small initial loans with the progressivity principle then provides the joint and individual economic incentives for careful mutual selection and monitoring. With time and in some of the more consolidated banks, the smaller clients can also access loans without the condition of group liability. In these cases, one or another durable consumer item (e.g. television set, bicycle,...) has to be pledged as collateral for the loan and/or the small clients have to look for a solvent (richer) guarantor with collateral who accepts joint-liability. Finally, the few richer clients that contract larger loans need to take a registered mortgage on land or (usually) buildings.

A crucial ingredient of enforcement policy is tenacity in the application of the 'rules of the game'. Local banks take a systematic hard stand towards delinquent debtors and an escalating battery of measures to pressure people to repay are put into action. This follows the slogan of the system that "there are no bad debtors, just bad collectors". In the first stage, the client is addressed by the credit inspector who usually had already noticed emerging problems before default. In some exceptional cases of accidental circumstances beyond the client's control, the inspector might support and submit an application for a restructuring of the due loan. If pressure from the inspectors does not result, additional visits by the local directors and sometimes of Nitlapán's bank official are made. These visits usually coincide with the period before the cancellation of the local bank's debts with the LBF when the collection of the delinquent loans becomes critical for compliance with the central institution.[14] If the visit by the directors still does not 'have an effect, group members or the local guarantor are contacted and asked to repay in the place of the debtor. When they do not want to pay or when there are no co-guarantors, the administrative team will visit the client together with a lawyer and threaten to go to court and ask for the sale of the pledged collateral. At this stage, clients are also automatically excluded from further loans in the near future. If all this still does not result in repayment, the bad debts are often written off without further legal action. There are, however, many cases of clear obstinacy and clients with larger loans that have been taken to court. A few times, pledged consumer durables, like television sets and bicycles, have been sold with much local publicity in order to set a 'psychological example'. Because of these actions, some people have condemned Nitlapán as a merciless institution without consideration for the difficult situation of the poor,[15] but in general these symbolic actions contributed decisively to the image of the seriousness and solidity of the system as a financial institution.

---

[14] This feature explains a cyclical trend in local repayment rates which are at the lowest at the time of cancellation to the LBF and tend to rise moderately during the year.

[15] For convenience sake, they often forgot that in general it was not the poorest of the clients that tended to be reluctant to repay.

6. On the Relation between the Institutional Environment and the Local Bank Network

By the end of 1996, the governance structure as described above resulted in a relatively favourable state of affairs: a substantial and increasing outreach of over 5,000 clients, a clear majority of smaller clients, a still not entirely satisfactory, but reasonable recuperation rate of 94,7 % and a close to break-even operation of the system in present-day financial terms. These results, however, were not obtained from the very beginning. The 1996 governance structure is the intermediate result of permanent institutional learning that has not yet come to an end. In this process of gradually learning, more effective ways were encountered to cope with the negative influence of the inherited institutional environment.

6.1. *Aspects of the historical genesis of the system*

When Nitlapán started to operate in the hamlets near Masaya in 1987, it refused to enter into any development project. The reason was that one was too much aware of the distortions generated by externally mediated aid flows enhancing clientelistic dependency and associated local division and jealousy. The initial endeavour was therefore to engage solely in popular education aimed at facilitating local problem identification and collective capacity building to solve the identified problems. Nevertheless, the severe economic crisis triggered by the economic stabilisation process forced the institute to engage in the local problem-solving process itself. Since the liquidity crisis made access to credit surface as one of the most pressing constraints, the institute started to promote village level revolving funds. With more questions than answers, the institute entered the dangerous ground of development projects, hoping that the provision of credit would be less tricky than the distribution of gifts.

The initial governance structure of the revolving village funds in Masaya and Carazo was gradually developed and at first relied primarily on a close collaboration with what were found to be 'locally respected natural leaders'. In line with the initial objective to enhance local collective capacity, the strategic choice was for assisted self-management by a local organisation under the direction of the identified leadership. Local leaders were brought together to receive training in banking affairs and democratic leadership. As to the

financial system, local self-managed banks were formed and provided with 'seed capital' in the hope that this would transform
Nitlapán's 'cold' external money into 'hot' local money. Despite policy options to the contrary, the local leaders turned out to emerge
almost exclusively from the Sandinista networks. Given the Sandinista predominance in the local polity at the time, it was leaders
from the Sandinista network that had met with the visiting promoters. It proved to be very difficult for anyone in the rural areas of
Masaya and Carazo to imagine an initiative that was not politically
linked to the revolution, and even harder to imagine that it would be
directed to all locals without any political or religious distinctions.[16]
In spite of their training and the general principles of the banking
network, the local Sandinista leadership saw no problem in restricting access to their political clients, friends and relatives. Worse still,
hoping to reinforce their sometimes shaky position as local leaders
they often presented the local bank as a gift for the village that was
intermediated by them.

Logically, the repayment rates were dramatically low (between
50% and 70%). It was inconceivable for local Sandinista patrons to
severely enforce compliance with repayment obligations. Many did
not even communicate the loan conditions to the people.[17] Incentive
mechanisms, such as the progressivity principle and the formation
of joint-liability groups, were not clearly explained nor properly
implemented, thereby losing most of their effect. Despite the commitment of Nitlapán to continue support in case of compliance, the
board members were often the least convinced of the advantages to
repay. First of all, they viewed their local prestige to depend more on

[16] In the pilot experiences, women of both Sandinista and (anti-Sandinista)
Catholic-charismatic families showed a strong interest in participating in a revolving
village chicken fund. Thinking and talking with others in their network, and realising that they would be joining a system together with the Sandinista women, the
charismatic women at the last moment decided not to show up at the first round
of the repartition of the chickens. The concept of a politically neutral project was
difficult to accept. (R. Mendoza, 1991, pp. 4-5)

[17] This problem is not particular of sandinista leaders, but applies to any traditional leader. In the network of Nitlapán, a variation on the problem emerged in the
interior region of Matiguas where in the first years the local structure of the parish
was used to intermediate loans. Rapidly, it turned out that the need to consolidate
the friendly relationship between the local clergy with the people in the villages
made it difficult for the same agents to take a hard stand on repayment. The local
governance structure through the parish structures had to be abandoned for this
reason.

their capacity to intermediate benefits and not on the improbable functioning of a sustainable financial system in the future. Their multiple previous experiences with official credit and development projects also played a prominent role in their absence of commitment to repayment. The reality that Nitlapán had not yet reached a minimum scale nor established its reputation, of course, did not enhance its capacity to make the people trust its commitments. Another important problem was that too often the leaders themselves were the least willing to repay. As predicted by the theoretical analysis of the patron-client relation, detailed examination revealed later that local leaders figured prominently among the delinquent debtors. Their control over information at that time and their power to avoid a potential imposition of sanctions provided them with an effective capacity for abuse. This abuse not only related to non-repayment and sectarian favouritism, but also took the form of more spectacular corruption in some cases. For example, one local leader in an isolated interior region used the money of collected loans for his own personal commercial activity and never repaid the entire sum when this was eventually detected and disapproved of by the LBF. In one urban bank, the local intermediaries, directors of local artisan service cooperatives, even engaged in a lucrative business of charging 'their' clients a substantial fee of about $10 for each loan they approved.

In this way it was impossible to construct any sustainable credit system. Consequently, corrective action was required. At first, Nitlapán tried to articulate better 'rules of the game' and to enhance compliance with these rules within the original framework of assisted local self-management. However, recuperation rates did not improve sufficiently, outreach continued to be 'politically' restricted and abuses by the local board members continued to be detected. Intents to promote a more stringent control of the leaders by a local assembly of client-members were not very successful, since the traditional patron-client pattern of social organisation did not support the idea of accountability of the leadership. The organisation of checks and balances in the local banks did not really succeed. Locals accepted any discourse of 'their' leaders and were not really interested in more participation. They remained confident that their leaders' benevolence and ability would guarantee them access to the loans or they did not dare to defy the local leadership openly by mingling themselves too actively in the affairs of the bank. The formula of giving 'seed capital' to constitute "local village funds for the benefit of all" also fell short of the initial expectation that it would promote collective interest and participation in the management of the system.

6.2. *External intervention as a means to remedy deficiencies of the institutional environment.*

Contrary to the emotional premises of the institution's strategic project, all this led to the inevitable conclusion that the high levels of trust and hope invested in the local leadership under the option for assisted self-management was not warranted. The pervasive impact of the sectarian and vertical governance structures invalidated any attempt to impose transparent and objective 'rules of the game', nor did they allow access for all clients independent of their network affiliation. It turned out that a strong active intervention of Nitlapán was required in order to provide for the necessary countervailing power to sectarian local leadership. As could be expected, this was not accepted by most of the initial leadership, who quite rightly felt that their position of power was being threatened. They demystified the discourse of co-management and protested against the shift from 'assisted self-management' to the top-down imposition of the 'rules of the game'.[18] However, many of the local leaders were delegitimised when Nitlapán, after having stipulated that no one could be a board member with pending debts, began to unravel and publicise the real situation of the leaders' delinquency. The erosion of the predominant position of the original Sandinista leadership under the Chamorro government, along with the growing disapproval of 'politics' in general, also contributed to weakening the influence of the politicised leadership. In this way, the profound change in the institutional rules of the game went together with a quite radical change in the members of the local boards of directors. This marked a definite turn in the nature of the functioning of the local banks and clearly contributed to a new perception of the local banks.

The change, however, was not primarily a change in local leadership. In fact, Nitlapán did not fundamentally contribute the governance problems to a lack of ethical or managerial quality of the

---

[18] This problem was evidently not present in the newer banks that were opened under the co-management system from the beginning.

leaders. Given the socio-cultural conditions under which they were functioning, they could not be expected to behave differently in a system that did not constrain their actions properly. As a popular Nicaraguan proverb says: *'En arca abierta, hasta el justo peca'* (with the strongbox open, even the just will sin). The problem is therefore mainly one of the design of the governance structure for circumventing behavioural deficiencies. Local checks and balances needed to be thoroughly enhanced, as well as supplemented with the consistent external intervention under the co-management system. Only in this way, would it be possible to create more transparency, to maintain discipline and objectivity in the operation of the system, and to impose sanctions without social distinction. The effect of the strategic turn towards the co-management system was impressive.

The repayment rates immediately increased from under 70% to more than 87% in the first year of the implementation of the new system. Moreover, with respect to outreach, corrective action was taking place so that the system managed to establish an unambiguous internal corporate culture of 'neutrality' as well as a gradually consolidating image in the same line. It is clear that the authoritarian intervention managed to restore local credit culture and to de-link access to credit from politically or religiously conditioned clientelistic intermediation

Given the critical role of external imposition of rules, one might wonder whether the whole idea of local participation in the financial system could not be abandoned altogether. Some of the analysts of Nitlapán's system saw a further indication of the redundancy of participation in the recent demand of the local volunteers to be relieved from their tasks by local professionals. For several reasons, we nevertheless believe that a participatory process is necessary both for the functioning of the financial system and even more for its ultimate impact on local development. It is the synergy between the external structure and the local organisation which will prove crucial for future prospects. First of all, the whole evolution in the banks has not only been a learning process for the central management of the system, but also for the clients in the villages. Without this process, the local banks would not enjoy the reputation and local legitimacy they have today and which are critical for their smooth functioning. It would be a dangerous illusion to take this gradually crafted local environment for granted. While today's evolution towards less involvement of non-professional locals in day-to-day operations testifies to the difficulty of sustaining substantial volunteer work over an extended time, it should not be interpreted as a prescription for forgetting about local participation altogether. An entirely external institution that would not pass through the initial phase of local confidence building cannot hope for a sound legitimacy basis, and will rapidly run into serious enforcement problems. In this context, it must also be stressed that in the more professionalised banks today the influential local directors are permanently consulted to obtain information about clients as well as mobilised in moments of repayment crisis to pressure delinquent clients. In the short run, we do not believe it can be a transaction cost-effective solution to rely exclusively on the legal mechanism to guarantee sufficient repayment.

Even more important in the argument for active local participation, however, is the longer-term development effect of the financial system. The provision of finance alone will indeed not be sufficient to generate the dynamic democratic rural development that is hoped for. In line with the conclusion of Hulme and Mosley (1996) on the impact of micro-credit systems on the conditions of the poor, recent research of the evaluation team of Nitlapán found only a limited positive impact on the income of the poorer clients mainly through increases in petty-commercial activities, not through substantial productive improvements (Nitlapán, 1997a). Their agricultural or artisan production and commercialisation systems remain largely unaffected by the availability of credit alone. Other improvements in their access to resources, knowledge and markets are therefore needed to generate a more substantial and sustainable improvement in their development prospects. Complementary commercial and technological innovations will thus be necessary to promote a more inclusive rural development. If these are to take place, a broader change in the nature and the capacity of local collective action will be needed. The vertical governance structures which hampered the organisation of a viable financial system will also obstruct the functioning and the dynamism of other market configurations. Therefore, the promotion of a transition towards a more civic, cooperative, transparent and reliable local environment, overcoming the development constraining deficiencies of the inherited vertical patron-client governance, represents the more fundamental development challenge. Losing sight of this challenge in the pragmatic organisation of the financial system might ultimately turn out to be self-defeating since the targeted clients will not be sufficiently supported to create a vibrant local economy. The organisers of a rural financial system must there-fore pay attention to the potential effect of the financial governance structure on the broader local environment. The participative articu-lation between the bank and local organisation is the way in which such an influence can be exercised.

The experience of Nitlapán indicates that this participative articu-lation needs to be organised correctly. A mutual learning process must be organised in a methodologically appropriate way. The initial approach of assisted self-management proves that an option for local participation should not be equalled with non-intervention or romantic optimism about local organisational capacity. The per-vasive influence of vertical governance structures requires a strong constraining, facilitating and even structuring through external inter-vention. An external development promoting agent, with the power over crucial resources for local development, can and must impose more civic, transparent and rule-based governance procedures as a condition for local participation in its activities. In this way, the local capacity for participative, horizontal collective action can be facilitated through the articulation of the external 'enterprise' with local society. Such a top-down approach can be effective for over-coming micro-macro incompatibilities and creating a positive syn-ergy between 'autonomous' local dynamics of transformation and supra-local initiatives.[19] The paradox is thus that the improvement and democratisation of local collective development capacity might require a firm external procedural intervention.

The co-management system in Nitlapán's banking network proves that even in the adverse context of Nicaragua it is possible to create an innovative corporate culture both within the enterprise and in its relations with the villages. In the system with its various central-local and local checks and balances, access to loans is no longer inter-mediated by sectarian patrons and objective rules of the game are enforced. This is not to say that vertical inheritance is easily circum-vented. It is worth noting, for example, that sometimes aspects of the practical operation of local banks articulate with traditional social mechanisms that do not necessarily enhance horizontal organisation.

---

[19] The argument is somewhat similar to J. Tendler's plea in favour of a demand-driven approach in the case of the organisation of technological-commercial links between government procurement agencies and small artisan villages, although she does not seem to emphasise the need to facilitate local civic organisation that much (Tendler, 1996).

Might the growing recurrence to a local guarantor with collateral providing bail for poorer clients then reintroduce a practical dependency of the latter to local 'patrons'? In the operation of some of the local banks, other potentially dangerous tendencies can be observed. For instance, one local division of a bank in Wiwili relies on the intermediation of loans by a traditional local leader-coffee trader. In this village, the bank intermediates the larger part of the loans through this patron in order to pre-finance smaller coffee producers in his sphere of influence. In this place, the smaller local clients will almost inevitably tend to have little direct say in the functioning of the bank. This cannot but foster the dominating position of the local trader. On the other hand, in a neighbouring village the local bank functions through a network of joint-liability groups of small coffee growers that are actively involved in the bank's operations. In this village, the local bank – with the approval of the small clients – also approved a larger loan to finance a local coffee trader. In this case, however, the outcome of future institutional development can be expected to be more democratic.

Another issue is related to the observation that clients are not so much interested in involvement in operational bank affairs themselves. A study by the evaluation team in 1996 revealed that more than half of the clients lacked substantial information about the 'rules of the game' of the local bank and were not all that interested to know about them. This might reveal two things. The first is that one should not try to foster maximum participation of clients in all the operations of the bank. The main issue is not the participation in the local bank, but the transformation of local organisation. Clients must not become bankers, but better local citizens, peasants, artisans, traders. What primarily interests them therefore is what the bank means for their development opportunities. Participation in the definition of strategic policies of the bank does not require full operational involvement nor complete knowledge of its internal functioning. Participation in the annual general assembly of shareholders and a good relationship with the elected board of directors can suffice to this end. The second point that might be revealed by the lack of knowledge on the 'rules of the game' is however that one has not yet sufficiently managed to transform the attitudes of a number of clients viz-à-viz their role and place in local society. In the perception of part of them, the imposition of the co-management system could just have meant the substitution of the old patrons with new ones, be they

Nitlapán's bank official or the local staff. In fact, one can observe a more individualised, dyadic relationship between the clients and the local bank. The idea of being a shareholder of a local member organisation or of being a full-righted local citizen altogether is not as evident as one would hope for. It is therefore not surprising that the participation of clients in the general assembly and their 'horizontal' relations with the board of directors is generally found to be weak.

A long way still has to be covered before local banks are raised to vibrant, civic local organisations. For this reason, Nitlapán is planning to invest more energy in the fostering of participatory local development debates in view of which it requires the definition of a local 'development plan' in the co-management contract. The bank official will also start to dedicate more time to direct information spreading and exchange of ideas with individual clients. In this perspective, it is clear that the growing professionalisation of routine banking should not be seen as a substitute, but more as a precondition for active local participation in banking policies. Another possible conclusion from these bank experiences might be that the initiation of complementary national-level activities in the field of commercialisation or technical innovation, repeating similar civic and rule-bound top-down governance structures, could be necessary to amplify the sphere of influence of the bank's corporate culture.

A final point to be mentioned is that one cannot but be impressed by what Klitgaard has identified as micro-differences in the socio-cultural 'soil conditions' between the different local banks (Klitgaard, 1995, p. 190). A great deal of relevant variation in the nature of the micro-institutionality in the different villages and even hamlets indeed seems to exist. For example, in the hamlets of Somotillo the members of the local board of bank directors are also the political representatives of the hamlet in the municipal council. Coordination between the local banks and the local political authorities is quite evident in this case. In other banks, the financial system and its organisation operates completely parallel, or sometimes even with some antagonism to the local authorities. We do not as of yet have systematised data on how and which of these differences impact on the nature of the local governance structures,[20] but differences do

---

[20] A research project trying to map these differences systematically and evaluate their impact on the local governance structures of both the financial system as well as the broader 'collective action' activities should start in the beginning of 1998.

exist and are reflected in variations of the co-management contract and even more in the real world practical operation of the various local banks. Not all villages are equally affected by previous experiences of clientelistic development aid of the government or NGOs. Some villages have relatively homogenous populations in socio-economic as well as politico-religious terms, others are strongly segmented with or without violent polarisation. Disrespect of the rule of law and mutual distrust are neither equally distributed among the villages. Some villages have a firmly established and legitimate leadership, others are much more disrupted. All these factors turn out to be quite relevant and should be taken into account when evaluating the effectiveness of approaches to local capacity building and development enhancing micro-institutional transition.

7. Summary and Conclusions

The experiences of Nitlapán's banking network demonstrate the difficulties of creating a viable governance structure for finance in the rural institutional environment of Nicaragua. Both repayment rates and outreach were negatively affected by the influence of sectarian patron-client governance. Through an appropriate institutional design, including firm external intervention and systematic checks and balances in the system, it was nevertheless possible to circumvent these problems and make the financial system work in a satisfactory way. The internal corporate culture of the banking network thereby represents a definite change compared to traditional vertical governance. Through a necessary participatory learning process the system also managed to transform the clients' perception and sustain a local credit culture with respect for the bank's disciplined and civic rules of the game. The bank's organisation therefore also had an impact on the nature of broader local organisation. To sustain future democratic development, this broader local environment should be further transformed in the direction of transparency, security and civic-mindedness, coupled with concrete socio-economic initiatives. Nitlapán's experience shows that one should not be too optimistic about the possibilities for such a transformation, but that – provided the correct methodological approach is followed – 'institutional entrepreneurship' is possible.

Annexes

Table 1: Stylised facts of the banking network of Nitlapán (end 1996)

Local bank	number of clients	number of man	%	number of women	%	extended loans (total in US $)	relative share	average loan/client/year
Urban Masaya	**724**	**295**	**41**	**429**	**59**	**288784**	**10.8**	**399**
Banarte	439	187	43	252	57	233157	8.7	531
Magdalena (*)	285	108	38	177	62	55527	2.1	195
Rural Masaya:	**960**	**606**	**63**	**354**	**37**	**448230**	**16.8**	**467**
Valle de la Laguna	285	144	51	141	49	101285	3.8	355
Quebrada Honda	215	144	67	71	33	129081	4.8	600
Los Altos	251	187	75	64	25	141584	5.3	564
El Comejen	191	123	64	68	36	68718	2.6	360
El Hatillo (*)	18	8	44	10	56	7562	0.0	420
Carazo: (**)	**1421**	**831**	**58**	**590**	**42**	**677736**	**25.3**	**480**
Fatima	869	467	54	402	46	470832	17.6	542
San José	293	226	77	67	23	87650	3.3	299
El Arenal (*)	103	49	48	54	52	13876	0.1	135
San Juan	156	89	57	67	43	105378	3.9	676
Rivas: (**)	**514**	**256**	**50**	**258**	**50**	**251418**	**9.4**	**489**
Nancimi	271	128	53	143	47	123206	4.6	455
Santa Cruz	243	128	47	115	53	128212	4.8	528
Somotillo: (**)	**630**	**483**	**77**	**147**	**23**	**277057**	**10.4**	**440**
Cayanlipe	258	169	66	89	34	93906	3.5	364
La Carreta	188	158	84	30	16	97897	3.7	532
San Ramon	184	156	85	28	15	85254	3.2	463
Wiwili:	**262**	**226**	**86**	**36**	**14**	**370325**	**13.8**	**1413**
Matiguas:	**177**	**131**	**74**	**46**	**26**	**362011**	**13.5**	**2045**
TOTAL:	**4688**	2828	**60**	1860	**60**	**2675561**	**100.0**	**571**

(*) These local banks' access to new loans from the Local Bank Fund was temprarely suspended. It are all small and poorly consolidated banks. In Magdalena and El Hatillo poor local organisation entailed deficient recuperation rates, which led to the decision to close them down and to integrate the good clients in neighbouring local banks. In El Arenal the local directorate refuses to take new loans in order to escape the imposed rules of Nitlapán;
(**) In these areas, new local banks will be opened in 1997: Diriomo (Carazo); Potosí (Rivas) and "urban" Somotillo.

Source: Nitlapán, 1996.

References

BASTIAENSEN, J. (1991), *Peasants and Economic Development: A Case-study on Nicaragua*. Ph.D. thesis in Applied Economics. University of Antwerp, UFSIA, Faculty of Applied Economics, 332 p. +annexes.

BASTIAENSEN, J. (1997a), 'Non-Conventional Rural and the Crisis of Economic Institutions in Nicaragua' in *Sustainable Agriculture in Central America*. Ed. J.P. DE GROOT and R. RUBEN. London, McMillan, pp. 191-209.

BASTIAENSEN, J. and B. D'EXELLE (1997b), 'The Consolidation of Agrarian Reform in Northern Masaya: Property Rights, Missing Markets and Perspectives for Agricultural Diversification' Paper presented to the XI Asercca Conference in Portsmouth, 19-21 September 1997. Workshop *'Markets and Local Governance for Rural Development in Central America'*.

EVANS, P. (1996), 'Government Action, Social Capital and Development: Reviewing the Evidence on Synergy' in *World Development*, 24(1996)6, pp. 1119-1132.

HOUTART, F. and G. LEMERCINIER (1992), *El campesino vomo actor*. Sociología de una comarca de Nicaragua. El Comejen. Managua, Ed. Nicarao, 175 p.

HULME, D and P. MOSLEY (1996), *Finance against Poverty*. London, Routledge.

KLITGAARD, R. (1995), 'Including Culture in Evaluation Research' in R. PIOCCIOTTO and R. RIST (eds.). *Evaluation and Development* (Proceedings of the 1994 World Bank Conference). Washington (DC), The World Bank, pp. 189-200.

MALDIDIER, C. and P. MARCHETTI (1996), *El Campesino-Finquero y el Potencial Económico del Campesinado Nicaraguense*. Tomo 1. Tipología y Regionalización Agrosocioeconómica de los Sistemas de Producción y los Sectores Sociales en el Agro Nicaragüense. Managua, Instituto Nitlapán, Universidad Centroamericana, 174 p., ill.

MARCHETTI, P. (1994), *Experimentación con Nuevas Modalidades de la Educación Popular para el Desarrollo Local*. Managua, Nitlapán-Universidad Centroaméricana, 30 p.

MENDOZA, R. (1993), *Las Garantías en el Crédito Agricola/Rural*. Una propuesta metodologica a partir de estudios especificos. Nitlapán-UCA, 34 p.

MENDOZA, R. (1991), *El Rostro Femenino del Campesinado: hacia un nuevo estilo de organización y liderazgo comarcal*. Evaluación del proyecto 'pollos' financiado por USOS y Broederlijk Delen. Managua, Instituto Nitlapán, Universidad Centroamericana, 27 p.

MOLENAERS, N. (1996), Investigating Political Culture in a Third World Setting' a working paper for University of Antwerp, RUCA, Institute for Development Policy and Management, 17 p.

NITLAPÁN (1994), *Financial Services Program*. Managua, Nitlapán-UCA.

NITLAPÁN (1997a), *Evaluación de Impacto Económico del Crédito en las Unidades Económicas Rurales*. Managua, Instituto Nitlapán-Universidad Centroamericana, 121 p. +annex.

NITLAPÁN (1997b), *Informe Anual 1996. Programa de Desarrollo Local*. Managua, Instituto Nitlapán, Universidad Centroamericana, 43 p.

PLATTEAU, J.P. (1996), 'Traditional Sharing Norms as an Obstacle to Economic Growth in Tribal Societies' a working paper for Centre de Recherche en Economie du Développement. Namur, University of Namur, 42 p.

PUTNAM, R.D. (1994), 'Democracy, Development, and the Civic Community: Evidence from an Italian Experiment' in *Culture and Development*. The World Bank, pp. 33-73.

PUTNAM, R.D. with R. LEONARDI and R.Y. NANETTI (1993), *Making Democracy Work. Civic Traditions in Modern Italy*. Princeton (NJ), Princeton University Press.

SCHROEDER, M.J. (1996), 'Horse Thieves to Rebels to Dogs: Political Gang Violence and the State in the Western Segovias, Nicaragua, in the Time of Sandino, 1926-34' in *The Journal of Latin American Studies*, 28(1996)May, part 2, pp. 383-434.

SCOTT, W.R. (1994), 'Institutions and Organizations: Towards a Theoretical Synthesis' in W.R. SCOTT and J.W. MEYER & associates (eds.) *Institutional Environments and Organizations. Structural Complexity and Individualism*. Thousand Oaks, Sage Publications, pp. 55-80.

TENDLER, J. and M. ALVES AMORIM (1996), 'Small Firms and Their Helpers: Lessons on Demand' in *World Development*, 24(1996)3, pp. 407-426.

UPHOFF, N. (1993), 'Grassroots Organizations and NGOs in Rural Development: Opportunities with Diminishing States and Expanding Markets' in *World Development*, 21(1993)4, pp. 607-622.

WILLIAMSON, O. (1994), 'Transaction Cost Economics and Organization Theory' in N.J. SMELSER and R. SWEDBERG (eds.), *The Handbook of Economic Sociology*. Princeton (NJ), Princeton University Press, pp. 78-103.

GLOSSARY

adverse selection: The problem created by asymmetric information *before* a transaction occurs. The people who are the most undesirable from the other party's point of view are the ones who are most likely to want to engage in the financial transaction.

American option: An option that can be exercised at any time up to the expiration date of the contract.

appreciation: Increase in a currency's value.

arbitrage: Elimination of a riskless profit opportunity in a market.

asset: A financial claim or piece of property that is a store of value.

asset management: The acquisition of assets that have a low rate of default and diversification of asset holdings to increase profits.

asset market approach: An approach to determine asset prices using stocks of assets rather than flows.

asymmetric information: The unequal knowledge that each party to a transaction has about the other party.

balance of payments: A bookkeeping system for recording all payments that have a direct bearing on the movement of funds between a country and foreign countries.

balance-of-payments crisis: A foreign exchange crisis stemming from problems in a country's balance of payments.

balance sheet: A list of the assets and liabilities of a bank (or firm) that balances: total assets equal total liabilities plus capital.

bank failure: A situation in which a bank cannot satisfy its obligations to pay its depositors and other creditors, thereby going out of business.

bank panic: The simultaneous failure of many banks, as during a financial crisis.

banks: Financial institutions that accept money deposits and make loans (such as commercial banks, savings and loan associations, and credit unions).

bank supervision: Overseeing who operates banks and how they are operated.

basis point: One one-hundredth of a percentage point.

basis risk: The risk associated with the possibility that the prices of a hedged asset and the asset underlying the futures contract do not move closely together over time.

beta: A measure of the sensitivity of an asset's return to changes in the value of the market portfolio, which is also a measure of the asset's marginal contribution to the risk of the market portfolio.

Board of Governors of the Federal Reserve System: A board with seven governors (including the chairman) that plays an essential role in decision-making within the Federal Reserve System.

bond: A debt security that promises to make payments periodically for a specified period of time.

branches: Additional offices of banks that conduct banking operations.

*Bretton Woods system:*The international monetary system in use from 1945 to 1971 in which exchange rates were fixed and the U.S. dollar was freely convertible into gold (by foreign governments and central banks only).

brokerage firms Firms that participate in securities markets as brokers, dealers, and investment bankers.

brokers: Agents for investors who match buyers with sellers.

bubble: A situation in which the price of an asset differs from its fundamental market value.

budget deficit: The excess of government expenditures over tax revenues.

business cycles: The upward and downward movement of aggregate output produced in the economy.

call option: An option contract that provides the right to buy a security at a specified price.

capital account: An account that describes the flow of capital between a national state and other countries.

capital adequacy management: A bank's decision about the amount of capital it should maintain and the acquisition of the needed capital.

capital market: A financial market in which longer-term debt (maturity of greater than one year) and equity instruments are traded.

capital mobility: A situation in which foreigners can easily purchase a country's assets and the country's residents can easily purchase foreign assets.

cash flow: The difference between cash receipts and cash expenditures.

central bank The government agency that oversees the banking system and is responsible for the amount of money and credit supplied in the economy; in the United States, the Federal Reserve System.

collateral: Property that is pledged to the lender to guarantee payment in the event that the borrower should be unable to make debt payments.

compensating balance: A required minimum amount of funds that a firm receiving a loan must keep in a checking account at the lending bank.

consol: A perpetual bond with no maturity date and no repayment of principal that periodically makes fixed coupon payments.

consumer durable expenditure: Spending by consumers on durable items such as automobiles and household appliances.

consumer expenditure: The total demand for (spending on) consumer goods and services.

consumption: Spending by consumers on non-durable goods and services (including services related to the ownership of homes and consumer durables).

costly state verification: Monitoring a firm's activities, an expensive process in both time and money.

coupon bond: A credit market instrument that pays the owner a fixed interest payment every year until the maturity date, when a specified final amount is repaid.

creditor: A holder of debt.

credit rationing: A lender's refusing to make loans even though borrowers are willing to pay the stated interest rate or even a higher rate or restricting the size of loans made to less than the full amount sought.

credit risk: The risk arising from the possibility that the borrower will default.

currency: Paper money (such as dollar bills) and coins.

currency swap: The exchange of a set of payments in one currency for a set of payments in another currency.

current account: An account that shows international transactions involving currently produced goods and services.

dealers: People who link buyers with sellers by buying and selling securities at stated prices.

debt deflation: A situation in which a substantial decline in the price level sets in, leading to a further deterioration in the net worth of firms because of the increased burden of indebtedness.

default: A situation in which the party issuing a debt instrument is unable to make interest payments or pay off the amount owed when the instrument matures.

default risk: The chance that the issuer of a debt instrument will be unable to make interest payments or pay off the face value when the instrument matures.

deposit outflows: Losses of deposits when depositors make withdrawals or demand payment.

deposit rate ceiling: Restriction on the maximum interest rate payable on deposits.

depreciation: Decrease in a currency's value.

devaluation: Resetting of the fixed value of a currency at a lower level.

discount bond: A credit market instrument that is bought at a price below its face value and whose face value is repaid at the maturity date; it does not make any interest payments. Also called a *zerocoupon bond.*

discount loans: A bank's borrowings from the central bank.

discount rate: The interest rate that the central bank charges banks on discount loans.

discount window: The central banks facility at which discount loans are made to banks.

disintermediation: A reduction in the flow of funds into the banking system that causes the amount of financial intermediation to decline.

diversification: The holding of a variety of risky assets.

dividends: Periodic payments made by equities to shareholders.

dual banking system: The system in the United States in which banks supervised by the federal government and banks supervised by states operate side by side.

duration analysis: A measurement of the sensitivity of the market value of a bank's assets and liabilities to changes in interest rates.

dynamic open market operations: Open market operations that are intended to change the level of reserves and the monetary base.

economies of scale: The reduction in transaction costs per dollar of transaction as the size (scale) of transactions increases.

efficient markets theory: The application of the theory of rational expectations to financial markets.

electronic money (e-money): Money that is stored electronically.

equities: Claims to share in the net income and assets of a corporation (such as common stock).

Eurobonds: Bonds denominated in a currency other than that of the country in which they are sold.

Eurodollars: U.S. dollars that are deposited in foreign banks outside of the United States or in foreign branches of U.S. banks.

European option: An option that can be exercised only at the expiration date of the contract.

excess reserves: Reserves in excess of required reserves.

exchange rate: The price of one currency in terms of another.

exchanges: Secondary markets in which buyers and sellers of securities (or their agents or brokers) meet in one central location to conduct trades.

exercise price: The price at which the purchaser of an option has the right to buy or sell the underlying financial instrument. Also known as the strike price.

expected return: The return on an asset expected over the next period.

face value: A specified final amount paid to the owner of a coupon bond at the maturity date. Also called *par value*.

Federal Reserve banks: The 12 district banks in the Federal Reserve System.

Federal Reserve System (the Fed): The central banking authority responsible for monetary policy in the United States.

financial crisis: A major disruption in financial markets that is characterised by sharp declines in asset prices and the failures of many financial and nonfinancial firms.

financial derivatives: Instruments that have payoffs that are linked to previously issued securities.

financial engineering: The process of researching and developing new financial products and services that would meet customer needs and prove profitable.

financial futures contract: A futures contract in which the standardised commodity is a particular type of financial instrument.

financial futures option: An option in which the underlying instrument is a futures contract. Also called a futures option.

financial intermediaries: Institutions such as banks, insurance companies, mutual funds, pension funds, and finance companies that borrow funds from people who have saved and then make loans to others.

financial intermediation: The process of indirect finance whereby financial intermediaries link lender-savers and borrower-spenders.

financial markets: Markets in which funds are transferred from people who have a surplus of available funds to people who have a shortage of available funds.

financial panic: The widespread collapse of financial markets and intermediaries in an economy.

fixed exchange rate regime: A regime in which central banks buy and sell their own currencies to keep their exchange rates fixed at a certain level.

foreign bonds: Bonds sold in a foreign country and denominated in that country's currency.

foreign exchange intervention: An international financial transaction in which a central bank buys or sells currency to influence foreign exchange rates.

foreign exchange market: The market in which exchange rates are determined.

foreign exchange rate: See *exchange rate.*

forward contract: An agreement by two parties to engage in a financial transaction at a future (forward) point in time.

forward exchange rate: The exchange rate for a forward transaction.

forward transaction: A transaction that involves the exchange of bank deposits denominated in different currencies at some specified future date.

futures option: See *financial futures option.*

gold standard: A regime under which a currency is directly convertible into gold.

government budget constraint: The requirement that the government budget deficit equal the sum of the change in the monetary base and the change in government bonds held by the public.

government spending: Spending by all levels of government on goods and services.

gross domestic product (GDP): The value of all final goods and services produced in the economy during the course of a year.

hedge: To protect oneself against risk.

hyperinflation: An extreme inflation in which the inflation rate exceeds 50 percent per month.

incentive-compatible: Aligning the incentives of both parties to a contract.

income: The flow of earnings.

indexed bond: A bond whose interest and principal payments are adjusted for changes in the price level, and whose interest rate thus provides a direct measure of a real interest rate.

inflation: The condition of a continually rising price level.

inflation rate: The rate of change of the price level, usually measured as a percentage change per year.

insolvent: In a situation in which the value of a firm's or bank's assets have fallen below its liabilities; bankrupt.

interest rate: The cost of borrowing or the price paid for the rental of Mods (usually expressed as a percentage per year).

interest-rate forward contract: A forward contract that is linked to a debt instrument.

interest-rate risk: The possible reduction in returns that is associated with changes in interest rates.

interest-rate swap: A financial contract that allows one party to exchange (swap) a set of interest payments for another set of interest payments owned by another party.

intermediate-term: With reference to a debt instrument, having a maturity of between one and ten years.

International Monetary Fund (IMF): The international organisation created by the Bretton Woods agreement whose objective is to promote the growth of world trade by making loans to countries experiencing balance-of-payments difficulties.

international reserves: Central bank holdings of assets denominated in foreign currencies.

investment banks: Firms that assist in the initial sale of securities in the primary market.

January effect: An abnormal rise in stock prices from December to January.

junk bonds: Bonds with ratings below Baa (or BBB) that have a high default risk.

lender of last resort: Provider of reserves to financial institutions when no one else would provide them in order to prevent a financial crisis.

leverage ratio: A bank's capital divided by its assets.

liabilities: debts.

liability management: The acquisition of funds at low cost to increase profits.

liquid: Easily converted into cash.

liquidity: The relative ease and speed with which an asset can be converted into cash.

liquidity management: The decisions made by a bank to maintain sufficient liquid assets to meet the bank's obligations to depositors.

liquidity preference theory: John Maynard Keynes's theory of the demand for money.

liquidity premium theory: The theory that the interest rate on a long-term bond will equal an average of short-term interest rates expected to occur over the life of the long-term bond plus a positive term (liquidity) premium.

loanable funds: The quantity of loans.

loan commitment: A bank's commitment (for a specified future period of time) to provide a firm with loans up to a given amount at an interest rate that is tied to some market interest rate.

loan sale: The sale under a contract (also called a *secondary loan participation*) of all or part of the cash stream from a specific loan, thereby removing the loan from the bank's balance sheet.

long position: A contractual obligation to take delivery of an underlying financial instrument.

long-term: With reference to a debt instrument, having a maturity of ten years or more.

macro hedge: A hedge of interest-rate risk for a financial institution's entire portfolio.

managed float regime: The current international financial environment in which exchange rates fluctuate from day to day but central banks attempt to influence their countries' exchange rates by buying and selling currencies.

margin requirement: A sum of money that must be kept in an account (the margin account) at a brokerage firm.

marked to market: Repriced and settled in the margin account at the end of every trading day to reflect any change in the value of the futures contract.

market equilibrium: A situation occurring when the quantity that people are willing to buy (demand) equals the quantity that people are willing to sell (supply).

market fundamentals: Items that have a direct impact on future income streams of a security.

maturity: Time to the expiration date (maturity date) of a debt instrument.

medium of exchange: Anything that is used to pay for goods and services.

modern quantity theory of money: The theory that changes in aggregate spending are determined primarily by changes in the money supply.

monetarist: A follower of Milton Friedman who sees changes in the money supply as the primary source of movements in price levels and aggregate output and who views the economy as inherently stable.

monetary aggregates: The various measures of the money supply used by the central bank (M1, M2, M3, and L).

monetary neutrality: A proposition that in the long run, a percentage rise in the money supply is matched by the same percentage rise in price levels, leaving the real money supply and all other economic variables such as interest rates unchanged.

monetary policy: The management of money supply and interest rates.

monetary theory: The theory that relates changes in the quantity of money to changes in economic activity.

money: Anything that is generally accepted in payment for goods or services or in the repayment of debts.

money market: A financial market in which only short-term debt instruments (maturity of less than one year) are traded.

moral hazard: The risk that one party to a transaction will engage in behaviour that is undesirable from the other party's point of view.

net worth: The difference between a firm's assets (what it owns or is owed) and its liabilities (what it owes). Also called *equity capital*.

nominal interest rate: An interest rate that does not take inflation into account.

nonsystematic risk: The component of an asset's risk that is unique to the asset and so can be eliminated by diversification.

notional principal: The amount on which interest is being paid in a swap arrangement.

off-balance-sheet activities: Bank activities that involve trading financial instruments and the generation of income from fees and loan sales, all of which affect bank profits but are not visible on bank balance sheets.

opportunity cost: The amount of interest (expected return) sacrificed by not holding an alternative asset.

option: A contract that gives the purchaser the option (right) to buy or sell the underlying financial instrument at a specified price, called the *exercise price* or *strike price*, within a specific period of time (the term to expiration).

over-the-counter (OTC) market: A secondary market in which dealers at different locations who have an inventory of securities stand ready to buy and sell securities "over the counter" to anyone who comes to them and is willing to accept their prices.

payments system: The method of conducting transactions in the economy.

Phillips curve: A relationship between unemployment and inflation discovered by A.W. Phillips.

political business cycle: A business cycle caused by expansionary policies before an election.

premium: The amount paid for an option contract.

present value: Today's value of a payment to be received in the future when the interest rate is *i*. Also called *present discounted value.*

primary market: A financial market in which new issues of a security are sold to initial buyers.

principal-agent problem: A moral hazard problem that occurs when the managers in control (the agents) act in their own interest rather than in the interest of the owners (the principals) due to different sets of incentives.

prudential supervision: See bank supervision.

put option: An option contract that provides the right to sell a security at a specified price.

quantity theory of money: The theory that nominal income is determined solely by movements in the quantity of money.

random walk: The movements of a variable whose future changes cannot be predicted (are random) because the variable is just as likely to fall as to rise from today's value.

rate of return: See *return.*

rational expectations: Expectations that reflect optimal forecasts (the best guess of the future) using all available information.

real interest rate: The interest rate adjusted for expected changes in the price level (inflation) so that it more accurately reflects the true cost of borrowing.

recession: A period when aggregate output is declining.

Regulation Q: The regulation under which the Federal Reserve System has the power to set maximum interest rates that banks can pay on savings and time deposits.

regulatory forbearance: Regulators' refraining from exercising their right to put an insolvent bank out of business.

required reserve ratio: The fraction of deposits that the central bank requires be kept as reserves.

required reserve: Reserves that are held to meet the central bank's requirement that for every dollar of deposits at a bank, a certain fraction must be kept as reserves.

*reserve currency:*A currency, such as the U.S. dollar, that is used by other countries to denominate the assets they hold as international reserves.

reserve requirements: Regulation making it obligatory for depository institutions to keep a certain fraction of their deposits in accounts with the central bank.

reserves: Banks' holding of deposits in accounts with the central bank plus currency that is physically held by banks (vault cash).

restrictive covenants: Provisions that restrict and specify certain activities that a borrower can engage in.

return: The payments to the owner of a security plus the change in the security's value, expressed as a fraction of its purchase price. More precisely called the *rate of return.*

revaluation: Resetting of the fixed value of a currency at a higher level.

Ricardian equivalence: Named after the 19th century British economist David Ricardo, it contends that when the government runs deficits and issues bonds, the public recognises that it will be subject to higher taxes in the future in order to pay off these bonds.

risk: The degree of uncertainty associated with the return on an asset.

risk premium: The spread between the interest rate on bonds with default risk and the interest rate on default-free bonds.

secondary market: A financial market in which securities that have previously been issued (and are thus secondhand) can be resold.

secured debt: Debt guaranteed by collateral.

securitisation: The process of transforming illiquid financial assets into marketable capital market instruments.

security: A claim on the borrower's future income that is sold by the borrower to the lender. Also called a *financial instrument.*

short position: A contractual obligation to deliver an underlying financial instrument.

short-term: With reference to a debt instrument, having a maturity of one year or less.

simple loan: A credit market instrument providing the borrower with an amount of funds that must be repaid to the lender at the maturity date along with an additional payment (interest).

special drawing rights (SDRs): An IMF-issued paper substitute for gold that functions as international reserves.

specialist: A dealer-broker operating in an exchange who maintains orderly trading of the securities for which he or she is responsible.

spot exchange rate: The exchange rate for a spot transaction.

spot transaction: The predominant type of exchange rate transaction, involving the immediate exchange of bank deposits denominated in different currencies.

stock: A security that is a claim on the earnings and assets of a corporation.

stock option: An option on an individual stock.

strike price: See exercise price.

swap: A financial contract that obligates one party to exchange (swap) a set of payments it owns for a set of payments owned by another party.

systematic risk: The component of an asset's risk that cannot be eliminated by diversification.

theory of portfolio choice: The theory that the quantity demanded of an asset is (1) usually positively related to wealth, (2) positively related to its expected return relative to alternative assets, (3) negatively related to the risk of its return relative to alternative assets, and (4) positively related to its liquidity relative to alternative assets.

underwriters: Investment banks that guarantee prices on securities to corporations and then sell the securities to the public.

underwriting: Guaranteeing prices on securities to corporations and then selling the securities to the public.

unexploited profit opportunity: A situation in which an investor can earn a higher than normal return.

unit of account: Anything used to measure value in an economy.

unsecured debt: Debt not guaranteed by collateral.

velocity of money: The rate of turnover of money; the average number of times per year that a dollar is spent in buying the total amount of final goods and services produced in the economy.

venture capital firm: A financial intermediary that pools the resources of its partners and uses the funds to help entrepreneurs start up new businesses.

theory of purchasing power parity (PPP): The theory that exchange rates between any two currencies will adjust to reflect changes in the price levels of the two countries.

thrift institutions (thrifts): Savings and loan associations, mutual savings banks, and credit unions.

trade balance: The difference between merchandise exports and imports.

transaction costs: The time and money spent trying to exchange financial assets, goods, or services.

transmission mechanisms of monetary policy: The channels through which the money supply affects economic activity.

wealth: All resources owned by an individual, including all assets.

World Bank: The International Bank for Reconstruction and Redevelopment, an international organisation that provides long-term loans to assist developing countries in building dams, roads, and other physical capital that would contribute to their economic development.

PERSONALIA

Johan Bastiaensen obtained Ph.D. in Applied Economics at the University of Antwerp (UFSIA). He is a researcher at the Centre for Development Studies, University of Antwerp. In collaboration with Nitlapán, a centre for research and rural development at the Universidad Centroamericana, Managua, he has published extensively on peasant production systems and the development of rural financial systems in Nicaragua.

Danny Cassimon obtained a Ph.D. in Applied Economics at the University of Antwerp (UFSIA) and MBA (Catholic University Louvain). He is a researcher and junior professor at the University of Antwerp (UFSIA and RUCA) as well as EHSAL (Brussels). His main fields of interest are financial aspects of development economics and corporate finance.

Guido Erreygers obtained a Ph.D. in Economics at the Université Paris X -Nanterre. He is Professor at the University of Antwerp (UFSIA), where he teaches micro-economics, history of economic thought, growth theory and foundations of economics. His main fields of research are history of economics, inheritance, and theories of production.

Dirk Heremans obtained a Ph.D. in Economics at the University of California (U.C.L.A.) and is currently senior professor of monetary economics and economic analysis of law at the Catholic University Louvain. He has published in the fields of economic and monetary policy, economic federalism, European financial integration, and law and economics.

Jef Van Gerwen s.j., obtained the degree of Ph.D. in social ethics from the Graduate Theological Union in Berkeley, USA, and is presently teaching economic and social ethics courses at the University of Antwerp (UFSIA) and at the Theological Seminar of Malines.

Luc Van Liedekerke holds degrees in Philosophy and Economics from the Catholic University Louvain. He is a researcher at the Centre for Ethics (UFSIA) and teaches business ethics at EHSAL (Brussels) and Handelshogeschool (Antwerpen). He publishes regulary in the field of applied ethics.

PRINTED ON PERMANENT PAPER • IMPRIME SUR PAPIER PERMANENT • GEDRUKT OP DUURZAAM PAPIER - ISO 9706

ORIENTALISTE, KLEIN DALENSTRAAT 42, B-3020 HERENT